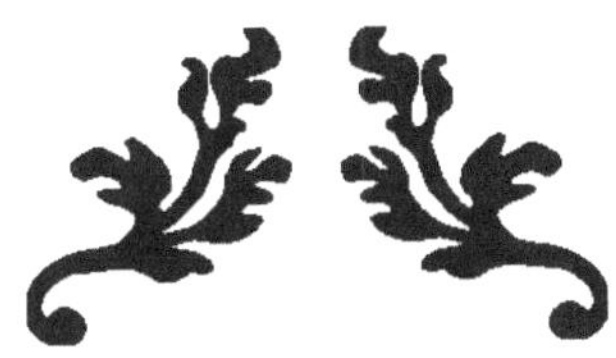

SILVER EYES ON SOUTH HOLSTON

TERROR ON THE MOUNTAIN

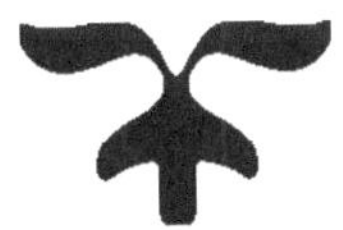

By

Jimmy A. Jones

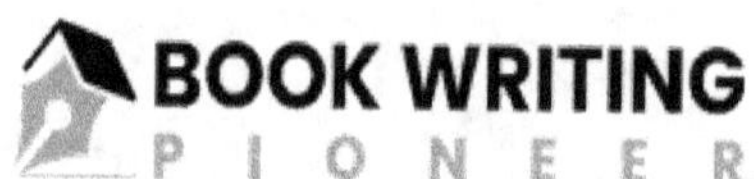
BOOK WRITING
PIONEER

TABLE OF CONTENTS

DEDICATION

I would like to thank my family for standing by me and giving me the courage to pursue my dream of becoming a true author. My mom, Patty Boggs, for always being there no matter what. And posthumously, my pop, Allen Boggs. The same goes for my wife, Leslie, and her never-ending support. I would also like to thank my brothers, John Jones, Ben Jones, and Kiser Boggs.

I especially want to express my gratitude and love to my girls, Katie Patrick, and our youngest, Jessica Stacy, my son Preston Nester, and my grandchildren, Amelia Patrick (little bit) and Elijah Patrick. Without all of you, my life would be empty.

ABOUT THE AUTHOR

Jimmy was born and raised in Bluff city, Tennessee, where he still resides with his wife, Leslie, and youngest stepdaughter, Jessica. Currently, he builds and remodels houses during the day and writes stories and books nights and weekends. He loves to fish, hunt, raise a garden, and spend time with his family.

PROLOGUE

1826 – CHEROKEE LANDS – EASTERN TENNESSEE

Black fox, War chief of the War Clan, had a lot on his mind as he prepared for this night's confrontation. He had to take a party of warriors to trap and then banish a Daemon to the Netherworld that had gone rogue.

Daemons are bloodthirsty, conniving spirits when control of them is lost. They are imbued with the ability to control the forces of nature in a small area. Most have their favorite animal forms to alter into, but all can appear as a dragon.

The only way to recognize them is through the eyes. No matter what form the Daemon takes, human or beast, the eyes are a constant, glowing silver.

As he went over his array of weapons, Black Fox was putting together a list of the warriors that would participate tonight. Chief Pathkiller had already made it clear that he was to be a part of it. After all, it was he who had summoned and then lost control of the Daemon.

Pathkiller had become deeply troubled by his decision to bring forth this particular Daemon. Chivas, as it/he was named. He thought that he was strong-willed enough to control it. In the end, he had lost control, and Chivas had become self-serving and full of bloodlust.

The Daemon began raiding the white settlements nearby, taking pleasure in whatever manor struck him, especially with the females. Afterwards, he would butcher entire families. Pathkiller knew it was only a matter of time before the Daemon turned its full attention on the tribe.

This morning, a young girl, Waterfall, had been at the river attending to this week's laundry. Chivas had appeared by the sixteen-year-old and accosted her. She had tried to run, but the Daemon had moved like the wind.

"SH, little one. I will make it fast, but I can't promise painless," he told her while slicing her clothing off.

He had sprouted Talons as sharp as razors where his fingernails had been. Waterfall moaned in agony as she felt the flesh part around her breasts, trailing to her inner thighs. It was at this point Chivas felt an arrow strike him in the ribs. The Hunting party had returned.

He knew that he could slay them all but decided to depart for now. Holding the still-squirming girl down, he Sliced her throat to send a message to the village. Pathkiller would know the Daemon was coming for him and his tribe.

After the hunters had brought Waterfall's ravaged body back from the river, he had gone to visit Mohe Stone. He was the Adewehi, or "medicine man" of the tribe. Stone turned, looked at the Chief, and shook his head.

"I foresaw this moment in visions the last few nights. The girl is only the beginning. You must stop Chivas from doing any more harm."

"How do we destroy something such as this?" Pathkiller asked.

"You cannot. You can only banish the Daemon back to the Netherworld. Listen to what I tell you. Then, you will gather your men. Time grows short."

A few hours later, there were groups of seven lying in wait. A line of runners, then the hunters, led to the seven warriors positioned up the top of the ridge. Within this last group, there were three black witches and one White witch stationed around an enchanted fire. Magical nets and vines lay at their feet.

Just inside the band of runners, Fawn, a young squaw of fifteen, sat on a tree stump. Waterfall had been her friend. The girl had volunteered to be the 'bait.' Though nervous, she bravely sat there singing a joyous lullaby as the night crept over the mountain.

Suddenly, a Crow call broke through the darkness. One of the men had spotted the Daemon. She kept singing. Her breath caught in her throat as she spied the silver eyes approaching not fifty feet from her. Chivas picked up on the song as if singing a duet with her.

As he got within arms-reach, she stopped singing. Sitting there staring at him, his appearance was that of a normal man other than the bright silver orbs. He said not a word as he reached out to stroke her hair, nails elongating into blades as he did so.

She gasped as he sliced her dress off in a single motion, deeply gashing her side in the process. There was no mistaking his intentions. He was simply going to take what he wanted and leave her for dead.

As Chivas pushed the girl down off the stump, he parted her legs with no resistance. Beginning to slice the tender flesh between her thighs, Fawn found her voice, letting out a long scream. She heard the answer returned in the war cry. The trap was sprung, and help was on the way.

Realizing this young woman had only been placed to lure him here, the Daemon became enraged. As Fawn rose to a sitting position, she felt a sharp pain in the center of her being. With her last breath, she was aware that Chivas had taken her purity after all. Talons fully extended; he had gutted her from her vagina up through her breastbone.

Weighing his options, the Daemon decided it would be better to face these men at the top of the ridge. There was a flat that ended in a cliff that dropped a mile into the river. He would fend his attackers off, throwing them over the edge to their deaths.

Dropping to all fours, his jawline protruded into a long snout, sporting six-inch fangs that ended in dagger-like points. Shedding the deerskin clothing as his back spread, hips and legs shifting, hands and feet became massive paws tipped in razor-sharp claws.

The runners were now chasing the largest wolf ever seen. Three times the size of any recorded in their history. This one, though, leading the way with its silver eyes, was not one to be trifled with.

As Chivas continued up the ridge, he did not realize that he had gone deeper into the trap. He passed into the wave of hunters who began to give chase as well. When the enchanted arrows and spears pierced his flesh, the Daemon understood that he might be in trouble after all. He had to shed some of his pursuers.

Further on up, Black Fox and his men stood at the ready. They could hear the chase underway. Standing prepared for what was to come, the sounds of pursuit changed to that of battle. He could hear the wolf roaring and men screaming. That told him the Daemon had transformed.

Seconds later, the fight was brought to him as Chivas burst into the clearing. Now, the beast was backed up into the final band of warriors. The enchanted nets and vines were at the ready, as were the three black witches to perform the banishment spell. The White witch would bind them all together, completing the ritual.

Within moments, the monstrous wolf was inside the inner circle, gnashing its teeth while using its claws as small swords. Black Fox's men were on the attack now as the Daemon changed forms once again. In the blink of an eye, the wolf disappeared. Standing in its place was a twelve-foot reptile resembling that of a dragon.

It was almost immediately that two of his fiercest warriors went down. The dragon had swung its tail, breaking one's neck while impaling the other on a large spike protruding from the end. Two of the hunters grabbed the nets and moved in.

Chivas backed up near the fire, hooking one with a Talon, using him as a battering ram. The ground was slicked with blood, causing a few of the men to lose their balance. One of the black robes began his spell-casting as the first of the nets were thrown over the dragon.

The Daemon, knowing the language of magic, caught on to what was happening and increased his efforts. Reaching out with his claws, he decapitated the mage. Blood erupted into the air, akin to a geyser, as the witch's body collapsed.

This move, however, gave the others time to engage the rest of the netting over the dragon. The remaining two black robes took up the incantation as the white witch used his sorcery to 'pull' the magically enhanced vines tight. This rendered the beast immobile.

Seeing Chivas bound and reverting to his human form, Black Fox and the others pushed him into the center of the fire. The dark witches completed their spell-casting, the white robe binding them and sending an electrical bolt into the heart of the Flames.

Chivas let out a furious oath as he sank into the ground. Once in the Netherworld, there should be no way for him to escape, as a man would lose the knowledge of Native American sorcery in the future.

As the Daemon vanished, the flames changed colors from orange to blue, then purple and yellow, dying into nothingness as if it had never been. Black Fox counted the number of men still standing. He noted with great sadness the cost of this endeavor.

Of the twenty-six that had begun this quest, including young Fawn, only nine were still alive. He and Chief Pathkiller were the only leaders remaining, and the Chief was missing an arm. Counting the total losses tied to this achievement, he hoped and prayed that no one would ever find a way to summon Chivas again.

Black Fox was long dead before that happened. It took almost two-hundred years before anyone became curious about the legend of the Daemon.

Chapter One:

Discovery

ONE HUNDRED NINETY-SEVEN YEARS LATER

As she pulled out of the Cherokee reservation, turning onto Blue Wing Road, Lisa Smallwood felt like screaming for joy. After years of research, traveling to various tribes across the country, and interviewing an endless number of people, she had finally found what she had been looking for.

"Now I'll show them who the bitch is. Years in the making, ripe for the taking." She laughed to herself.

Lisa was headed back to her hometown of Bluff City, Tennessee. She had been planning this for what seemed like forever. Her patience had run thin, but now that she had all the information needed, the plan could be put into motion. Revenge would be so sweet.

She had been raised with the common idea that mixing of the races between pure-blood Cherokee and the white man had never been a good combination. Too many Native Americans were brought up in poverty on the reservations, and in one way or the other, the blame led back to the light-skinned ones.

It was them that had introduced hard liquor and man-made drugs to the Indians. Before the English had "discovered" this land, the only so-called drugs were natural. There was Peyote and certain mushrooms used in the vision ceremonies; Marijuana was used in the peace pipes and for its vast medicinal properties in healing.

Now, it seemed as if most of the past couple of generations on the reservation only wanted to draw a government check and stay "buzzed" in one way or the other. This was not the actual case, only a small percentage made up this group. But it was the general opinion of those elders who honored the history of their ancestors.

It came as a surprise when she found herself attracted to a pale skin boy in High school. The two had been friends from the time Lisa's parents had moved from the Reservation to Bluff City when she was in kindergarten.

Playing games together after school, he had taught her the basics of baseball and basketball. And she, in turn, had tutored him in the traditional Cherokee games of stickball, chunkey, and the blowgun shoot.

To hear his name as an elementary and junior high student meant playtime to her. As she got older, however, she kind of had a funny feeling when he was around. Lisa knew she was falling in love with Kevin Miller.

This changed during the deer season, their Senior year. Her younger brother, who would forever remain twelve, had asked to go hunting with Kevin, to which she had informed him to say no. She didn't want Leeland to be in the wilderness with so many men carrying guns. There had been too many accidents with the locals involving liquor and hunting combined.

He had taken the boy anyway, vowing to keep him safe. When the hour struck ten that night, without sight or a word of them, she knew something was wrong. The police showed up around midnight. Leeland had dropped his rifle out of the tree stand. It had gone off as it hit the ground, and the bullet made a direct path through the boy's head, killing him instantly.

Of course, she blamed Kevin. He had taken him against her wishes, ignoring her pleas not to. Love became hate in an instant. Lisa had physically attacked him during the funeral, vowing to see him perish by her hands. After the burial, she went back to the reservation to help recondition the old school to reopen.

Lisa was gone for two years, not even visiting her parents' home, loathing to run into Kevin. No one spoke of him or mentioned his name to her. It was upon her return that the hatred burned anew and turned into something else.

It seemed like Lisa had been the only one to put the full blame on the Miller boy's lap. What she couldn't understand was the news that her sister Angie was engaged to be married to him. She had been seeing him for the past year and a half. How her family could do this, she never understood. Nor did she want to.

There's an old saying that "Hell hath no fury like a woman." Hell couldn't have come close to the rage and hatred running through Lisa Smallwood's soul that day. From that very moment, she was a different person. She set upon the path for revenge she had been relentlessly seeking these past twelve years.

Some say Lisa went so far as to try and make a deal with Satan himself. No one knows how that worked out or if it was even true, but she did start digging through the old myths and legends of the Cherokee. She began to find bits and pieces of different legends that led her to her latest discoveries.

After spending years traveling and interviewing old medicine men, Tribal historians, and teachers, she had found her legend. She spent many more months digging up forgotten spells and ceremonies. She had just gathered the final piece to her puzzle.

Amazing that after all the miles traveled and out-of-state trips made for this knowledge, the final bit of information had resided not three hours from home. An old white witch had what she needed to set her plans in motion.

What had taken so long for her to track him down was the fact that Native American witchcraft is not like that practiced in the outside world. The Cherokee had pretty much relinquished its practice and use to the underground.

This was due to the progress the settlers had made. They were beginning to mix and mingle with the Indians and started conforming to a lot of the community. Native American and white marriages became a semi-common happening, resulting in mixed bloodlines and loss of heritage. This still dismayed the elders and those who held strong in the practices of the old ways.

The old man, who went by the name of Thomas Keeler, claimed to be a twenty-third-generation white witch. He knew of and engaged in both life and death magic. Said to be a strange man who rarely left his home, he was known not to welcome strangers for any reason.

Mostly, he stayed to himself unless one of the tribal heads of state wanted his advice or some piece of history confirmed. Some noted that on certain nights, under a full moon, he could be heard in the woods behind his house chanting strange vocations and witnessing an ever-changing, multi-colored fire.

Lisa was a little nervous after hearing these things about the witch as she pulled into his driveway. Shutting off the F-150, she reached into the glove box and removed the pipe. "HER peace pipe," as it was referred to. It was loaded with some of the best Kush to be found. If this shit didn't get him to talk, it would at least calm her nerves.

She started up the sidewalk when the door abruptly opened, and an old man stepped onto the porch. He was regarding her as if she had been expected.

"I had a vision last night," he said with a calm voice. "The spirits told me I would have a visitor full of questions today."

She could only stand and stare. Her mind went blank as her body was covered with chills.

"I am inclined to welcome you in to test your curiosity and how much you really want to know." He continued. "It is rare for the Death spirits to communicate with many for any reason these days."

Death spirits? Those words rattled her nerves, flying through her mind like a streak of lightning. "What the hell am I getting into with this?" she asked herself.

"My name is Lisa Smallwood and I have traveled far seeking much information." She announced. "If you are Thomas Keeler, the White witch, then I have arrived at the right place, and hopefully, this is the end of my long journey."

"Come. Come inside, where you will gain the knowledge that you seek. If it is as I understood it in my vision." Thomas said. "However, I doubt that it will be the end of your journey. For it is only the beginning."

"What do you mean?" Lisa asked.

"The scales of balance have been tipped in the Life spirits' favor far too long. It takes a toll on both human and nature's souls if balance is not regained." He replied.

"The spirits told you this?" She inquired.

"It is time for something to nudge the scales in the direction of Death in order to make things right once again," Keeler answered.

"Okay. I only want to complete the task I have labored for these many years." Lisa stated.

"The information is yours for the taking. Along with it comes a warning." He continued. "Great harm will come to mankind if you lose control. For good or evil, this burden will lay heavily on your shoulders as well as mine."

"I accept," a simple reply.

"Then sit and know that you are welcome. For you are the first person invited into my dwelling in three decades." Keeler informed her.

All of a sudden, the old man was smiling.

"What?" she asked. "Is something funny?"

"Now," the old man said with laughter in his eyes. "If that pipe your holding has something good in it, let's make peace and then begin the lessons.

****

Lisa ended up staying with the old man for two days. During that time, they combed through old manuscripts and faded handwritten notes, compared the pre-civil war maps with the up-to-date ones, trying to pin-point the exact location of the banishment ceremony that had taken place one hundred and ninety-seven years prior.

According to the old witch, she had to be at nearly ground zero when she tried to break the banishing. In order to summon the Daemon Chivas to this plane of existence once more, everything had to be near perfect. It was drilled into her head that she could not, by any means, lose control of him.

"Look here, little one," Keeler said. "According to my ancestors' maps, this took place on what was once called 'Wolf-Runners Ridge.' At the highest point on a flat overlooking the river."

"Yeah, but what is it named now? And where is it located?" Lisa asked.

"If we apply this overlay of the newest TVA map of that area… See? It seems to be at the top of the Flint Mill Trail near where it intersects with the Holston Mountain Trail." He pointed out.

"Damn. Right outside of my hometown." She observed.

"It seems to be about a two-mile hike off Camp Tom Howard road. Do you know where that is?" The old man asked.

"Yes," Lisa replied. "I know it very well. We used to ride the mountain road all the time just to party and have fun. A lot of people hunt there."

"Good hunting?" he asked.

"There used to be some real good deer until they got spooked by a Hippie convention they held there a few years back." She said.

"Hippie convention?" he raised his eyebrows.

"Yeah. Cars and busses for miles. They had tents and campers set up, running around stoned out of their damned minds for a month." She answered. "If I were a deer, I would have gotten the hell out of there too."

Keeler looked at her with an amused expression on his face. Lisa liked the old man. She was learning a lot in a short amount of time. Not only about the Daemon and the summoning but about the way it truly was in the past histories of the Cherokee. Not the crap they teach in public schools either. In essence, she was learning her true heritage.

She could also tell as Thomas spoke of the traditions and the 'old ways' that he enjoyed teaching real history. Plus, she knew he was still trying to determine if she was serious or not. Lisa felt as if he were taking her under his wing as he would a grand-daughter or niece.

They had dug out an ancient ceremonial cup and historical dagger to be taken and blessed by the holy man. Both blade and cup were made of gold lined with silver. Images of wolves and serpents were inlaid into the knife handle and the chalice, with cedar grounds sealed with bronze.

After dropping the items off to the holy one for blessings, they shaved cedar bark into paper-like parchment for her to write three names upon. There had to be three sacrifices to appease the Daemon. Without them, Lisa would have no control over whom he tortured or killed, or the number of victims he would take.

Keeler handed her a total of seven of these cedar pieces. His purpose was simple.

"In case you think of anyone else that has done the Cherokee wrong that so deserves such a punishment." He told her.

"What do you mean?" She asked.

"Yours cannot be the only revenge taken. Avenge the tribe while you have the resources to do it." He stated.

This somewhat bothered her. Not what he said, but the tone in his voice and the expression on his face uncovered an eagerness she did not understand. A few seconds later, it was forgotten. He was back to his old self.

The old man was meticulous in teaching her the words to the spell. The ingredients had to be mixed in precise order and amounts in the chalice. He gave her a deerskin of water from the river that had been spoken over by the medicine and wise men for the base of the mixture.

To this base, she was to add a bit of hair from the main targeted person, Spruce granules, Laurel root, and half of the herbs and spell components from the hex bag given to her. These were to be stirred with a thin rod of silver and heated by the ceremonial fire.

The fire itself must be laid out in a seven-foot circumference of cedar as this was the most sacred of wood. Lisa was to say the first of the incantation, inflicting and annunciating each syllable correctly. Thomas had made her go over this what seemed like hundreds of times until he was satisfied she had them perfect.

"There can be not one little slip of the tongue, one mispronounced word. Chivas will flay the flesh from your bones." He informed her.

Lisa knew from the look on his face that this old witch was not joking at all.

On her second full day, she rehearsed the final part of the ceremony. After the first half of the mixture began to boil, she was to add ginseng, snake skin, wolf hair, and the remainder of the hex bag. Remove the chalice from the heat. She was then to use the dagger to cut herself diagonally across the back of her hand.

Blood streaming into the mix, drop the cedar pieces into the cup. On these were written the sacrifices' names. In the end, speaking the final words to the enchantment, pour the blend onto the fire.

"As he arises from the flames, make sure that you stand your ground. Let Chivas know that you are in control. You are the one whose blood arose him," Keeler instructed.

"Then what? He'll bow down before me or something?" Lisa asked.

"No, he will not bow. Chivas will not be as a child that cowers or as a slave that's humble. He is a Daemon after all." The old man told her.

"Then what do I do?"

"Tell him that you are granting him a certain amount of freedom for a time. You take control." He said.

"And…?" She looked at him expectantly.

"And what little one?" Keeler asked.

"When I'm finished with him, how do I send him back? I'm sure not going to turn something like that loose on the public. On innocents." Lisa stated.

"Oh. That. I have prepared a way for you in that endeavor also. This second spirit bag I will give you. When the time comes, rebuild the fire in the same location." He told her.

"Okay. I'm listening."

"Just repeat these seven words, seven times," He said, handing her a slip of paper. "Then throw the hex bag into the fire. This will revoke the summoning, sending him back to the Netherworld."

As Lisa packed to leave the next morning, bidding the old witch farewell, one thing kept nagging at her. She never thought to ask him, *If the spell was so easy to reverse, why in the hell didn't Pathkiller do that one-hundred ninety-seven years ago?*

CHAPTER TWO:

FRIENDS

Work was the last thing on Neil Baines' mind as he turned down Beaver Creek Road. He was looking forward to the three-day weekend scouting for a place to set up a couple of hunting stands. The archery season for deer opened up the following weekend, and he was late getting things set up in the mountain.

He already knew the general area in which he would hunt but not the exact spot or which trails he would watch over. Neil had waited on archery season all year with great anticipation. He was almost like a kid going to the county fair.

Usually, he started preparing as early as the end of May for the September opening. This year, though, he had worked overtime and just about every weekend all summer. When Kevin Miller and Jeff Bishop, his bosses, had told him the plan was to build eight houses over the summer, he had thought they were joking.

The joke turned out to be on him. They couldn't find dependable or knowledgeable enough help to form an extra crew, so overtime had been the answer. Sure, they had an extra helper now and then, but hard, skilled labor wasn't for everyone.

Right now, though, his mind was in two other places. South Holston Mountain and Shady Valley, the two places he had hunted every season since a teenager. As usual, he planned to hunt Shady opening weekend, then move to the mountain the next. Unless he saw a lot of big animals there, then he would stay in Shady Valley.

His dad and grandpa had raised him on the mountain. There wasn't a trail, valley, or ridge that he hadn't seen on this side of Mountain City. It had been a good, wholesome place to grow up. Not many young people did things like that anymore. Too many damn video games or social media.

When he wasn't hunting, hiking, or riding his horse, Neil fished the river. Plentiful in both Rainbow and Brown trout, it offered some of the best angling opportunities in the state. Lord knew he had caught enough in his lifetime to feed a small country. So this was what he was thinking as he turned into the Fox Meadows subdivision to begin the day.

His thoughts shifted gears and went into work mode the minute he pulled up at the job site. However, Kevin and Jeff were busy unloading tools and setting up the work station for the day. Anson wasn't here, yet he noticed, but that's no different than any other day. Kevin's younger brother had been stopping by the other job to get the subs started. He would roll in around seven-thirty.

Rick Harris was cutting the bands off of a stack of half-inch plywood. Neil knew he was going to be up on that damn roof all day. What a way to end the shortened week. They had worked twelve-hour shifts just to have this three-day weekend. Jeff and Kevin were going scouting as well.

"Should have named this company 'Hunters Building' instead of 'Bishop and Miller Construction,'" he mused.

Between Neil and Rick up on the roof and Kevin on the ground cutting the boards, it was sheeted and felted by lunchtime. Jeff and Anson had spent the morning roughing in the electrical. Everything was moving along at a good pace.

As the four of them stood around Jeff's truck eating, the subject on everyone's mind came up, "Deer season and where each of them planned on hunting." Anson had decided to break off on his own this year and go over to Iron Mountain, foregoing the usual spots of Holston and Shady. Some friends of his had told tales of seeing some huge Bucks over there.

Rick was going to look around the same areas as Jeff and Kevin, so he was meeting up with them at about four or five in the morning. Neil informed them he would be scouting in the Flint Mill and Holston trail areas. Only a couple of miles up the mountain from them. They all expressed hope that the deer were continuing to move back in after that "Hippie Convention" of a few years back.

"All that noise and activity up there scared the shit out of the animals," Kevin was saying. "But I didn't mind driving through looking at all the Boobs, I mean women,"

"I hear you. You better not let Angie know you said that, though," Rick laughed.

"Okay, guys. All joking aside. The roof's sheeted, and the electrical rough-in is finished. I say that's a good week. Let's call it." Kevin said.

"You read my mind," Jeff chimed in, "Let's load the tools up and get out of here. Start fresh Monday morning."

"What time do you want me to meet you guys in the morning?" Rick asked.

"Four-thirty at The Store on Hwy 421," Kevin told him. "Don't be late."

"I'll be there."

As Kevin drove Jeff home to Hickory Tree, they decided to take their wives to dinner. The men figured that would be best since once deer season opened, there would be no weekends out.

"Where are we taking Angie and Casey to eat at? The Longhorn?" Jeff asked.

"Yeah. Then maybe go down to the Tavern and dance a little while. Or, at least, listen to the band for a bit."

"Sounds like a plan," Jeff agreed as they pulled into his driveway. "Casey and I will meet you at your house around five. Is that okay?"

"Great. We can drink a cold one or two while the girls finish getting ready." Kevin answered.

Backing out of the drive, Kevin's thoughts glazed over the past years. He and Jeff had been friends ever since grade school. Neil

Baines had hung out with them a lot until he went into the Air Force. As soon as he was honorably discharged, he had gone straight to work for them.

Lisa Smallwood had rounded out the circle of friends until her baby brother was accidentally killed during a hunting trip while with Kevin. She had been against the trip to begin with, and of course, Kevin was blamed for the accident. She had left town for a couple of years after that.

She had blown her top when she came back to learn that not only had her family forgiven Kevin but that he was engaged to marry her middle sister, Angie. There was a bouquet of black roses sent to their wedding. Lisa had, more or less, disowned her entire family.

She still stopped by Neil's place now and then to have a drink or smoke a little. At least she hadn't ended all the friendships over it. Neil had told him that there were times when she got a good buzz going; all she could talk about was revenge for Leeland's death. If she was going to act on it, she would have done so by now. Fifteen years was a long time to hold a grudge.

****

As Kevin drove, lost in his thoughts, Lisa was coming down interstate I-81. She was running every detail of her time with the old witch, Thomas Keeler, through her mind. He had drummed it into her head that one little mispronunciation, one thing out of order, and she could die a horrible death. It had to be perfect in every way.

She didn't want to do this alone, however. Her best friend for the past few years, Becky Combs, had helped her with researching the old myths and legends. She was the one who had found Keeler for her.

If it hadn't been for Becky's time and extra effort, Lisa might not have found the legend of the Daemon, and her revenge may have been put on hold. When Lisa had first set her mind to this project, she had been too outspoken. She had made more than a few Cherokee leaders disgruntled, closing doors to herself on a lot of reservations. She was sure that Becky would want to be a part of the finality of this long journey.

About the time she hit exit sixty-nine into Blountville, her phone rang. A glance at the caller's I.D. showed that it was Neil.

"I thought you were at work. What did you do? Lay out today, asshole?" she said, laughing.

"No. We called it a day early. Taking a three-day weekend to do some scouting, " he said.

"Oh yeah. Deer seasons coming up," she remarked.

"Yeah. We've all got a case of deer fever. Say, are you anywhere around? I was going to see if you could drop me off a little smoke for the weekend. My guy's out." Neil asked.

"I guess. I can't stay long. I have a lot to do and a short time to get it done in. I'll be there in a bit," she told him.

"Alright. Do you need any help with what you're doing?" he asked. "I was going to shoot my bow for a little while, but I'll help if you need me to."

"No, Becky's going to help me. This is private stuff anyway. I'll see you shortly."

While Kevin was at the grocery store in Piney Flats, Lisa was hurrying to his house, hoping that he had driven Jeff home as usual. It was a stroke of luck that Neil had called when he had, or she would have never known they had quit work early. She would have either gotten caught or had to delay the summoning of the Daemon a few weeks or even months.

Slowing as she pulled into Millers' driveway, Lisa came up with an excuse in case someone spotted her. She would simply say that it was time to check up on her sister. Not seeing any vehicles in the drive, she drove right up to the door. She discovered that her sister still had the same habit of leaving the spare key under a flowerpot.

Lisa inserted the key into the lock, jumping back in surprise as Kevin's black Lab, Token, jumped up on the glass. The dog knew her from previous unknown ventures here when no one was home. She kept an eye on her sister, whether she wanted anybody to know it or not. Just because she hated Kevin didn't mean there was no sisterly love for Angie.

She knew that she had to hurry. Time was of the essence. Angie would be at the school until three-thirty, but knowing that he was off work worried her. He could pull in at any time. Lisa ran to the bathroom and grabbed the brush that had the shorter hair entangled in it. All she needed was a few strands of Kevin's locks.

Making her way back out of the house as fast as she could (giving Token a good head rub on the way out), she locked the door behind her. Firing up her F-150, she was backing down the driveway as fast as she dared. In and out in less than two minutes. Good.

With that small mission accomplished, she turned toward Bluff City and Larry Blacks' house. He always had the best smoke and plenty of it. He was kind of weird in her books but always seemed like a nice guy.

While on the way there, Lisa called Becky and informed her that she should be ready in about an hour. And also that it would be best to wear jeans and some comfortable hiking boots and that it was going to be a long day and evening. If this thing was going to get done, it needed to be now.

She had also called Larry on the way and told him she would be there in fifteen minutes. He was waiting on her with her order ready when she pulled in. Exchanging the money for the bag, she made a little small talk and told him she had to go. She didn't have time to waste; had things to do. And she was losing the afternoon.

It took around two hours to hike to the top of the Flint Mill trail. The fire had to be made, ingredients set out, and things put in the correct order before dark. Of course, she still had about eight hours of daylight left. She was growing nervous with each passing minute though.

Reaching Neil's place on River Road, she saw him in the field by his house. He had his bow out, drawing it back to aim at a target forty yards away. Lisa climbed out of the truck picking up his 'order' as well as her bowl as she exited the cab. She stood there quietly until he had made his shot.

Men could be touchy about being disturbed when shooting. She remembered a time when Kevin and Jeff would have been right there shooting with him. She was glad they were not. In the back of her mind, she knew that if things had been handled differently, alternate words said, the situation may have let her be forgiving. But they were not.

Yes, Lisa realized that things had escalated this far because of her unwillingness to forgive. But hell, her brother was killed. And Kevin was there. It boiled down to blame. And Kevin got the brunt end of it as far as she was concerned. But that was then and this was now. You can't change the past.

"Kill shot!" Neil announced as the arrow hit the target. "Where have you been the past couple of days?"

"Visiting some people back on the res.," she answered.

"I tried to call you yesterday evening. I had a gift card from Outback and was going to take you out to dinner if you wanted to go." He told her.

"Thanks. But I had my phone turned off. I'll go with you tomorrow night or Saturday if you still want to," she replied.

"Can't this weekend. You know the routine. Week before the season begins, three solid days of scouting, hiking, and setting up stands. Sorry. Maybe Wednesday." He said.

"Sure. Sounds fine. That is, if the two jackasses don't work you to death between now and then."

"Yeah. Wednesday it is then," he stated.

"Listen, I was going to smoke one with you, but I've got to go. Time's flying by, and I have a lot of things to do this evening," she said.

"I told you on the phone that I will help you if you need it. I can always make time for a friend."

"No. That's alright. Becky's helping me and between the two of us, it will be fine. So, here's this," she said, handing him the bag, "and I will call you later, or you can call me Sunday evening when you're finished with your little scouting expedition."

"Okay. I'll give you a yell. And, hey," Neil hollered as she walked away, "Whatever it is that you're doing, be careful."

"Always. See you later," she yelled as she backed down the driveway.

"Damn! Damn! Damn!" She cursed herself for not thinking of the upcoming deer season before. The mountain's going to be busier than usual this weekend. She knew for sure now that the summoning must take place tonight. Hunters in the woods would make for a big chance of her being discovered. Then she would have a lot of explaining to do.

Lisa saw Becky standing at the end of the gravel drive as she negotiated the sharp curve on Ryder Church Road.

"Dang girl, you're ready for this, aren't you?" Lisa said as Becky climbed into the passenger side.

CHAPTER THREE:

CALM BEFORE THE STORM

"Yes. If you don't mind though, I'd like to stop by the store on the way up." Becky said.

"I was going to anyway. I've got to get a couple of waters and some Pepsi for a chaser," came the reply. "I have a bottle of Evan Williams for a little pick-me-up."

"God, you've got to tell me what went on with Mr. Keeler. I've been pacing the floor the past two days." Becky stated.

"He gave me what I needed to know. It was a worthwhile trip," she said.

"Well, you haven't called or anything. I was starting to get worried. Some people had told me that Thomas Keeler was not a very nice man at all or trustworthy."

"People just say that junk because he doesn't socialize much. He don't like company and keeps to himself for the most part," Lisa told her.

"I was still worried."

"I'm not saying that he doesn't give people the impression that he's, well, eccentric. Once you get to know him though, he's a nice man. But all business." Lisa continued.

"Nothing weird about him?" Becky asked.

"He talks to himself a lot. I could hear him from the other rooms. He claimed that he was conversing with the spirits." Lisa said. "He also claimed the Death Spirits informed him of my coming and instructed him to teach me the ritual."

"Seriously? That's messed up. Was he a real medicine man?" Becky inquired.

"White Witch. There's a difference," Lisa replied. "According to him, he's twenty-third generation. His Great, great something or other was the witch at the original banishment of this Daemon."

"Does the Daemon have a name, or what do we call him?" Becky asked.

"His name is Chivas. He was supposed to have caused all kinds of trouble in the early 1800's." Lisa informed her. "Some Chief Pathkiller lost control of him somehow, and they had to send him back to the Netherworld."

"You're talking as if you are not taking this as seriously as you should, Lisa," Becky said. "if we're messing with the demonic forces and talking this nonchalantly about it, maybe we should just leave it alone."

"I am taking it seriously. The old man told me what could happen if I fuck up. It's life and death. I'm trying to calm myself by downplaying it a little," Lisa replied.

"You do know what happens if this works. Right?"

"People are going to die. You and I will never be the same again. Hell, life around here will never be the same." Lisa said.

"Are you prepared to accept the consequences of this?" Becky asked.

"Even to the point of my own death. The anger and hurt have grown to where I can't live with it, knowing there was something I could do to at least avenge Leeland's death," came the reply.

"'Will you be able to live with yourself when this is finished,' is what I'm really asking, I guess," Becky said.

"Somehow, I believe that I will. Now," she said as she pulled into Hickory Tree Grocery, "Let's go in and get our drinks so we can be on our way."

"Wait a second. There's something I have to tell you." Becky grabbed Lisa's arm. "I know physically or mentally there will be some price to pay. But I have a name I would like to add to the sacrifices."

"Are you kidding me?" Lisa looked at her, surprised. "Who?"

"My father, Leonard. I'm tired of him abusing Momma and Jenna. Every day he comes home shitfaced drunk and yells at mom for no reason, or he slaps her around. I'm sick of it." Becky told her.

"Why didn't you tell me this before?" Lisa asked her friend.

"Shame, I guess," was the answer. "But, now he gets that look in his eyes at night when Jenna gets ready for bed."

"Oh no!" Lisa gasped.

"She's the same age as I was when the bastard started sneaking into my room at night. I won't let that happen to her. He deserves to die." Becky stated as tears began down her cheeks.

"Come on. Easy on the tears. We'll add him. Let's get our stuff and head up there to get this thing underway." Lisa said, getting out of the truck.

She had gone to the store on the reservation before leaving for home and picked up some extra things she thought might be needed. She had bought an axe, saw, lantern, extra backpack, and a few other small hand tools that might come in handy. And, of course, a bottle of Bourbon for the nerves.

These, she had already distributed between the two backpacks in the bed of the truck. While making this last stop, however, she picked up some extra batteries for the lantern and another hunting knife. It never hurt to be prepared for any contingency.

After paying for the items and loading them in the F-150, she pulled out of the parking lot onto the mountain road. She was feeling more confident as the pavement gave way to dirt and gravel. Lisa turned the radio on, tuning in 101.5 WQUT. Neither young woman caught the irony of the song playing. It was "Highway to Hell".

****

When Kevin turned into his driveway off Allison Road, he noticed that Angie's Blazer was gone. He started wondering where she was when he realized it was only one-thirty in the afternoon. She was at school. Angie was an English teacher at Sullivan East High. He wasn't used to getting home this early on a weekday.

Angie had gone on to college to pursue her teaching degree while he stayed and went to work for his uncle building houses. By the time she had earned her degrees, he and Jeff Bishop had gotten their contractor's licenses. They had formed Bishop and Miller Construction with a little financing help from the Bank of Tennessee.

To begin with, they had bought quite a few lots and built new homes for sale in the vicinity of King College and the Bristol Country Club. Those sold well even when the market was down some. Their hard work and reputation kept them busy when a lot of carpenters had been sitting at home.

Now that the business was in the profit margin, they had bought a dozen lots in Fox Meadows. It was a middle-class subdivision that was selling homes rather quickly because of its location at the racetrack.

When they had first started out, it had only been the two of them with some occasional help from Kevin's younger brother. Now, Anson was full-time and a crew leader with carpenters Neil Baines and Rick Harris, along with several subcontractors doing a variety of work for them. Things were looking up.

Kevin got out of the truck and unlocked his storage shed so he could unload the tools that were in the back of the vehicle. He wouldn't be needing any of them over the weekend. He began to get a couple of tree stands out but figured those wouldn't be needed until Saturday. Why take a chance on someone stealing them?

When he shut the door to the building, he heard scratching noises coming from behind the house door. He walked over and unlocked it with a knowing smile on his face. Can't get anything by Token. He was a good dog.

Kevin reached inside the entrance, picked up one of the tennis balls lying there, and threw it across the yard for Token to chase. This daily ritual went on for a good twenty minutes. He was breaking a sweat again. With his companion on his heels, he went into the house, retrieved a cold beer from the refrigerator, and sank into his favorite recliner.

Opening the Budweiser, he clicked on the TV and tuned into the Outdoor Channel to see if he could find a hunting show to pass the time with. A re-run of Mossy Oak's hunting the Country was on. Good enough. He saw an ad for a new cover scent from Buck Nuts Deer Scents. He had heard that this new outfit was one of the best for attractants. He would have to get some.

About that time, his cell phone began ringing. The caller ID showed it was Larry Black. He and Neil were close friends, but to Kevin, Larry was just a decent guy who hung around sometimes. He wondered what in the hell he wanted on a Thursday afternoon.

"Hey, Larry. What's up?" Kevin answered.

"I heard you guys were off for the rest of the week. Just wondering if you needed any smoke for the weekend before you get tied up looking for Bambi." Larry said.

"I haven't been home an hour, and words spread that we quit early for the week? News travels fast. Next thing you know, the town's gonna know what color underwear I have on before I leave the house." He replied.

"No. It's not being advertised. Lisa just stopped by the house to pick some up for Neil. That's how I knew." Larry told him. "Could've figured it out for myself once I realized it was the weekend before deer season."

"Lisa, huh? What's she up to besides being Neil's errand girl? None of her family hears from her." He said. "Other than Neil mentioning her once in a while, Angie wouldn't know if her sister was alive or not."

"Just that she was busy. You know I don't talk about anyone's business. Especially hers. That bitch would just as soon kick a man in the nuts as to look at him." Larry replied.

"I get what you're saying. As far as the smoke, I'll take my usual. Will it be alright if I just have Jeff stop by and get it? Save us an extra trip."

"That'll be fine. Tell him I'll be leaving around six or so; try to get here before then."

"He'll be there. Appreciate it, Larry. Talk to you later."

Kevin hung up and called to inform Jeff of the stop on the way that evening. Taking a long pull from his beer, he closed his eyes. He hadn't a clue that Lisa had been in his house not fifteen minutes before he arrived home. Angie was waking him up an hour and a half later.

****

Lisa rounded the curve near the Flint Mill Trailhead and breathed a sigh of relief. There weren't any vehicles in sight. Alone. For now. She pulled to the side of the gravel road and cut the engine. Sitting there for a moment to gather her thoughts.

She knew that once she and Becky began up the trail, there would be no turning back. Be it for bad or good, this was happening. She was the type of person that when she started something, she damn well finished it. This had been in the works for nearly fifteen years. No way was she backing out now.

"Hey, if you're sitting there having second thoughts, I'll understand," Becky said. "Because the way I see it, if this works, people we both know are going to be hurt and killed."

"No. I'm not having second thoughts. Are you?" Lisa replied.

"I'd like to see it through. Too much time was spent to chicken out. At least we can find out if the legends are true or if it's all just bullshit." Becky stated.

"I'm trying to wrap my mind around the fact that after the years of research, all the dead ends, it's here. Time to make it happen for real." Came the response.

"Okay. But how let down are you going to be if we do all as instructed, the fire, the spell, and dance around like messed up little Indians, and nothing happens?" Becky asked.

"First of all. I'm full-blood Cherokee, so if I ever hear you say any smart-ass remark like 'messed up little Indians' again, I'm going to beat the shit out of you."

"I'm sorry. I didn't mean it like that." Becky said.

"Second. I know it's going to work. And hell yes, I know death is coming for some." Lisa continued. "I want Kevin to know what real pain is. I want him to die horribly."

"But what about the others?"

"My sister will learn what it means to be un-loyal and unfaithful to family. It's obvious that you want it to work. You're all hyped up to throw your drunk, abusing father to the Daemon." Lisa stated.

"Yea, yea. Fine. Let's go." Becky said, opening the passenger door.

Lisa shook her head as she began checking the gear and spell components, making sure they were secure for the hike. She double-checked the Canister of blessed water. It wouldn't do to get to the top only to discover she had no base for the mixture. Most of the sturdy equipment and supplies were in Becky's pack, while the most important was in hers.

They shouldered the backpacks and began across the road only to hear a vehicle approaching from the opposite direction. Lisa stepped back beside her truck, acting out an animated conversation with the other woman, waiting to see if the automobile stopped or went on.

If they stopped, she would have to come back in a while and try again, which would mean working in the dark. And that she did not want to do considering what it was. Her fears were abated as soon as the vehicle rounded the curve. She spied the Zombie Apocalypse tag on the front of the black Jeep.

Mark Canter and Jake Ellis. Two good old boys out for an afternoon cruise through the mountains. They were either out to do some scouting, catch a buzz, or both. She waved at them as they drove by while walking across the road to the trail entrance with Becky on her heels.

Glancing at her watch, she saw that it was two-thirty. Lisa figured that would put them at the top where they needed to be by four-thirty or five. Four if she could push Becky hard enough. It still left her plenty of time to prepare the ceremonial area. It didn't get dark until eight-thirty or nine. And she couldn't begin the spell casting until precisely midnight.

Thomas Keeler had impressed upon her that any sooner or later, the spell would not work. And if some part of it did, it wouldn't have the expected outcome. That was way too dangerous a game to play with the forces of nature and the Death spirits, even if the timing was off by a mere minute.

CHAPTER FOUR:

THE ASCENT

Flint Mill started off with a slight upward slope for about seventy-five yards or so but began to increasingly steepen soon thereafter. It didn't take long for Lisa to come to the conclusion that Becky wasn't in marathon shape.

She could see the other woman huffing and puffing inside the first few hundred yards. So, she slowed the pace down a bit. There wasn't any point in killing her before they arrived at their destination, and the real work began.

"Are you alright, Becca? Need me to slow down some more?" Lisa asked.

"No. No, I'm fine. Really. Let's just get to where we're going, and I can rest there. How much further is it, by the way?" Becky inquired.

"All the way to the top," Lisa replied, laughing as she heard Becky groan.

****

Jeff and Casey showed up at Kevin's right at five o'clock that evening. The screen door was open, and as usual, when they visited, recognizing Jeff's truck, Token ran circles around it. The dog was barking and jumping sideways until Jeff got out and reached down to pet him. Casey climbed out of the passenger side and went in to find Angie.

The men walked to the garage, where they cracked open a couple of beers. They stood around Kevin's classic 1967 Ford Mustang, talking about the restoration job he had done on it. The old car was in mint condition.

It didn't take long, however, for the conversation to turn to tomorrow's scouting and the upcoming archery season. The two discussed which trails or ridges they were to look at the next day. It was decided they would hit the Josiah Trail early and try to make it back to what the old timers called "Harriers Ridge."

Kevin's grandpa used to swear that was where the biggest bucks always traveled between their bedding and feeding areas. The only trouble was that if you harvested one that far back, it was a hell of a drag back out to the mountain road. At least most of it was downhill.

They were hoping to get in there and find a couple of good locations to set their stands up the following day, on Saturday. Jeff stated that he would like to be heading back down the mountain before the heat and humidity got too high.

Rick hadn't told either one of them in which direction he would be breaking off. Both had an inkling of an idea he would go straight to the crossroads and circle back around to the furthest edge of a cutout where Neil had taken a nice eight-pointer the year before last.

If he did that, at least between the three of them, they would have that whole area covered by the grape vines all the way past the cutout. No deer should be able to get by them. In theory, at least.

"Hey, did you stop by Larry's and pick that up for me?" Kevin asked.

"Sure did," Jeff said, handing him the smoke. "Are we still going to eat at the Longhorn? I'm starting to get a little hungry."

"Yeah. Then I figured we could stop by the Tavern for some drinks and maybe some dancing. If the girls want to." Kevin said.

"A FEW. I don't want to be walking those trails half-drunk or hungover in the morning. I'm going to only get a couple hours of sleep as it is." Jeff replied.

As the last sips of beer went down, the women came on out and joined them. Taking their husband's hands and leading them to Angie's Blazer, they let it be known they were ready to go. Food, drink, and dancing were the main objects for the remainder of the night.

After a relaxing steak dinner at the Longhorn, the foursome made their way back to Bristol and a favorite bar and grill aptly named The Tavern. At dinner, Angie had mentioned that one of her favored local bands, Soul Collision, was playing there tonight. It had been a while since the four of them had heard that particular band.

Soul Collision had always played great music and put on a good show. Kevin and Jeff had worked with one of the off-and-on-again drummers, Kevin Bullen, for a while. This was before the business when they were working for Kev's uncle.

Kevin pulled into the parking lot, and, noticing the fullness of it, he figured the place was packed. This band always pulled in a great crowd. As they got out of the vehicle, you could hear the music loud and clear. Yeah, the beat was going on.

The group walked towards the doorway with smiles on their faces, anticipating a great night. Once inside, the two couples had a few drinks, a few dances, and some laughs, calling it a night at eleven. If they had known how everyone's life was about to be drastically changed, they would have stayed a little longer. Would have laughed a little harder and enjoyed the evening for as long as possible.

****

It had been years since Lisa had done any real hiking on Flint Mill. She had forgotten just how steep the latter part of this trail was. It seemed as though it was a good forty-five degrees or more. They were about three-quarters of the way up. She had been climbing and hiking this mountain most of her life, and she was getting winded. Becky was gasping for air, sounding ragged.

"Hey, Becca, let's take a short break when we get to that small rocky area. It looks like a good place to sit for a few minutes." She said, eying a half-level appearing spot.

"Sounds good to me." Came the reply. "I'm hot, sticky, and out of breath. I could use about ten."

Five minutes later, both women were kicked back against some rocks in the shade. The two were passing a water bottle back and forth between them, looking down the hill from where they had come. Seeing it from this angle, it didn't look quite as bad as it felt coming up.

It would make you think that the trip back down was going to be easy. Lisa knew that would not be the case. The trek back would be by flashlight and they were going to have to pick and choose their footholds. One wrong step, and BAM! It was all over but the crying, if you were still able.

She glanced over at Becky and wondered if they should take a different route out after this was finished tonight. Flint Mill crossed the Holston Mountain trail near the top and angled off to the right at a normal slope. Or, they could walk the top of the ridge until it ran into the old Josiah Horse trail, which was an easier way down.

Either alternate route would take longer, but it would be a whole lot safer, and she didn't really want Becky to end up hurt. Or, worse. Tightening the lid on her water bottle, Lisa looked at the other girl. Their hair was disheveled, clothes dirty, and sweat poured down her face.

"Becca. Are you alright? We're getting close. Do you think you can make it?" She asked.

"I'll make it. I look worse than I am. Plus, there's no way in hell am I going to miss seeing if this works or not." Becky replied.

"Let's get on with it then. The sooner we get there, the more time to rest we'll have." Lisa stated.

Shouldering her pack, Lisa began back up the trail with a determined Becky on her heels. A half-hour later, the two young women rounded a curve in the trail and were rewarded with a leveling of the ground. The trees were thinning out a little also.

They also noticed an increase in signs of life. The wildlife inhabiting this area was obviously sticking to the top of the ridge where it was easiest to move around. Observing the trails, she could tell the animals were using this steady ground to move back and forth between bedding and feeding areas.

Lisa knew that they didn't have much further to go when the girls arrived at the crossing of the Holston Mountain Trail. Maybe only a couple of hundred more yards. Then, they could take a half-hour or so break in which to catch their second wind. She also knew that Becky needed that rest. The other woman could be heard gasping for air twenty yards behind.

When things got quiet all of a sudden, she turned around and saw that Becky had given up and sat on a log. More like laying on it was what it appeared. She couldn't help but shake her head and giggle to herself, remembering the first time she had hiked this trail to the top. Lisa could still hear her daddy poking fun at her for being the slow poke.

Later, after a few outings, she learned that it all had to do with the pace you set as well as stamina. It had been her turn to give Pops some good-natured ribbing the next morning when he could barely stand straight.

She turned and walked back to Becky, sitting next to her and handing over the water bottle. Hell, it couldn't hurt to sit a minute; they were going to have time to rest at their destination anyway. And, it was just up ahead. If it wasn't for the fullness of the trees she would have been able to see it from where they sat.

"Just breathe deep and slow. And don't drink the water too fast; it'll give you cramps." Lisa told the other girl. "We're only a couple of football fields distance from it."

"If I had known it was that close, I would have kept going. Sorry." Becky answered.

"Don't worry about it. We had a better time than I thought we would. We're going to rest for a bit, nevertheless." Lisa told her.

"Then what? Wait until midnight?"

"No. Before dark, we need to get the cedars cut for the fire. There's plenty of them right there around where we'll be." Lisa told her. "There won't be much walking and hauling to it."

"That's a good thing." Becky laughed. "I can make it now that I know it's that short of a distance away."

"Alright. Let's go," Lisa said, extending a hand to help her up. "Let's get this thing started."

****

Neil spent the rest of the day shooting at various targets at different yardages, fine-tuning his sights as he went. The short visit from Lisa earlier that afternoon had left him puzzled, partly because she was so abrupt in cutting the visit short. And the excuse of having things to do without elaborating. She always told him what was going on. Never hid anything.

Every time she had come over before, she would at least drink a beer or a soda. Something. Or, she just stood around and talked for a while. If it was something serious, she sat on the front porch. Never had she kept anything from him. Nor had she ever been that anxious or hurried before.

He had known that she was out of town for a few days. The day before yesterday, he had been trying to get ahold of her, and no one that she would see several times a week had heard from her. Rebecca at least always knew where to find her. He thought she was covering up something when telling him that she had no idea where Lisa was.

He just had the nagging feeling that whatever it was that she was up to, Rebecca was there right in the middle of it. "Oh well, it's none of my business anyway." He thought to himself as he gathered up his targets to be put away. Between his grandfather and the military, he had developed the habit of "leaving it clean." He was walking to his shed when a thought hit him.

Every time that Lisa had stopped by before, she had always inquired what her sister and Kevin were up to. Although not directly, but in subtle hints or asking questions about events that she would know they were a part of. This time however, Neil realized that not once had she asked about anything going on at school or about her parents.

She didn't even ask if the "asshole" worked him to death that day. Not a word of the normal conversation. Thinking back, all she could say was that she was in a hurry. Had things to do. No sir. Not like her at all.

Then he started thinking about all the past talk of revenge against Kevin over the years. At first, when she had begun saying things to that effect, he blew it off as the fact that she wasn't over the accident. And the fact that he knew before the tragedy she was in love with him.

Neil had thought that after fifteen years and some maturity, Lisa would call it what it had been. An accident. Since his return from the military, people had told him that she had only become a bitter person. But he knew the real Lisa, and to him, she seemed fine. Angry still, but fine.

He knew that whatever she was doing, she would be careful. All he cared for at this moment was the hunt drawing closer. His passion had always been the outdoors. It cleaned the soul to be out in the fresh mountain air, and if you were lucky enough, you got some fresh meat for the freezer.

As he was hanging his Mathews single-cam bow up in his man cave, he had an idea. Since he was just counting down the hours until time to hit the woods tomorrow, why not take a nap now? Then, he could rise about Ten or so and take a little ride across the mountain. Just to see what was moving.

Maybe he would call Rick in a little bit and see if he would be interested in going. Something to do anyway. Yeah… He might just do that.

****

Lisa and Becky had made it to the top and were leaning up against a fallen pine, relaxing for a few minutes. When first sitting down, Becky had thought that there was no way she would be able to get back up. Fifteen minutes had passed, and she was beginning to feel normal again.

"You want a drink to take the edge off?" Lisa asked, reaching into her pack. "I'm gonna have one or two myself. We're going to have to get started laying out the fire soon."

"Please. But I think it's going to be more than one drink." Becky laughed. "How long are we going to have before we need to begin doing all the prep work?"

"We have a little while. Maybe thirty or forty minutes. I don't want to rush through this." Lisa replied.

"Right."

"Well, it would be too easy to forget something or make a mistake. This is not some kid's game. This is some major shit." Lisa said.

"I know. If we really summon this Daemon or whatever he is, is it like going to destroy the area or leave a path of destruction?" Becky asked.

"No. I don't think so."

You never did tell me what you learned from the old witch. I don't want to be responsible for it getting out of control and hurting innocent people. Ones that have nothing to do with this." Becky said.

"Look, Becca. We both knew what we were researching for when we started. At least I did."

"I did. Sort of. In a way it was something to keep you occupied. But, as we found more, I hoped that it turned out to be true." Becky confessed.

"I was clear in my purpose when you joined me in the search for the ancient legends and rituals. Was I not?" Lisa asked her.

"Yes. I can't say any different." was Becky's answer.

"Well. As long as we do everything exactly as Keeler instructed me, things should be fine." Lisa said. "Chivas will arrive, hit our sacrifices, targets, whatever. Then I call him and send him back."

"To Hell?"

"Keeler called it the Netherworld. But I guess it's the same thing. Don't worry. I've memorized the ritual so I could do it in my sleep." Lisa told her. "Do you trust me?"

"Yes. I trust you. If I didn't, I would have never gone this far." Becky replied.

"That's my girl. Okay. Let's split up and get some cedar logs. Cut them as close to seven feet as possible. He didn't say they had to be exact. Only that they were to be 'about' seven feet." Lisa said.

"Right," Becky said. "I mean, they didn't have tape measures two hundred years ago when this was first done. Did they?"

"No. of course not. But make good guesses." Lisa smiled.

CHAPTER FIVE:

SECOND GUESSES

About the time Angie was waking up Kevin, Jeff and Casey were getting ready to go to the Miller's, Neil was just laying down for his nap, and Lisa was searching for cedar logs; the White witch, Thomas Keeler, was packing his own summoning bag of tricks.

He had done as he believed he had been instructed to. Now, he felt as if he must confer with the Death spirits once more. The first time he had had a dream, or vision of resurrecting the Daemon Chivas, was many months ago. Dreams were the easiest way for the spirits to communicate with the living.

To ignore the dreams did not bode well with those of the other realm. He had conversed with both the Life as well as Death Spirits many times in the past. His being a White witch gave him the advantage of being sought after equally by both. At the same time, the Black Witches could only deal with death and necromancy.

Thomas usually listened to these omens without question. When he was told that certain things must come to pass, he always took into account that it was decreed by the Masters. Who was he to doubt the veracity or importance of these matters?

There was just something about the way all these circumstances with the young woman from Bristol had been presented to him. The first feeling of doubt crept in when the Death Spirits became interested in the whims of vengeance by a girl of no worldly importance.

They had first told him that a young squaw from the Eastern edge of the Tennessee mountains would come seeking him. She was searching for a way to avenge the death of a family member. That her soul was of great importance to the spirit realm and until it was settled, things would be in turmoil.

Their instructions had been for him to teach her the ways of raising a Daemon. They had specifically chosen Chivas. Their reasoning behind this had been that this particular Daemon had been used here in the "center" world before. That it had been proven Chivas could and would do what was necessary without prejudice.

Thomas had heard varying stories of this one off and on all of his life from the elders of the tribe. None of it had been offered. He had had to ask, had to push the issue until his questions had been answered.

Years ago, when Cherokee history, the real history, had become mandatory to his training as a witch, tales of Chivas were one of his main studies. Most of what he learned was of nothing but a path of chaos and destruction that had been left behind in the Daemon's wake.

Thomas knew the truth about how hard it would be to send Chivas back to the Netherworld. He had only told the woman that it was as simple as a hex bag because he had been ordered to do so. The Spirits said that they would draw him back when the time came. Keeler knew how hard it would be for any human to banish this one a second time.

Months went by after the initial contact, and he had almost forgotten about it. Surprised at first when Miss Smallwood arrived at his home, he quickly remembered it all and greeted her at the door. Sure enough, she had come seeking knowledge of the Daemon to avenge a brother's death. He was obligated to teach her as commanded.

Secretly wishing that this directive had fallen to someone else, he began not to teach her these things to turn her away after a good history lesson. But to disobey an edict from either the Life spirits or the Death spirits was to forfeit his soul. And their punishment was far worse than anything imaginable.

With this on his mind, he slid into his pack and began up the trail behind his dwelling. This led to the talking stones and sacred fire pit. This was his communication portal to the other realms. This time would be different. He would not listen without question. He would ask them.

* * * * * * * * * * * * * * * *

Neil awoke from his nap around seven that evening. He turned on the coffee pot as he made his way to the bathroom. A minute later, he was wide awake, clothing himself in the camouflage he had picked up on sale at a new outdoors shop down the road. The lightweight ones were good for the warm temperatures of early fall.

He toyed with the idea of calling Larry Black instead of Rick to go ride through with him. However, logic told him that Rick, being an outdoorsman like himself, would be the better company on a night ride across the mountain.

Hell, Larry was probably already hanging out with some girl half-stoned out of his mind. Grabbing his phone from the nightstand, he dialed Rick's number. It was answered on the third ring.

"Hey, buddy. This is Neil. What are you up to this evening?" he asked.

"Nothing much." Came the reply. "I came home and lay down for a bit. Now I'm up getting my gear together for tomorrow. I thought about taking a little ride after a while."

"Well, now. It seems like we were on the same page. I was fixing to head up to the mountain road myself. That's what I was calling about." Neil said.

"Since we were thinking the same thing, are you picking me up, or am I getting you?" Rick asked.

"I'll be at your house in about an hour," Neil stated. "Mine's already got a full tank of gas. Just be ready."

Ending the call, Neil sat down in his rocker and pulled his boots on. He rose and strolled over to the gun cabinet, picking out a sidearm to carry. He couldn't take a loaded gun with him in the truck, but he could keep the ammo close enough for a quick load if the need for defense arose.

He always had his Winchester 30-30 and a Remington twelve-gauge pump shotgun on the rack in his Silverado. The shells of each were in the glove box. This time around, he decided to take his Ruger nine-millimeter in a shoulder holster with him. Clips in his pocket. He never chambered any round unless he had full intentions of pulling the trigger.

A few years ago, a man could ride across the mountain day or night without the worry of getting in a predicament. Nowadays, though, there were more than a few drug deals and several robberies up there. He liked being prepared for any circumstance.

Neil got out his small backpack and loaded it with a few goodies, snacks, water, and such. You never could tell what could happen to get you stuck. Flat tire, overheating, wreck, etc. Finishing up by packing an extra flashlight and a few batteries, he zipped it up and went out to his trusty old Chevy. Backing out of the driveway, he made a beeline for Rick's house. It was eight o'clock.

****

Lisa and Becky had cut and gathered plenty of Cedar. They had the logs placed slant-wise side by side and "X'ed" until they had a circle three stacks high. The sun was going down so they had laid out a smaller fire pit twenty yards away from the ceremonial one.

Lisa had decided on the second fire instead of the lantern to see by. Remembering what Keeler had told her about everything involved in the or near this spell was to be all-natural. She did not want to mess anything up, especially by something so simple as using artificial light.

The women had dug away all the vegetation and dry leaves from the larger fire pit, surrounding it with large stones. This was to keep the flames from spreading and maybe starting a forest fire. They did not need that.

On the outer rim of the stones, they had stacked boughs of laurel to add to the sacred fire when it was time. The secondary fire also cleared and lined with rocks; they went ahead and lit.

Sitting a short distance away, backed against a large Pine, Lisa dug through her pack for the bourbon and a semi-hot Pepsi to chase it with. It wouldn't hurt to have a shot or two. Taking a long, slow pull on the liquor and almost choking on the chaser, she handed the bottle to Becky.

"I don't know if I want any of that stuff or not." Becky laughed. "From the grimace on your face, it almost makes sense not to take it."

"Pepsi's a little warm. It still does the trick, though. Go ahead; it'll calm your nerves." Lisa told her.

"I don't know"

"Don't tell me that the closer the time comes, the more antsy you feel. I can see you shaking. Besides, I'm somewhat anxious myself," Lisa stated.

Becky neither agreed nor disagreed with Lisa's observations as she took a mouthful, followed by the warm Pepsi. Gagging a little bit, she began to pay attention to the details of the landscape around her. She noticed that Lisa was doing the same. Just sitting in silence, taking it all in.

"Let's say this spell works. And, we bring this Daemon back from Hell…"

"Netherworld," Lisa interjected.

"Right. But, say we get him here to do our bidding. After he's set free, how do we get him back up here to this very spot and convince him that he has to go back?" Becky asked.

Slowly turning her head in Becky's direction, as if taking the time to run the question through her mind, Lisa replied.

"I don't know. I just assumed that Chivas would return of his own accord when his tasks were achieved. I'm sure if there were something special to be done, Keeler would have instructed me in that as well."

"Yeah. You're right. I don't think a White witch would endanger innocent people for no reason." Becky said.

"Everything's fine. He instructed me as I should have been. Hell, he had me repeating all of it until I could recite it in my sleep." Lisa stated.

"What now," Becky asked.

"Let's get some of these ingredients out. We can do some of it beforehand, get them laid out in the order I need them to be." Lisa replied.

She reached into her pack, removing the chalice and blade, admiring the inlaid wolf and snake images. Next, she withdrew the hex bag of spell components Thomas had prepared for her use. Along came the Laurel root, a section of rattlesnake skin, a zip-lock baggie containing wolf hair, and another with the hair from Kevin's house.

She removed the final two items needed, which were the paper-thin cedar shavings and the deerskin containing the water blessed by the Holy Man. Laying these on a small cloth, Lisa took stock of her components, moving them around in the order they were to be used.

"I don't guess it would hurt to go ahead and mix the first part together. The old man didn't say I couldn't have that ready." Lisa said more or less to herself as Becky quietly stood aside, watching her.

Lisa took the deerskin, opened it pouring half the blessed water into the chalice. Setting this down, wedging it between two rocks so as not to turn over, she added ground spruce and part of the crushed

Laurel root. Then came half the ingredient from the hex bag, with Kevin's hair completing the first sequence.

"That's all we can do for now. We'll light the main fire around nine-thirty or ten and put the mix on to boil about eleven." Lisa told her.

"Eleven?" questioned Becky.

"Yes. Everything must culminate to a climax by exact midnight. So, it appears we have some time to kill." Lisa said.

"Speaking of climax," Becky stated as she put her arm around Lisa, guiding her towards the other blanket.

****

While Lisa and Becky were preparing for their beginning later that night, Thomas Keeler was laying out his own summoning fire. The 'speaking ring' was located on a completely different mountain in North Carolina by a stream in a small cove not known by many.

He had gathered his thoughts together on the hike here trying to sort out how to question the Death Spirits without offending them. One did not challenge their authority lightly, for the judgments and justice from them were swift and firm.

Being a White Witch, it was possible that Thomas could call upon the Life Spirits in dire need. He could practice every level of sorcery, from the healing arts to Necromancy. Most of the time in the past he had dealt only with Life and Nature magic. As of late though, the darker spirits had begun to demand more of him.

It may have been because he shunned the outside world, deeming it irresponsible and unable to see the truth of the path mankind was traversing. They were using and destroying more and more natural resources and beauty to build structures made of concrete and steel.

Once he had the fire burning and the flames shooting as high as they would get, he threw bone fragments and pieces of deer hide into it. Closing his eyes, he began casting the spell that would bring the Death Spirits to him.

He was only a few lines into his incantation when he felt the wind pick up. The chill of the grave crept into his bones as it did when the lifeless ones were near. However, he did not stop as most would. Thomas Keeler knew that it took more coaxing than this to bring the Masters forth.

Normally, one felt the calling and was drawn to this spot by them. You did not call them at your own behest. To do so was chancing their wrath for disturbing them. But, he felt as if he were in their favor and would come away from this unscathed.

A few moments later, sweat on his brow and a chill in his bones, he heard the snapping of fallen limbs. The rustling of leaves came at him from different directions. He felt the hot breath against his neck, accompanied by the smell of putrefying corpses.

Thomas opened his eyes upon five decomposing wolves that seemed to have left this world long ago. It was through these cadavers the Death Spirits communicated. Or, worse case, tear him apart if they were dissatisfied with his reason for summoning them or his line of questioning.

"Why did you awaken us from our slumber? You were told what to do about the inquiring one, were you not?" The wolf in the center spoke.

"We know that she came to you as intended when we set events in motion that would guide her to you." A second one continued.

"Yes. She came to me. As you said, she would." Keeler stated. "I also instructed her as you commanded. I have never doubted your wisdom or questioned you. But, this one has me bewildered, great ones."

"What about it confuses you?" A third spirit chimed in. "We informed you of our wishes, and instructed you as to the way we wanted them carried out. Did we choose the wrong man for the job?"

"I have served you in the past with great loyalty. This one, though. To enable a young woman, without any prior knowledge of magic, to summon a Daemon as destructive as Chivas?" Thomas asked bravely.

"Our reasons are not yours to know or understand." The lead corpse stated.

"Forgive for my doubts. But, you had me to instruct her in a way that guaranteed her to never have any control over the Daemon. Why would you have me turn this scourge loose on the world?" Thomas continued. "I must, at this, question your reasoning and motives."

At this, all five wolf corpses began howling and gnashing their teeth simultaneously. This went on for about thirty seconds, quieting down only when the lead in the center spoke once more.

"It is not for you to continue this line of questions, and it is not necessary for us to explain our motives."

"We are setting the balance right once again, for the scales are tipped too much in Life's direction. It is not good for the universe for it to be this unbalanced for long." The second one was added.

"How does this end, though? Once Chivas is freed to act on his own, there's no stopping him." Thomas said.

"We will handle that." The leader spoke again. "This we have decreed. Do not interfere in this undertaking from this point forward."

"It is not in your best interest to question us further or involve yourself in any way. Our judgment on you will be harsh if you do." The fourth one stated. "This matter is over."

Before Thomas had taken another breath, he was alone. The fire was extinguished, and he was shivering from the nearness of death. He gathered his belongings and packed them for the walk back home.

As he ascended the trail, his mind was running in high gear. He considered everything he had heard and more truth that had been picked up between what he was told and what he read in the wolf's eyes.

Making his decision on what to do and knowing that he would perish doing it, he picked up his pace. Arriving back home, Thomas began packing a suitcase. He had some traveling to do.

****

After Neil had picked up Rick, they decided to go the long way around. Up Hwy 421, by Observation Knob Park, and on across the bridge at South Holston Lake. Even this late in the year, there were still plenty of people at the boat ramp and picnic areas.

As they drove by, Rick realized that he had not put his boat in the water all summer. There had been too much work to do to fish. He would have to remedy that after he (hopefully) filled his deer quota.

The ramp was lined with those waiting to either load or unload their boats. He also noticed that even this time of evening there was a family of four grilling burgers and hot dogs. The two boys played as if there wasn't a care in the world while Mom was hollering at the dad. He was burning the meat. Good, country family time.

They rode in silence, taking in the changes in scenery as the leaves turned to deep oranges, reds, and golds. Some were beginning to fall, creating a light 'blanket' on the shoreline. Homes that were hidden from sight during late spring and summer, becoming visible again with the thinning foliage.

By the time they turned onto Camp Tom Howard Road, it was beginning to darken. The sun had set and was disappearing below the horizon. The moon was already bright and full in the sky. The display on the dash stated that it was eight-thirty-five. He could slow the pace and begin animal watching. Neil crept along the gravel at five miles per hour.

The two co-workers and hunting buddies each studied the area on their sides of the road, paying the utmost attention to any signs of movement. Looking for fresh trail crossings, scrapes, and horned trees within sight. Both anticipated catching one crossing the road, traveling to a feeding area or watering hole.

When they passed the Josiah Trail, where he, Kevin, and Jeff would be scouting in the morning, he was relieved to notice there were no fresh tire tracks in the small parking area. This meant that no one else had thought of hunting here yet. Fewer people traipsing around only increased their chances.

As Neil took the fork to the right, driving up to the entrance to Little Oak Campground and turning back, they spied a couple of bear cubs. He sped up a hare to get by them. Most bears, on their own, will shy away from humans. But getting between momma and her cubs was just asking for trouble.

Later on, across the top, as they came down the other side of the mountain, Neil recognized the F-150 parked off the edge of the road. This truck that he knew so well was sitting across from the Flint Mill trail entrance. He eased his pick-up to a halt in front of the other. Rick exited the passenger side and walked over to the Ford, laying his hand on the hood.

"It's still warm," Rick said. "Isn't this Lisa Smallwood's truck?"

"Sure is. She was just by my house earlier. Said she had some things to do. Never mentioned that it was up here." Neil replied.

"What would she be doing here this time of night? It's damn near ten o'clock." Rick asked.

"I don't know. Unless she decided to go camping or something. Look towards the top; that's the glow of a campfire." Neil observed.

"Yeah. I'll bet Becky Combs is up there, too. They're always together," Rick said.

"I know Flint Mill is a steep hike, but you want to go up and surprise them?" Neil raised his eyebrows. "They might enjoy a little company.

"Sounds good to me. Except, in case we run into a bear, I'm taking my .380 with me loaded." Rick replied.

Neil nodded, holstering his nine-millimeter and slipping an extra clip into his pocket. The two of them grabbed their packs and started up the trail. It was ten-thirty-five.

CHAPTER SIX:

THE SUMMONING

At precisely eleven o'clock, While Keven and Jeff were taking their wives home, and Neil and Rick were a few hundred yards up the trail, Lisa set flame to the ceremonial fire. After the flames began shooting higher, she made her way back to Becky and the smaller blaze.

Leaning against the tree, she gathered the parchment made from Cedar that Keeler had given her. Also brought out was a small bowl, the dagger, and the enchanted quill. These she placed next to herself.

Taking the blade in her right hand, she slowly cut across her left, the heart hand. She held it over the bowl, letting the blood drain into it as Becky watched in silence. The younger girl's eyes were wide; her mouth hung open in a state of surprise.

"What the hell did you do that for?" Becky asked.

"Didn't I mention that the target's names had to be written in blood, the summoner's blood? My blood." Lisa answered.

"No. You didn't. What else have you not informed me of that I might need to know?" Becky continued. "Am I to be the human sacrifice to the Native Gods or something?"

"No. Nothing you should worry about. The words to the spell are a little disturbing to me, although you won't be able to understand half of them." Lisa told her.

"Why? Is it in a different language?"

"Yes, they have to be spoken in the old Cherokee dialect. The pitch, inflection, and pronunciation of each word are a certain way. Otherwise, the spell won't work." Lisa said.

Shaking her head in confused understanding, Becky watched as she took the quill in hand, dipping the end in the blood. Lisa wrote each name in order on a piece of the parchment, like cedar. Of course, the first name was that of Kevin Miller.

The second name given up was Jeff Bishop. Hadn't he accompanied them on that fateful hunting trip as well? For her, the final name was Anson Miller. Take them all out. She then handed a piece to Becky, freshening up the blood as ink on the quill.

"Are you sure about this? Once it's done, there's no taking it back." Lisa asked, a stern expression on her face.

"Becky just nodded her head as she wrote the final name. Leonard Combs. A single tear ran down her cheek. Other than that, there was no show of emotion or regret at the fact that she had just condemned her father to death. It was the only way she could be sure to protect her mother and baby sister. Even if this project failed, he would be forever dead to her.

With that task completed, Lisa took the chalice containing the pre-mixed potion and carefully placed it at the edge of the fire. She wedged it between two rocks so as not to turn over. Now glancing at her phone, she realized that there were only thirty minutes left until everything came together. Twenty minutes and this part of the mixture should be boiling.

"Take your clothes off," Lisa told Becky as the minutes wound down.

"Why?"

"Because the ritual itself has to be performed in the nude, expressing the barest form of ourselves to nature," Lisa responded.

"What does nature have to do with the Daemon?" Becky asked.

"I'll be calling on nature for assistance more than you think. Nature is in the raw. So, the participants must be bare of all trappings with clear and translucent thoughts and form." She explained.

"Okay. But I'm not actually taking part. I'm just an observer." Becky argued.

"You became part of this the minute you set foot on the trail. I have to focus on the immense power of the Earth, and I don't need to worry if your clothing's going to mess it up." Lisa told her.

Six minutes till Midnight.

With a piece of deer hide in her hand, Lisa grasped the Chalice from the coals. She lifted it in a salute to the fullness of the moon. Becky, naked and shivering from nerves, backed up, watching in silence.

"Brother Moon. To the brightness that you bring to me on this night. You wrap me in your loving light. I beseech you to grant me a portion of your magic, your power to aid me in this undertaking."

Five minutes.

Bringing the chalice to her bare breast, she began speaking the phrases that would gather the forces of Upper, Middle, and Lower Earth. Phrases that had not been spoken together in the Cherokee language for almost two hundred years.

Words that, when used in a certain combination with each other, would call forth the energies of all three levels of Earth. Mixing together to form a massive burst of sorcery no person of the last two centuries could fathom.

Repeating these phrases several times, a change in pitch and inflection at each interval, she dipped her fingers in the liquid, flicking it into the fire. Each droplet produced an explosion of sparks, the flames changing to a deeper yellow-orange. She then proceeded to pour out the remainder of her blood from the wooden bowl onto the fire. Again, altering the blazes' colors.

Having never witnessed anything compared to this in her life, Becky stood speechless, unable to catch her breath. She was trembling with both excitement and a fear that had every bone, muscle, and nerve twitching beyond her control.

The Flames danced wildly now, an ever-changing cascade of colors. Oranges, yellows, blues, and reds reached for the sky. Sparks being propelled into the night air as the Cedar popped and crackled.

The wind was picking up, blowing Lisa's hair around her, resembling a picture Becky had once seen in a magazine.

For Becky, the clock stopped ticking, and time froze. She did not know why she was really here. Her mind went blank, all body movements restricted to a point where even a minuscule twitch cost an extreme amount of effort and energy. She was lost in the enchantment, realizing they were on the verge of another realm of existence.

Three minutes to go.

****

Something was happening here in his prison. Something of importance for him began to feel a pull. Other than the screams and moans of the tortured, the only sounds Chivas had heard since being cast into the Netherworld were those of his masters.

They had come speaking to him in hushed tones of an approaching assignment. He wanted no task, needed no task. His only goal was to be set free. Free to wreak havoc on mankind, maiming, raping, and murder causing uncontrolled chaos and destruction to everything in his path.

It was what he had been born to do, if you could call his creation a birth. He had been created and summoned into existence in a magical and spiritual petri dish. The overseers had combined bewitched DNA along with tortured souls from mystic animals such as the Mammoth Wolf and the Dragon of Old.

Bind these together with the destructive forces of nature, and the Daemon had been born. He was an almost indestructible killing machine that could also collect and deliver the souls of his victims to those in the underworld.

Chivas could metamorphose into either animal, the wolf, or the dragon. He had the ability to call upon nature to aid him in whatever assistance he may require. The Daemon could move as silently as the serpent and could strike with the force and speed of a lightning bolt.

Very seldom had he been put to use, however, as he was almost uncontrollable and left far too much damage and destruction in his wake, even for the Death Spirits that held this realm. They desired only a slight balance in their favor over the Life Spirits, not the complete desolation of the world.

Middle Earth, where the humans dwelled, was overseen by that known as Mother Nature. She held sway in the end balance of power. She let things tip one way or the other every now and then, but, not too much nor for too long. She was also a formidable rival. One they could ill afford to go against.

Chivas was restrained and magically bound to an iron, grill-like wall. Chains were attached to each arm and leg, spread tight, as well as by the neck and forehead to immobilize his range of vision. For an extra precaution, he was strapped to the wall by a solid steel band. He had not opened his eyes since arriving back here two hundred years ago.

"It is time, my son." A voice whispered in his ear.

"We will be with you every step of the way," said another.

He heard the click of a lock being released and felt the chain removed from around his throat. With a second snap of a lock, the chains vanished from his arms and legs. A third and his torso were freed. When the weight of his bonds disappeared, two bright silver orbs appeared as he opened his eyes.

"Others are being freed as we speak. Each with a specific task, a different location, and a certain amount of souls to gather." The first voice said.

"Do not exceed this number, including the sacrifices that are named by the humans that are opening the gate for you." The second one was added.

"And what if I do?" Chivas asked defiantly.

"The consequences will be disastrous for you. You will feel the full torment of the damned upon your return." Came the answer.

"You each have assigned territories in which to wreak your havoc. When your goal is obtained in one section, move to the next in a short fashion." He was further instructed.

"How many do I get?" Chivas asked.

"Thirteen for each region. You have four total regions in which to complete this. Then, return to the gate where we will retrieve you." The first Master said.

"What about the one that is raising me up?" Chivas questioned further.

"It is a female. She has a few 'sacrifices' named already. You will take those as payment for her help in attaining our goals." The first Master continued. "However, you may kill her first if you wish. Her soul would make an excellent addition to our collection."

At that moment, he felt the heat of the fire. He heard the ancient Cherokee language of magic being spoken and began to smell the odors of Center Earth. He stepped forward.

****

Neil knew they were near the top when the trees began thinning out somewhat. He motioned for Rick to slow it down and extinguish the flashlights. The moon was bright enough in its fullness that they could see to sneak on around the bend.

From there, they should be able to see the flat area leading to the drop-off well. He hoped to get an idea of what the girls were up to before barging in on them. The closer they had gotten, Neil had heard Lisa's voice, but not Becky's. That made him curious as to whom she did have up here.

He thought that she had said something about the moon. Or, on second thought, it sounded as if she were talking *to* the moon. He knew she wasn't a user of any kind of heavy drugs, so this had raised his curiosity a bit.

Both could see the glow of a campfire through the trees. As they moved further up the path, rounding the last bend, Neil saw not one fire but two. One was a normal size; the other, however, was three times larger, flames shooting high in the air. What had kept the Forestry Service or Game Wardens from investigating, he had no idea. They had reached the final bit of cover between them and the two women.

Neil pulled Rick behind an uprooted tree, kneeling so as not to be seen. Yet, this position allowed a clear view of the clearing. Both men were intrigued and confused as to the reason the girls were completely naked, Lisa standing close enough to the larger fire to fall in.

He noticed Becky was standing off to herself, looking lost and out of place, hands clasped in front of her. He watched as Lisa lowered some kind of cup or container to her bare breast and noticed the changing colors of the flames as she flicked her fingers toward it. The fire changed once again as she poured some liquid from the bowl onto it.

He put his index finger to his lips in the gesture of silence, stopping Rick from rising and walking in plain view. Motioning at his watch, he let him know to wait a few minutes and find out what was happening. Looking at Neil's watch and nodding his head in agreement, Rick saw that it was Eleven-fifty-seven.

****

Lisa motioned for the other woman to bring the remaining ingredients, which were combined to the last half of the mix one at a time. Ginseng, snake skin, wolf hair and the rest of the hex bag in that order. She then added the strands of Kevin's hair, speaking his full name three times in concession, changing the tone and inflection with each.

Two minutes remain

Becky became further nervous and frightened, if that were even possible, as Lisa moved a step closer to the fire. She began chanting the locutions once again that would establish a link with the Netherworld and Daemon that would summon Chivas to this world as once before.

She watched with fascination as the flames expanded and contracted, only to increase in size again. All the while producing a flow of ever-changing colors, faster and faster with each variation of the phrases. Lisa then turned her back on the fire and faced the woods, speaking as if to the mountain itself.

"Mother Nature. We as a people, and I myself as those and one who worships the true beauty and majesty of your blessings – The open air to breathe, firm ground to trod upon, and the plants and animals for nourishment."

"You give us the wind to cool us and the sun to warm us. I humbly beg of you to thrust upon me a taste of your power to aid in the raising of one of your own, a Spirit Wind walker. Grant me this power, and I will forever be in your debt."

For a moment, Becky thought she had heard someone gasp, dismissing it as she stood in awe at the raw power Lisa had called upon Mother Nature for. The wind had picked up considerably.

Jumping in fright as a bolt of lightning was unleashed from the sky to strike at the very heart of the fire, sending sparks high into the air.

It was then that she noticed the outline of Lisa's body was surrounded by a glowing aura as she turned back to the flames. The area was suddenly fading in and out of her vision, being replaced with blurred images of others moving about. One, in particular, was being guided towards the threshold into this world. Her world.

Surrounding the one who advanced were tall, black shadows, ever-changing in form and posture. Sounds of chains being unbound reached her ears, the smell of rot and decay touched her one moment only to change to a sweet, earthly odor the next. Her world slowed as it came back into full existence. Her voice was non-existent as she tried to warn Lisa to stop. She went numb.

One minute remained.

****

Neil was watching all that was happening, unable to comprehend just what in the hell Lisa was doing. This had to be what was so important to her and the reason she had been in a hurry when she had left his house. Finish something, she had said. When did she start this, and what was it?

He didn't understand any of it. He had not known she could speak another language, for one thing. And he sure couldn't figure out what kind of crap she was acting out. And in the nude at that! The two women looked as if they believed in what they were doing, though.

When he had at first noticed the women were unclothed, all he could do was stare at Lisa's well-defined form glistening with a slick sheen of sweat in the firelight. As he observed her actions, though, he became mystified.

He could see her holding the cup, motioning to the flames, speaking in a dialect he had never heard before. He had watched with the bewilderment of a child as Lisa had turned towards the wood, facing them without knowing they were there.

Whatever she was doing, whomever she was trying to communicate with had held her full, undivided attention. He probably could have risen straight up from his hiding place and walked right at her; she never would have noticed.

It was at this second she had begun asking Mother Nature for her blessings. Mother Nature? Was there such a person, an entity? The women believed there was from the way they were carrying on.

He was suddenly aware of the wind picking up in a dramatic fashion. As Lisa continued to speak, the surrounding trees began bending towards her as though bowing to her. It was then he heard Rick's sharp intake of breath and had to pull him back down into cover.

Neil could feel the vibrations of his heartbeat throughout his extremities. He took notice that Rick appeared as if he were ready to jump out of his own skin. At this point, a lightning bolt shot from the sky, striking the larger fire. He could feel the electricity in the air. That was when both men stood, not caring if they were seen or not.

CHAPTER SEVEN:

THE ARRIVAL

As Lisa finished asking Brother Moon for his assistance, she began to lose her sense of reality. Nothing that went on around her other than the summoning caught her attention. By the time she had conversed with Mother Nature, she had lost herself in the magic. Only she had heard the reply to her request in the wind.

Nothing to her existed in this time and space, she was being torn between the two realms. Devoid of all feelings and thoughts except for the ecstasy of this dream-like state, it was becoming hard to concentrate.

It was as though an ancient soul had taken control of her mind and body. Each movement she made, each word pronounced in the forgotten Cherokee language of magic, came not from her but through her.

Turning back to face the fire, Lisa motioned for Becky to step forward and hand her the parchment-like Cedar shavings. These she dropped into the flames, reciting each name as it caught blaze. Beginning with Kevin's and ending with Leonard's. As they first touched the fire, they burst into multi-colored billows of smoke.

The final parchment piece released was shaved from Locust, not Cedar. On this one was written the name of the Daemon, Chivas. When it began to burn, it did not immediately turn to ash as the others had done but slowly blackened around the edges. The letters flared up in a glowing white.

At this juncture, Lisa poured what potion remained in the chalice onto the Locust as the edges still darkened. It was also the exact second when one day retires to the next. Midnight. The Locust erupted in a bright sliver flame shooting over eight feet high. A dark grey fog, thicker than ever seen before, enveloped the clearing, only to be dispersed by the winds.

The brightness of the moon increased ten-fold, shooting a beam akin to a spotlight on the ceremonial fire. Lisa felt some of her senses returning to her when she felt Becky's hand on her shoulder. The other woman was pointing to a dark human outline in the center of the inferno.

Becky retreated a few steps as the figure emerged from the blaze making a downward sweep of its hands, vanishing the fire as if it had never existed. The knowledge that she had succeeded entered Lisa's mind. She approached the large male form, viewing it from head to toe, admiring her handiwork.

Since vanquishing the flames, the Daemon had not moved an inch, nor had he opened his eyes, she noticed. She took in the long black hair flowing halfway down his back, large muscular arms and chest, and powerful legs. The figure before her had the stance of a caged animal that had just been freed. He looked as if he was ready to pounce.

"Ancient Daemon of the Cherokee," Lisa began, "I have summoned you from your prison for a season to perform four tasks for me."

The Daemon stood, still not moving. Appearing as if he were not even breathing.

"I believe these tasks will be, to your liking, enjoyable for such a creature as yourself." Lisa continued.

She was slowly walking around him. Inspecting him as if he were her personal property.

"When you arose back to this Earth, when I *Raised* you back up, I bore in your mind four names. You have their scent and images embedded into your senses. These are your four sacrifices." She said.

She reached out a hand to caress his strong chest as she made this circumference of his being, expecting some movement on his part. There was none. Stopping in front of him to stare at his face, she continued.

"Punish those men in any fashion that meets your pleasure. When you have completed this, you are to return here. I will meet you to restore you to your slumber. Do not touch or harm any other. Slay only these four that I give you permission." Lisa finished.

Becky's breath caught in her throat as Chivas finally opened his eyes, taking in his new surroundings. The Daemon's eyes were an intense, bright silver that glowed with a mesmerizing ferocity. There was no emotion shown on his face as he stared first at Lisa and then at Becky.

Haltingly, he turned in each direction, seeming to make quick calculations in his mind to gauge his position on the mountain. Realizing where he was, he moved back to stare Lisa in the eyes, showing a mixed bag of both respect and loathing.

"I am Chivas, both savior and destroyer of the human race." He spoke. "I was sent to the Netherworld from this exact place One-hundred ninety-seven years ago."

"I know this," Lisa said, taking a step back.

"It took many warriors, much stronger than you, and wizards of great power, to banish me there. There were many deaths." Chivas spoke on. "Why did you, a puny nothing of a female human, think that you could control me?"

That statement being made, Chivas stretched to his full height of around six-foot-six, extending his arms out and down to his sides. Shaking out his mane of hair and spreading his fingers apart, he sprouted razor-sharp claws. Bringing them around, he struck Lisa in both the face and chest at the same time.

The blow knocked her fifteen feet backward against the fallen tree. It was all she could do to maintain consciousness. With blurred vision, she saw the Daemon approaching. He towered over her.

"You never had a chance at controlling me. This was doomed for you from the beginning. The Death Spirits prepared the way for me. Not the likes of you." He said.

Lisa's first thought went to the old witch Keeler. "He tricked me."

"The summoning spell given you were laced together with a chaos enchantment," Chivas informed her. "With gratitude for unleashing me from my prison, I will let *you* live. If only to witness what you have brought into this world."

Half-dazed, Lisa saw movement emerging from the tree line, appearing as if someone were running towards them. That could not be. Believing herself to be dreaming, she had the vague recognition that Rick Harris was coming into the picture.

"Please, no," were the only words to pass her lips as she lost all consciousness. She was out cold.

****

Neil and Rick had stood watching in awe as Lisa poured a liquid onto the blaze creating the pure silver eruption of flames that temporarily blinded them with a thick, acrid fog. As it cleared out, neither man could grasp the meaning of the man standing in the middle of the fire.

Both were paralyzed with fear, accompanied by a feeling of great evil growing over them as they observed the man stride out to stand a mere foot from Lisa. The men heard every word of the short conversation between her and Chivas.

Neil could plainly see that the man appeared to be a full-blooded Native American. He became angered and horrified at the same time as the man struck Lisa with what seemed to be small knife blades. He saw the blood cascade down her chest as she was flung backward by the blow.

Rick broke his paralysis of fear and took off in a dead run towards the scene, drawing his hunting knife from the sheath on his side. Neil's horror only mounted as Rick drew near the man, plunging the blade deep between the man's shoulders.

The invasion of the knife seemed to have no effect other than to piss the attacker off. Chivas turned with an uncanny speed, burying his claws into Rick's stomach. With one quick jerk, the Daemon lifted him high off the ground, shaking him like a ragdoll. Disemboweling Rick, he flung his body to the ground as if it were nothing.

Neil overcame his fear enough to crouch back down behind the tree before he was spotted. At this moment, it was as far as he could think about moving. His body was numb with the realization of what he had just witnessed. All he could do was hide.

He was thinking that maybe he could either slip away and get help, or, wait it out until this thing left. As Neil squatted behind cover, praying like he had not done since he had been in Iraq, he saw Chivas turn towards Becky. She screamed.

****

Becky was trying to figure out what was going on as the Daemon dealt Lisa a tremendous blow. She then noticed the fresh blood running in small rivulets down Lisa's jawline and chest on down to her waist. Desperately running the events through her mind, she was attempting to determine what had gone wrong with the spell.

Everything was happening around her so quickly that it was hard for her to keep up with what was transpiring around her. Her mind was in a jumbled mess. She became aware of a figure running at them from the trees. "Was that Rick Harris?" she questioned herself. "How in the hell did he get here? Why was he here?"

Becky saw the Daemon stab at Rick with his hand, lift him high off the ground, and gut him. Rick's body hit the ground at her feet. His entire midsection had been sliced open and emptied. She knew that she was being driven insane when her first thought was that Rick wasn't going to be at work on Monday.

She looked up at the Daemon as he moved towards her. He had a grim smile on his lips and laughter in those eyes of silver. It was then that she tried to will herself to flee, but her legs would not move. As Chivas circled, feasting his eyes upon her, he had a malevolent tone in his voice as he said, "You are mine." It was then that she screamed.

****

It had been almost two hundred years since he'd had any fun and games with a female. Chivas noticed how well-built this one was, with curves in all the right places. Sweet. He decided to start from behind, running his Talons up the outside of her thighs, across her butt cheeks.

Not too deep. Just enough for her breath to halt for a second as small, glistening red streams began to run down the backs of her legs. He could hear the sobs coming from within her being, which turned him on even more. Chivas had always liked it better when they cried and pleaded with him to spare them.

He moved to stand in front of her, roughly grabbing the woman by the arms and throwing her on the ground. Becky knew at this point that she was not going to make it off of this mountain unscathed. When he lay on the ground beside her, she detected the scent of rot and decay on his breath, the smell of death rising from his skin.

All thoughts in her mind were suspended as he began to run his hand around her breasts, along her ribcage, leaving gashes an eight-inch deep. The blood was trickling down on the leaves, forming small pools, spreading as he parted the flesh of her abdomen.

Becky tried to focus all of her attention on the night sky, intending to put the pain in the back of her mind. But when the moon came into view, she asked it over and over, "Why?" For she knew that the moon had lent its forces to bring forth this abomination. Of course, she received no answer.

Pure agony washed over her as the Daemon spread apart her legs with such force that her hips were dislocated. He grabbed her by the head, guiding her eyes to stare into his. Chivas did not like it when they tried to mentally absolve themselves from his considerations.

He wanted them fully aware of what he was doing to them, wanted them to feel and experience every slicing caress, every thrust of his manhood, every ounce of pain. He slid his talons through her shoulders, pinning her to the ground as he drove himself deep within her, stretching her wide and pushing as far into her body as he could.

To her, it felt like she was getting laid by a foot-long icicle. She had never felt a coldness like this inside of her before, or outside, for that matter. Somehow, her pain dissipated as she brought to mind a picture of Frosty, the snowman on top of her, pounding away. That made her laugh. Even with the pain, she began laughing in the Daemon's face.

That must have upset him tremendously, for he began pumping harder and more violently. He removed his hand from her shoulder, and with every thrust of his hips, he sliced away more flesh. Becky started screaming again.

****

Lisa had passed out for a few minutes after being struck so fiercely by the Daemon. She awoke in confusion and blurred vision but was entirely able to make out the sounds of someone screaming in pain. The voice was that of a woman.

"Shit, Becky." Her mind was slow to register.

She moved herself to a sitting position, back against a tree, trying to focus her sight in the direction of the screams. Her vision cleared some just as Chivas entered Becky, and the girl began to laugh. It didn't take but a few seconds for the laughter to turn back into screams of agony.

Tears flowed down Lisa's face as she watched her friend's body being hammered and torn apart. She was frozen in place by fear, unable to provide any aid to the other woman. The scene in front of her unfolded like a bad horror film fest, somewhat along the lines of a Nightmare on Elm Street deal.

Only now, here, the blood was real, the pain genuine, and the fact that it was happening not forty feet from her made it all too clear that this was real. She had never witnessed anything such as this before. Nor had ever dreamt that she would.

Just when it seemed that Becky's body couldn't take any more torment, the Daemon arched his back and thrust as deep as he could, holding his position as if he were having an orgasm. If that were even possible, being that he wasn't of this world. Stranger things have happened, though.

Lisa cringed when Chivas climbed off of the young woman, finishing her off by cutting her throat. He stood up beside Becky's inert form, magically acquiring the appearance of being clothed in modern-day attire. Jeans, t-shirts, belts, and hiking boots completed the picture. How he had accomplished this, she had no idea. She didn't care. She only wanted him to leave.

She became afraid that what had just happened to Becky was about to happen to her. But her fears of this disappeared as Chivas stopped a few feet in front of her and only stared at her. It seemed like an eternity.

The Daemon stood still, looking at Lisa as if trying to decide what to do with her. After all, she was the one that had freed him from his prison. As he lingered, gazing at her in her nakedness, the defiance showing in her eyes, he came to his decision, believing her to be at least a true warrior, if not a Cherokee princess.

"When I arose from the flames, I told you that I would let you live, and I will. I do so only as another form of torture for having the audacity to believe you could control a being such as myself." He stated.

She tried to rise, but he motioned for her to be still. Then he continued.

"You will punish yourself at the news of each unnatural death heard of, each house that is razed, and every family torn apart with grief. You will know that it is of your doing by resurrecting me." He said. "The four named by you will be the first among many."

The sound of twigs snapping and leaves rustling drew all attention to the figure of another man emerging from behind the tree line. As Chivas shifted his position to view the new intruder, Lisa locked eyes with the man. She recognized another of her friends, Neil.

"Run." She screamed at him.

Hearing the panic in her voice, Neil turned and took off back down the trail as fast as his feet could carry him. The Daemon only looked at her, smiling, and followed, leaving Lisa alone with the bodies of two of her friends.

CHAPTER EIGHT:

NEIL'S DESCENT INTO DARKNESS

Neil was horrified at the murder of Rick, sickened at the ravaging of Becky. He was so full of terror that all he did was hide and watch, waiting for the chance to run and try to get some help. He almost vomited as the thing climbed off of Becky and slit her throat. When he saw the full damage done to her, he threw up.

When he heard the Daemon tell Lisa that he was going to let her live, yet many more lives would be lost, he jumped up. Staring Lisa in the eyes, he didn't know whether to try and help her or to flee. She answered that question herself. When she yelled at him to run, he didn't hesitate. It didn't take a fucking genius to realize when it's time to go into a situation such as this.

Neil had run about a hundred yards when he remembered his nine-millimeter and stopped. He drew it, made sure there was a bullet in the chamber, and took the safety off. Kneeling behind a rock, steadying his arm across it for a truer aim, he decided that he was just going to blow the things ass back to hell or wherever it came from. A couple of seconds later, Chivas appeared, following his trail, sniffing the air as a hunting dog or a predator would.

As soon as he got a decent aim on the Daemon, Neil pulled the trigger in rapid succession, emptying the clip. He knew for a fact that Chivas had taken most of the rounds in the chest and abdomen area. The huge figure kept coming at him anyway, as if he hadn't been touched.

He had never in his life witnessed anything get shot multiple times and not go down. "Screw this," he thought and began running back down the mountain once again. Soon, he decided to cut to his right and go parallel to the top of the ridge. He could angle towards the road, double back, and rejoin the Flint Mill further down.

If he remembered correctly, there was a stream flowing down that he could follow. Wading through the water might mask his trail better. The stream should cross under the road where his truck was parked. He hoped so anyway.

As close as that thing was when he shot it, he wondered why it hadn't already climbed right up his ass and taken him down. The thought crossed his mind that he may have wounded it after all. If this were the case, then just maybe he had a chance to get away and alert the sheriff's office. His hope was destroyed a second later as he heard loud laughter. The sounds of pursuit picked up again.

Neil had done everything he could to gain some extra speed, only a modest amount is all he wished for. "Not happening, not in this lifetime," he thought. Hell, he hadn't even jogged around his field in four years or more like he used to. Had, in fact, not performed any real exercise other than work since being discharged from active duty.

Years ago, he could have doubled this pace, but that was back when he ran high school track, then boot camp. He was scanning the area as he ran. Looking for both obstacles and a landmark that would tell him exactly where he was and how far he had to go. It was just so damn dark. He had dropped the flashlight long ago.

He pushed on ahead and began angling away from the main trails, intending to cut back in a half-mile. This would either bring him back to the Flint Mill close to the road, or he would run into the stream and follow it as he hoped.

There were an awful lot of things that could happen between here and there; his pursuer catching him was one he wished to avoid. Neil knew one thing, though: he was going to have to find a place to hide for a short period, and soon. It seemed as if he had been running forever. In reality, it had only been three minutes.

His legs were beginning to cramp; breathing was a chore coming in ragged bursts, and his lungs felt ready to explode. No doubt about it, if he didn't rest soon, that thing was going to catch him. "Probably laying out here dead of a heart attack or stroke," he thought. Wouldn't that be some bullshit luck?

He forced himself to slow enough so that he could look around the area. Maybe he would find some cover where he might rest for a bit, at least until he caught his breath. With a little luck, his followers would pass right by without noticing him. Then he'd take the opposite direction down.

Neil doubted that was going to happen, though. He had made enough noise crashing through the trees and underbrush that it was probably heard the next county over. By the moonlight that filtered through the trees, he spotted an outcropping of rock that had some limbs hanging over it. It might be the entrance to a small cave.

The rocks had an abundance of moss growing along the top, dropping to blanket the sides. Looking back the way he had come to make sure he was in the clear, he made his way towards this hiding place as quietly as possible so as not to alert his stalker to his position. So far, so good, it seemed.

Praying that he wasn't crawling into a copperhead or rattlesnake nest, Neil got on his hands and knees, scooting under and behind the overhanging moss and limbs. He realized this cave only allowed him to tuck in four or five feet before it narrowed to an opening of roughly twelve inches wide.

Being all the way back, the opening covered by the foliage, he figured to be okay long enough to recoup some of his energy.

Having only just settled into a halfway comfortable position, the snapping of twigs reached his ears. The sounds came from the direction he had just traveled. Lying flat as he could, Neil inched up to the small opening, silently moving a few leaves to afford him a view of the area. He was hoping the man would pass by without a glance in his direction.

Gazing out, he saw the silhouette of his pursuer. The man was looking around leisurely, all the while sniffing the air as if trying to get a scent on him. As his pursuer got within seventy-five yards, it stopped and turned in a complete circle like it had lost the trail.

Neil, believing that he had fooled it for a few moments, breathed a sigh of relief and relaxed a bit. He had not thought it possible to throw the man off his trail. His moment of elation came to an abrupt end however, as the man image faced back in his direction.

Dropping to its hands and knees, it turned its head skyward. Letting out a low moan that quickly altered in volume and pitch, becoming a hair-raising howl, its body began to change. The face elongated into a snout with a mouth full of vicious teeth, and bones snapped and reformed as legs and arms changed both length and girth. The hands became large paws with bladed talons protruding.

In mere seconds, Neil was looking at the biggest wolf he had ever seen. Easily three times the size of a normal one. With the canine standing six feet tall while on all fours, he could see the rippling bulk of muscle thick on its legs, chest, and shoulders. These had the appearance of steel cables that had been knotted together.

Thick neck attached to a large head that ended in a long, powerful snout full of teeth, dripping saliva as though it could already taste its prey. And it was staring directly at him.

****

Thomas Keeler had begun some heavy thinking about this last meeting with the Death Spirits. What had they meant when stating that Lisa had been guided towards this moment leading her to him?

It wasn't what they had said exactly, but how it had been said. He could read between the lines.

A person had to watch the spirits very close. Sometimes, they spoke in riddles that confused most men. The Death spirits had been known to speak in half-truths, and if you didn't pay attention, you could end up in a world of trouble.

This last conversation had left him not only unassured but troubled as he read more into what he felt were their true meanings. Running every word spoken through his memory, he looked at each statement made from every direction he could. Each way he took them didn't add up, and he did not like the conclusions he came to.

Keeler was a wise man. I'm not saying that he was smarter than most; he just had a way of looking and listening not only to things said but *to* them. It was with this approach that he decided the best course of action would be to try and stop Lisa from performing the ceremony at all.

He was positive that it was too late for that, though. Thomas had felt the energies that dwelt in nature spike in abundance at the stroke of midnight. Strong enough waves with enough momentum that he'd had to use an alternate invocation than normal when he called the Death Spirits. One that didn't involve nature's forces.

The old man often spoke to himself in times of deep inspiration, but now it was as if he were having a full-blown conversation. He was lost in the possible ramifications that could occur trying to impede what the spirits had intended.

Taking a second carry-all out of the closet, he began to fill it with tools of arcane nature – spell components and other "accessories" that might be needed. Without realizing it, he had already chosen his preferred course of action in this matter. Stop the Daemon and lure him back to the sacred grounds, bind him once again, and send him back to the Netherworld. Both would be damn near impossible.

"There," he thought as he took inventory of his travel cases. He had thrown it together so quickly that he had to go back through it to make sure he had a suitable array of implements. Enough to suit his need in any foreseeable occurrence that might be thrown his way. Thomas did not like surprises. This event, he knew, had been caused by himself and the trusting of the specters.

He took his cases and 'equipment' out to his old Dodge, throwing everything in the back. There was no telling how long he would be gone if he made it back at all. Thomas was positive the old truck would make the trip. He kept it in excellent running order, though it was rarely driven.

He went to his water meter, turned the main valve off then proceeded to the main breaker box at the rear of the garage, where he then shut off the main power to the house. He always disabled these whenever trips were taken without an exact return date. If he made it back, he didn't want to find that his home had burned to the ground.

Locking the house up tight, he made his way to the fenced-in backyard, lifting Dakota's leash off the peg by the gate. He would take his only true companion to the veterinarians for boarding on his way off the reservation.

Thomas put the German Shepherd in the passenger seat and then climbed behind the wheel. He sat there for a moment longer, staring at his home, wondering if he would ever step foot back in it again. The knowledge was there that this likely would be a one-way trip.

In the case that he perished in this endeavor, he had only one nephew left to carry the bloodline of the White witches. There were no sons or daughters to pass everything to as his ancestors had done the last forty or so generations. He had never married. All of his time and devotion had been spent on his love of magic.

The magic had utterly consumed his life; now, it looked as if it would also devour him in death. There were no regrets, no sorrows. With a heavy sigh, He turned the ignition, and the old Dodge roared to life. Shaking his head, he shifted into first gear, pulling away from the house.

With a rare smile, he looked in the mirror. "Why not? I've never been to Bristol."

CHAPTER NINE:

REALIZATION/ NEIL'S DEATH

When she saw Neil spin and take off down the mountain and the Daemon leave in pursuit, Lisa felt as if she needed to do something. But she was stunned by the events that had taken place in such a short amount of time and how they had all gone wrong. It was all she could do to straighten herself up from the slumped position she had been in.

Lisa sat looking around at what was left of the ceremonial fire. Nothing but charred earth. The implements used were scattered, chalice blackened and cracked. The dagger had been broken in two, separating the blade from the handle.

Glancing down, she saw the backpacks within arms reach, most of the contents strewn upon the ground. Her eyes lit upon what was left of the bottle of bourbon and a hot Pepsi. She picked these up, opened the whiskey, and downed a mouthful, bypassing the chaser. Maybe it would help clear her head some.

The fiery liquor burned all the way to her stomach, almost making her wretch. It did seem to wake her up a bit, though. Most of the things that had happened from the time she inquired of brother moon, to Chivas making his unnatural appearance, seemed like a dream. She couldn't recall anything in the first-person sense. It had been as though she were watching a movie.

She did know that she needed to get the hell up and find her way back to the road to get some help. Taking one more drink, she screwed the lid on and set the bottle down by her pack, looking around in search of her clothes.

Locating them under some brush, she crawled over to them. Knowing she needed to hurry, but her body nor mind were cooperating much at this point. Picking her jeans up, she lay back and slid them on. Forget the panties.

Grabbing the shirt, she gingerly worked it over her bruised shoulders with the same opinion of the bra that she had with her underwear. To hell with them. She was too sore and too tired to mess with them. Pulling on her socks and boots, she finally worked up enough courage to look at Rick. His body was face up as though observing the pre-dawn sky.

His left arm was resting across his chest while the right sprawled out beside him, broken in at least two places she could tell of. The shattered end of his forearm stuck out about four inches through the skin at his elbow. Worst of all was his abdomen, split wide open, revealing every bit of his intestines and internal organs as if on display in a biology classroom.

Holding on to the nearest tree trunk for support, Lisa stood upright and moved around some, easing into it to make sure everything worked correctly. After a few seconds of this, she walked over to stand above the inert body of her best friend. Tears running unchecked down her face, she kneeled and gently lifted Becky's head. She scooted her legs under, easing the girl on her lap.

"I'm sorry. So, so sorry," she muttered over and over while brushing Becky's hair out with her fingers. "It's all my fault. I never should have gotten you involved in any of this."

At that moment, Lisa heard extreme cries of pain coming from halfway down the mountain. Two more casualties that were her fault. How many more would she have to bear the weight of?

"I never would have believed Neil would have gotten that far," she numbly thought. "I've got to go."

Easing Becky's head upon a pillow of leaves, she stood up and stared at the heavens, asking for one more favor.

"Lord, please watch over my friends and make them feel at home when they get there. I know after the things I have done, I won't be joining them, but let them know I love them. For good or bad, I'm going to fix this."

With that being said, Lisa set off walking towards the Holston Trail, trying to avoid the Daemon. She would make her way back to the road a different route. It'll take a little longer, but she felt safer this way. Then, she hoped to find help in one fashion or the other.

****

Neil knew that he had been spotted. The wolf was glaring at him with a look of intense hatred in its eyes of silver. It hadn't moved an inch yet. Only staring. He reasoned that he only had two choices. He could stay where he was hoping it was only suspicious of the rocks and overhang, or burst out running, take it by surprise, and maybe lose it again.

Opting for the latter, he leapt up and out between the limbs taking off at full speed, still heading in a diagonal direction. He was going downhill trusting that would help speed him up to take a quick lead while the thing was still standing there.

His instincts told him that this reckless pace in the dark was liable to cause injury to himself before it caught him, and he knew it would. What did he have to lose? A few minutes of adrenaline-pumping terror?

Tree branches smacked him in the face, leaving whelps and scratches. That didn't bother him so much as the knowledge of what was behind him. What did annoy him, was looking back to see that he had not gained one second by exploding out of cover. As a matter of fact, he had lost ground. The beast seemed to be loping along at a leisurely pace yet still closing the gap.

The moonlight showed through an opening in the treetops, illuminating what Neil recognized to be the lower half of the Flint Mill Trail. He had come back around. Guessing he was two-thirds of the way down, he glanced in the direction of the road. There, a single pair of headlights is shown through the brush for only a moment. Oh, how he wished he were in that vehicle safe and sound.

"That's not in the cards tonight, buddy," he said to himself.

Neil tried to get his legs to move faster, but there wasn't enough energy left in him. He began side-stepping in and around trees and brush, trying to at least throw the beast in a slowing zig-zag pattern. Always changing direction which, to his dismay, did not impede it one bit. If anything, the wolf sped up, bypassing the brush and second-guessing his next move.

He finally came to the conclusion that he was caught. The only thing to do was to stand and fight as best he could, hoping to injure it somewhat in order to buy some more time. Maybe enough to make it to the road. If he was lucky enough to get to his truck, he had it made.

As he continued on as fast as possible for a man his age and physical shape (God, he wished he had worked out more), he made a mental checklist of anything that could be used as a weapon. There were only two on his person, his nine-millimeter with two extra clips and the hunting knife strapped to his side. Figuring that if worse came to worse, there were usually some sticks with sharp ends lying around.

When Neil stepped foot onto the Trail, he came to a sudden stop, unholstering his pistol as he spun around to face his attacker. He ejected the empty clip from before with his right hand as he grabbed a full one with his left. As the empty hit the ground, he was already slamming the new clip in place, taking aim in the direction he had just come from.

Moving the barrel from side to side, trying to find his pursuer, he found, to his confusion, that all was quiet. Nothing in his line of sight, nor was there any noise. It was as if he had never been chased down the mountain at all. He knew for a damn fact that he hadn't been hallucinating the past couple of hours.

If that were the case, then all he had witnessed at the top had been his imagination. Rick would still be alive as well as Becky. They would be fine, standing around waiting for him to regain his sanity. But that was not the reality of it. He felt as if he were in Hell.

Wiping the sweat from his forehead, he continued to watch everything in sight. Both straight ahead and in his peripheral vision. Listening to the quietness surrounding him paying attention to the slightest snap of a twig, the scuffling of leaves.

Nothing. That was all he heard. The nothingness of the mountain in the eerie darkness of the morning hours. It seemed as if all of nature were waiting. Watching to see who would be the victor. Or, maybe he was losing his mind. It could be that simple.

A split second later, Neil knew that he was completely sane as he felt the hot breath on the back of his neck. Damnit, while he had been standing here second-guessing himself, the wolf had circled around and snuck up behind him. How, without making a single sound, he didn't know.

It hadn't struck him yet, although it was only a matter of time. Afraid to turn for a look, he just stood there feeling breath after breath heat his back up. It was toying with him. Gathering every nerve in him, he spun around, taking no aim, pulling the trigger four times in rapid succession. It had disappeared. He was staring at empty space. What the fuck?

Now, he was getting agitated and angry. "If you're going to kill me, let's just get it over with," he yelled into the darkness.

As Neil stood at the ready, something hit him from the right. Hard. The blow slammed him into a large rock beside the trail. Feeling as though he had been pulverized by a wrecking ball, he looked up, expecting to see the death blow coming. There was nothing.

However, this time, the wolf wasn't as silent as before. He could hear it roaming back and forth behind him. He rose to his knees and started to stand when the beast smoothly walked in front of him. It bent its head to stare him eye to eye.

Neil began to raise his right hand when he realized the gun had been knocked away from him when he was hit. He stood the rest of the way up, plucking his knife from its sheath. As the wolf leaped for him, he brought his hand around in a sweeping motion, burying the blade in its shoulder to the hilt.

Expecting to at least stagger the beast, he withdrew the knife and plunged down with it again. This time, the blade entered the beast's neckline while he wrapped his left arm around its head. He was hoping to hold it still long enough for another thrust. Instead, the animal's powerful jaws clamped down on his bicep, crushing bone. It twisted its head, slinging him against the rock once again.

Neil let out his first sound of pain as he hit, both hearing and feeling his collarbone snap. He was finished. There was no fight left in him, he thought as the wolf made its way to him and smacked him across the face, slicing his cheek to ribbons.

He had heard that when you're facing imminent death, your life flashes before your eyes. Well, Neil didn't know about that, but a hundred memories flooded his mind in those last few moments. Almost all of the happiest times in his life had been spent on this mountain. Now, he was going to die here.

"At least I'm where I should be," he thought as the beast sunk teeth deep into his throat, destroying his jugular vein and crushing his spine. He drew in his last breath and tried to voice his final words. All that came out was a gasp.

****

Kevin Miller had agreed with Jeff when it was mentioned that it might be best to wait until six in the morning to leave for the mountain. They weren't doing any actual hunting, only scouting the woods, searching for the trails most used by deer. That would give them a couple of hours of much-needed rest.

Arriving back at the Miller's residence, they had said their parting goodnights, Jeff and Casey heading back to Hickory Tree. Angie was getting ready for bed while Kevin kicked back in the recliner for one more beer.

He thought he had better call Rick and leave him a message as to the time change. He picked up the phone and dialed the number.

Sheila, Rick's wife, answered sleepily on the fourth ring. She informed him that Rick had left earlier with Neil, but she would make sure he got the message.

Hanging up the telephone, he wondered why the two would get together. Neil had plainly stated that he was hunting Shady Valley this year while Rick would be on Holston with them. Hell, maybe they were just out cruising across the mountain having a few beers together, talking about how Jeff and I work their asses off, he thought.

Nah, they were likely pumped up about archery season coming in, couldn't sleep, and wanted to go see what was moving in the dark. Rick had better be getting home to rest soon though. He didn't need him dragging ass and lagging behind.

He heard Angie come to the bottom of the stairs and turned to look at her when she cleared her throat. She always did that when she wanted his attention. When he saw her standing there in a see-through negligee, motioning him to come to bed, he killed the rest of the beer.

He kicked off his shoes as he rose from the chair; seconds later, he was by her side. Not saying a word, she took him by the hand, leading him up the stairs to the bedroom. The lights were cut off on the way.

He sat on the edge of the bed as she made her way around the other side, climbing on the mattress to ease up behind him.

Playfully, Angie began kissing along the side of his neck, nibbling on the tip of his ear.

Kevin moved around, rolling onto the bed and pulling her down. He removed her nightgown as she unbuttoned his jeans. He reached over to the lamp on the nightstand, turned the knob killing the light, and rolled back over to his wife.

CHAPTER TEN:

CHIVAS/ THE DREAM

Chivas, still in his wolfen form, sat back on his haunches to stare at the man who had so dared to intrude upon him as he was having the most fun in centuries. This man must have been very brave to have faced off with him the way he did. Most humans would have kept fleeing until he ended their lives.

Most would have carried the smell of cowardice, but not this one. Yes, he could smell fear on this man, only it was mixed with the scent of determination, courageousness, and cunning. The human had turned to fight even when he knew there had been no hope.

And what of the other one that had run to him, attacking him with the knife after witnessing his rise from the flames of the Netherworld? Or the woman who had boldly attained the courage to summon him to this world without fear for herself or the one standing with her. She certainly was no witch, and there hadn't been a single one dressed in the garments he would have expected.

Time had passed while he had been banished, and the world had moved on. It was as simple as that. He would have to adapt. But in these times which he arose, were there warriors at every turn? What advances in power and knowledge had there been? In the woman, though not one of the arcane arts, Chivas had felt a true power emanating from her soul.

Although she did not complete or perform the summoning spell correctly, he knew that it had been in the way that she had been instructed. Maybe she did not realize that she had a natural grasp of the spiritual and magical capabilities that he had strongly sensed in her being.

Taking in his surroundings, the Daemon began to recognize the area he was in. Things had changed so much over the last couple of hundred years that most of the landmarks were gone. The path he was on at this moment reminded him of the trail that Chief Pathkiller's tribe had taken to the long man or river.

He knew that following it on to the water and bear to his right would bring him to a white man's settlement that he used to visit. After all these years, it must have changed remarkably so. He decided he would have a look.

As he pushed to a standing position with his hind legs, he morphed back into human form. He stretched to relieve the mild bunching of his muscles as they changed mass. When he took on another form, he preferred the wolf persona over the dragon because he felt more agile. Whereas, with the reptile form, he could do much more damage and take on more adversaries at once.

The dragon was also a mythical creature to humans, so when he used it, it threw them into a state of confusion. This caused them to lose their perspective of battle for a minute, giving him the extra advantage.

Chivas pondered a moment where to start besides making his way to the river. The four names the woman had used in the ceremony suddenly rushed to the front of his mind. No matter if she had not performed the spell exactly, those sacrifices were mandatory.

He identified Kevin Miller as the main target, so still being his rebellious self, he decided he would get around to it *after* he had made his own agenda. Once he'd had some fun, this man would be the first to find.

"If this one is as fearless as the others, it will make for a great battle if I were to stay in human form." He pondered out loud.

Chivas began walking down the trail, trying to get used to the feel of this new footwear. His masters had clothed him when he had finished with the girl. Normally, he hardly ever wore moccasins, much less these heavy, thick boots.

As he descended, the landscape began to change drastically from what he remembered, and then, he came upon the gravel road. Here, it lost him; he had no idea what could have made this path until his wonder grew as he spotted the horseless wagons. Of course, he knew nothing of motorized vehicles.

He figured that what was needed was for him to go somewhere to gain the knowledge of these times. He hoped the settlement was still where he remembered it to be. Turning that direction anyway,

Chivas whistled an old tune as he walked carelessly onward. The Daemon looked into the woods on both sides of the road, trying to spot anything he recognized from the past.

All this surrounding him had been thick with Oaks, Hickory, spruce, and cedar. Now, it was easy to see that most of the land had been cleared somewhat. It had been thinned out so many times only to grow back into new thickets, leading to different clearings. Some of the old trails were now as wide as this gravel one.

After he had been walking for an hour, he came around a bend in the road when a smaller, horseless conveyance came into view. At this one, there were two men standing at one end of it. One of them was smoking, the other lifting a bottle of brownish liquid to his mouth. When they had spotted him, both men waved him over.

****

Kevin had just climbed into his tree stand and strapped himself in the safety harness he had removed from his backpack. He turned, settling in the seat, admiring a beautiful sun rising over the crest of the ridge he was watching when suddenly, he heard something walking the path he had come up moments before.

He froze in place, not moving a muscle. Moderated his breathing making as little sound as possible. He was hoping for a look at the animal coming towards him without spooking it. If it was the buck that he had spotted while scouting, he was taking it.

Ever so silent, he turned his head inch by inch until he had a clear view of the small animal trail he had hiked in to his stand on.

He could hear the leaves crunching under the feet of whatever was approaching. The slow, steady pace led him to believe it was either a human or a bear. Black bears were plentiful on the mountain. They were moving, foraging for food before their long winter hibernation.

He had, in the past, seen several bears at the forks of the trail where the Josiah split into two directions. The path off to the left leads to a big feeding area cleared out by the TWRA long ago. It amounted to a three-acre field surrounded by greenery, wild fruit, and nut-bearing trees.

When they weren't eating from the trees, the field supported grasses akin to hay. The deer loves to graze here as well as bed down in the tall greenery as it provides plenty of cover. You had to be careful if you hunted around the field, though. Startle them enough times, and they expect you to be there, diminishing the chances of seeing one at all.

The path to the right led deeper into the mountain, all the way past the wild grapevines, which was one hell of a hike in itself. If you reached the furthest ridge beyond the vines, you came to road number ninety. Ninety was another gravel road that was cut off for public use. The only vehicle traffic with access to it were the TWRA and the Game wardens. Certain logging companies gained limited use with the right permits.

Sometimes, during the archery season, the barricades were unlocked for temporary hunters' use. Not many took advantage of this opportunity for fear of someone locking the gate on them. Then you were just stuck until the TVA or Wardens came out to unlock it.

From the point where the Josiah split, there was a "cutout," an extreme stand of small trees and brush growing back from being logged out years ago. It was so dense that it was impossible to fight your way through it without sounding like a thrashing machine.

That ran to the left for about three hundred yards. Kevin's stand was on a knoll to the right of this, where he could watch both, it and the flat leading up to a small ridge in front of him. Both bear and deer loved the cover of the clear-cut, so he figured one had followed him out, curious from the little noise he had made.

The noise quieted as if the person or animal had stopped. Maybe it had seen him and was having second thoughts of advancing any further. He turned his attention back to getting settled in the stand for the day, hanging his pack on a hook screwed into a branch on his right.

He then drew an arrow out of the quiver attached to the side of his Mathews bow, nocked it, and suspended it on a hook screwed in on his left. With that finished, he could sit back, relax, and watch the area for any deer traveling within his range.

After a few minutes of enjoying the sights and sounds of the woods, waking up, and coming to life in the morning sunlight, he heard it again. Whatever or whomever it was had begun moving along the path behind him again; he set his gaze upon the trail, waiting to see what had decided to move on his way.

He first saw a head, then shoulders appearing over the small knoll, becoming a full silhouette of a female dressed in jeans and a t-shirt. As the woman approached the tree which housed his stand, full recognition set in bringing his mind into a state of confusion.

It had been many years since he had been in this close proximity to her; he knew this woman. Knew her well. For at one time, she had been as close to him as any sister could have, and now, legally, she was his sister-in-law. Looking at her on the ground, he noticed that her clothes were in disarray.

One leg of her jeans had been torn, as well as parts of her shirt, which seemed to be soaked in what looked like blood. It ran from her neck, down the left side, along the rib cage, across her stomach, and onto the waist of her pants.

She only stood there, staring up at him with her arms hanging loose at her sides, tears flowing down her cheeks. It was obvious to him that something bad had occurred, and she or someone was in trouble. But how did she know where to find him?

"Lisa," Kevin spoke. "What's happened? Are you alright?"

She continued to stare up at him, almost as if looking through him, which only served to puzzle him more. He was almost beyond worried, and now he was starting to get angry at her silence. She had not uttered a sound since coming into view. Had not given any explanation as to her appearance or the reason for being here, period. Just that damn accusing stare.

Before he could question her again, she raised an arm, finger extended, and pointed at the top of the ridge he had been watching. She spoke one word. "Hurry."

Turning his gaze in the direction she was pointing, he swept his vision from left to right and back again. He looked at the entire crest of the ridge that was within his eyesight. Nothing. He brought his scrutiny further down, scanning the hillside.

"Hurry," he heard again.

"Damnit, I'm looking. There isn't anything. What the hell are you trying to show me?" He replied while overlooking the hillside a second time, then a third.

Taking a quick glance down at Lisa again to make sure he was searching the area she was pointing to, he noticed there was blood trickling down her forehead now. It seemed to be coming from her hairline. Becoming more worried by the minute, he turned his vision back to the ridge.

This time he did see some movement on the left, just a few yards below the top. The figure appeared to be that of a tall, muscular man of Native American descent. His waist-length hair swayed in the breeze as he casually walked along as if for a morning stroll.

"Hurry," Lisa repeated.

Reaching for the clip that would release him from the safety harness, his eyes caught movement cresting the peak of the ridge. This one appeared to be female, and she was walking straight towards his stand, not noticing the male approaching her position.

This one he recognized also. It was Angie. She was wearing her solid white sundress, one of her favorites. It was decorated with light blue butterflies. He had bought this one for her just this past Easter.

"Hurry."

As Angie descended the hill, coming right at him, the long-haired male altered his course to intercept her. While he watched on, Kevin noticed the fingernails on the man's hands elongate into gleaming razor-sharp blades. He looked at Kevin with a pair of bright silver eyes, such as he had never before seen.

He stood up, trying to get the harness unclipped, but it was stuck. Raising his head up, he screamed for Angie to run, but she acted like she didn't hear him. The male was closing in on her fast. He began to laugh, still staring at Kevin.

"Hurry." Lisa's voice came again.

Yanking on the release clip as hard as he could, he watched in horror as the man came up beside Angie. The stranger grabbed his wife by the hair and jerked her head back, exposing her throat. Kevin looked down at Lisa, wondering why she hadn't run to help her sister but merely stood there staring up at him and pointing.

Just as the clip let go, he heard a ringing sound. Something hit him in the back, knocking him out of the tree stand. As Kevin fell towards the ground, he closed his eyes only to open them a second later to Angie laying over and poking him.

"Are you going to answer the phone?" She sleepily asked.

He had been dreaming… Shit.

****

Kevin answered the phone, still half-asleep, the dream weighing heavily on his mind. The memory of it triggered a deep uneasiness as he tried to erase it from his now-awakening consciousness. It had seemed all too real to him. He felt as if he could have acted upon any aspect of it, and it would have developed into reality.

Though fully awake now, he could still smell the outdoors and feel the roughness of the tree bark on his hands. Still faintly, yet nevertheless, I hear the birds chirping and the leaves crunching underfoot.

"Hello?"

"Hey Kev. It's Jeff. I was just making sure you were up. I'm getting my things together, so I'll be heading your way in about forty-five minutes."

"Yeah. That'll be good. It will give me time to get some coffee in me and talk to Angie for a minute. My stuff is already in the back of my truck. You can park yours here, and we'll take mine." Kevin replied.

"That's fine. Are you going to call and get Rick up, or do you want me to?" Jeff asked.

"Hell, I called last night, and Sheila told me that he and Neil took off riding through the mountain road. She said she'd tell him of the time change in plans." Kevin told him.

"What were they doing out riding together? I thought they could barely stand each other at work. Never mind. I'll give him a ring and let him know we'll be on our way shortly." Jeff said.

"Alright, buddy. See you soon."

Ending the call, Kevin got up and walked over to a small closet in the corner of the bedroom. He had built this to store nothing except his hunting and other outdoor clothing. As he opened the closet, he could smell the aroma of fresh coffee permeating the house. Angie had gone on and started the brew for him instead of going back to sleep.

"Hey, Ange," he hollered down at her. "Don't fix anything to eat. I think Jeff and I will just grab a couple of sausage biscuits at the store on the way."

"Okay," she replied. "Just the coffee, then."

The weather forecast for the day was the prediction of the sun with the high temperatures in the upper seventies to eighty degrees. He chose a thin pair of Realtree camouflage bib overalls covering an ultra-thin long-sleeve shirt.

Grabbing his water-proof Redhead hunting boots, he went to the rocking chair beside the door and sat down, sliding them on. He sat back for a moment and closed his eyes, reliving parts of the dream. He couldn't figure out what triggered that type, though. His entire life, Kevin had never had nightmares, so to him, this was disturbing.

After a couple of minutes had passed, and not coming up with any explanation, he rose from the chair and went to the bathroom to relieve himself and brush his hair. Noticing a few strands of gray on his head, he pulled them out with a grimace. His grandpa had always told him that if you pulled one out, two more would grow in its place.

Looking in the mirror, he shrugged to himself, walked out, and headed downstairs. As he passed through the living room, Kevin stopped by the gun cabinet and unlocked it, picking out his Glock forty-millimeter and two extra clips to go with it. Then, after strapping on the shoulder holster, he attached his Gerber Knife and sheath to his side.

Closing and relocking the gun cabinet door, he then continued into the kitchen, sitting at the table as Angie placed a cup of coffee in front of him. Thinking things over, he decided that maybe he would feel better if he told of the dream and got her opinion on it.

"Sit with me a minute," he asked her.

"Baby, I have a wild idea," she said, sitting in the chair facing him. "Why don't you call Jeff back and postpone your little exploration for the day? I'll call in sick, and we can lock ourselves in the bedroom all day like we used to."

"That sounds nice," he replied. "But then the school would have to get a last-minute sub, and your classes would go all to hell. Then we'd have Jeff beating on the windows and doors all day just for meanness."

"Yeah, you're right." She agreed. "You have something on your mind. I can see it plain as day. Do you want to tell me about it?"

"Well, it's kind of both a question and a tell. First of all, I want you to be careful and aware of your surroundings today. Promise me that." Kevin said.

"Why? You've never asked me to do something like that before. What do you know that I don't?" She asked.

"I had a dream. No, call it what it was. A nightmare. Now quit smiling; I'm not joking." He told her.

"Okay. Tell me about it. Maybe going back over it will ease your mind." Angie replied.

So, he started from the very beginning. By the time he had finished describing the dream to her in detail, Angie had a thoughtful but bemused expression on her face. Kevin sat there in silence to give her a few minutes to mull things over in her head. She stood up, picking the cups up, noticing they both needed a refill.

She stood at the coffee pot and looked out the window for a moment. He could tell that she was trying to take him seriously. Angie was like that. She didn't make fun of anyone no matter how silly something may sound., there was a reason behind everything. That was the Full Cherokee blood in her.

"Why do you think that after all these years, you dreamed of Lisa?" She asked. Her back was still to him.

"I don't know. That's not my main concern. What worries me is that maybe this nightmare was a warning or a sign that she will be in trouble and you'll come to her aid." Kevin said.

"That's what sisters do you know." Came the reply.

"I know that. But the thing is that according to the dream, you will be attacked on your way to her." He continued. "I still can't figure out the man or why he would harm you unless it was only to stop you from helping her."

"Have you heard something from Neil or Larry that led you to believe she's in some kind of trouble?" Angie inquired.

"No. Look, it was probably just a dream, and my subconscious was throwing in random people from my past. It might be nothing." Kevin said.

"Maybe," Angie said with hesitation in her voice.

He could tell that she was assessing the implications of the dream. Her parents had raised her with most Cherokee beliefs, and to them, dreams were visions of things yet to come. They all had a reason and meaning behind them.

They saw the headlights turn up the driveway and heard the horn blow. Jeff had arrived. Gathering the few things on the table, he finished his java and put his arms around her. He gave her a kiss on the lips, pat on the ass, and started for the door. Before closing it behind him, he looked at her and smiled.

"It's probably nothing. You know how I let my imagination run wild sometimes. Don't let it consume your day. I'll be home right after dark, if not before then. Love you."

"Love you too," Angie replied as he pulled the door shut.

Turning around and pouring herself another cup, she stared at the wall. Lost in her thoughts, replaying the vision she had just described.

****

CHAPTER ELEVEN:

RUNNING INTO AN OLD FRIEND

Jeff had backed his truck in beside Kevin's and was busy transferring his gear over to the Z-71. Kevin strode out to the vehicles to help finish.

"What did you bring the stand for?" he asked.

"Just in case I find a good spot early enough to set it up for an alternate site. I'm still going to do my main hunting near the grapevines." Jeff replied.

Both men climbed into the cab, strapping into their seatbelts. Kevin's Glock forty and extra clips were deposited into the center console safely tucked away. He took one last look at the house with an uneasy feeling as he turned right onto Allison Road. Why, he didn't know.

"Did you talk to Rick?" Jeff asked.

"No. I called twice. Sheila answered the second time and said that he never came home. She guessed they went ahead and waited on daylight, then went on in the woods." Kevin replied.

"That's fine. He should have at least let us know."

"Yeah. Which way do you want to go in?" Kevin asked. "The Hickory Tree side or up 421?"

"I don't care. We're not pushed for time, so let's stop at Pardners and get some breakfast." Jeff answered.

"Alright. Then we'll go around the river and check if any deer are out in the fields this morning. We'll hit the mountain on the Hickory Tree side." Kevin stated.

He reached into his pocket and drew out a cigarette, lit it, and rolled the window down to let out the smoke. The sun was beginning to crest the horizon brightening up the morning as the fog began to lift. He just knew it was going to be a beautiful day. If they could get in and find a few spots to place their stands and be out on the way home before dark, that would be perfect.

Pulling into the restaurant, he noticed there were more customers there than normal for a Friday morning. The parking lot was almost full. Having to park in the lower gravel lot, he and Jeff took their time walking to the entrance, allowing Kevin to finish his smoke. Entering the dining area, they were glad to see one of their favorite tables empty.

Ellen, their preferred waitress, had seen the boys walk in and was already pouring coffee into the two cups on the table. She had worked here for over twenty years and knew her regulars well. They looked at her expectantly.

"The usual?" Ellen asked.

"You got it," Kevin replied, adding cream and sugar to his java.

After the waitress had left for the kitchen with their order, Jeff looked up at him. In the full light of the restaurant, Kevin appeared as though he had more than just eating and scouting on his mind. Actually, he looked as if he hadn't slept well.

"Hey. You look a little preoccupied over there. Something bothering you this morning?" Jeff asked him.

"Not really. I just had this strange dream that I can't shake. It seemed all too real." Kevin replied as he took another sip of his coffee.

"Nightmare, or just plain strange?"

"Forget I said anything. It's just bullshit anyway." Kevin said.

Shrugging, Jeff started to pick up his phone when Ellen brought their plates out to them and placed them on the table. As she re-filled their coffee she asked if there would be anything else.

"No. Give us about ten minutes then bring the check. Thanks." Jeff told her.

While eating, Kevin looked around the dining room at the unusual Friday breakfast crowd. He noticed there was a lot of camouflage being worn today. Most of the guys he knew. Clarence and Bobby in the last booth, Danny and Jacob Fleenor two tables down, men who ran their own businesses like he and Jeff. They could take the day off without question.

He also knew the Fleenor boys hunted on some private land next to Iron Mountain while Clarence and Bobby would be heading over to Shady, where Neil said he was hunting. Ellen brought the bill as he was finishing his last bite to which Jeff took it from her and stated he was buying. Kevin left a five-dollar tip and stopped by the Fleenor's table, wishing them a good day.

Jeff had beaten him to the truck and was already seated and ready to go. He fired up the Chevrolet, pulled onto the road, and turned in the direction of Bluff City, then onto River Road. The pair would be hitting the gravel mountain road in twenty-five minutes. He turned on the radio for a little John-Boy and Billy, laughing when a snoozing Jeff jumped at the sudden noise.

Yep. It was going to be a good day.

****

Lisa had left everything where it lay at the top. She didn't even bring the flashlights. After all that had happened, the hell that had broken loose, she wanted nothing to do with any of it. It only would have served as a constant reminder of the past few hours.

The deaths, what she had freed on humanity, were all on her. Now, though, all she needed to be thinking of was getting some help. Maybe contact Keeler again? He was the one who had instructed her wrong to begin with. Why would he help her now?

The knowledge at the forefront of her mind was the fact that three of her friends were now dead because of her and her stupid ideas of revenge over something that happened long ago. An accident, that's all it had been, yet she had blamed Kevin and those in the hunting party with him. God had simply decided it was time for her little brother to leave this world.

The going was slow. She was having trouble negotiating the trail in the pre-dawn light. If she wasn't careful, an ankle or leg could be broken, leaving her stranded up here for days. She had told no one where she was going. Another dumbass move.

Crossing over onto the Holston trail in order to cut down the chances of running into the Daemon, she found the going was a bit easier. This way would take her longer, but it was a moderate slope instead of the steep, rocky Flint Mill. She began to try and think of someone whom she could trust to help.

If Lisa went to the Sheriff's office with a tale like this, she would be charged with the murders herself. That, or they'd lock her up in a mental institution somewhere. Hers was not a believable story to be told, and no amount of sugarcoating could make it sound plausible.

The first person she thought of that would've given her the benefit of the doubt and at least come check it out was Neil. But it was too late for him. He was laying somewhere over on the Flint Mill or near it anyway, dead that she was sure of. Larry? Maybe? Hell, he was probably still out with some ladies, stoned off his rocker.

As she thought of this predicament she was in, the sun made its way skyward, providing her with some much-needed light. She was able to increase her pace quite a bit. After what seemed like days to her, she spied some stretches of the gravel road through the breaks in the tree line. At the sight of this, she amplified her speed, bringing herself to a fast jog.

Finally, she was able to stop, feet firm on the road, hands on her hips. As she caught her breath, she looked up and down the road, hoping to catch a ride the mile or so back to her truck. Not seeing anyone, she began walking.

Lisa had made it a hundred yards when the sounds of an approaching vehicle drew her attention. She already had a story made up in explanation for her rough appearance. Claim that she had been hiking and became lost in the woods after dark. It happened.

After hitching a ride to her F-150, she could determine where to go for help. Maybe as far away as the reservation again. She could try Nate Duncan first. He was a friend of her father's and also a Game Warden. His territory was over in Carter County, but they had jurisdiction in the entire state.

She stopped and turned, looking in the direction of the oncoming vehicle as it made its way around the curve. Lisa recognized the Z-71 almost immediately.

"Shit," she thought. "Of all people, it just had to be him."

****

Kevin had turned off of Flatwoods Road onto Camp Tom Howard, the actual name of the gravel mountain road. He slowed to a speed of ten miles per hour, thus giving them a better chance to see any movement back in the brush.

Neither man said anything as they rode. They didn't have to, both had been riding together, watching for animals on this road for years. And when they were on foot in the woods, they communicated with a few hand signals and a series of low grunts. The two of them understood each other well whether anybody else did or not.

This morning had proved noteworthy so far, having had three deer cross mere feet from the front bumper not even a half-mile in. They snapped a few pictures and drew a crude map of the location. Noted the time, temperature, and weather. All these had varying effects on deer and their movement.

Continuing on, they spotted more places that had been used as road crossings for the animals. Eight miles into their journey, they rounded a curve to see a lone female walking along the side. The woman carried no equipment at all. Then she turned and looked at them.

Kevin recognized who it was before the girl's head turn was completed. The dream from the night before came rushing at him like a freight train. He slammed on the brakes in momentary panic. Jeff's knees hit the dashboard, causing him to let out a string of profanities.

Sitting there, staring at her, Kevin broke out in a cold sweat. He was trying to sort out the connection between dream and reality. What was she doing here? This happenstance coming on the heels of the nightmare had left him speechless. He knew that it meant something. Occurrences like this did not happen often or without meaning.

Jeff had no idea what was going on. Oh, he knew enough of the history of these two and that this was Angie's sister. He knew of the accident that had taken their brother Leeland's life. He had also heard rumors that Lisa had been vowing to exact revenge on Kevin for that accident but just chalked that up to talk. Too much time had passed.

However, Kevin's reaction to her being here, seeing her for the first time in years, spoke volumes. His buddy looked as if he had seen a ghost. He was pale, sweating, and his hands were shaking like a leaf.

"Hey Kev, are you alright?" Jeff asked. "Is that who I think it is?"

"Yeah. It's Lisa." Came a weak reply.

"What do you think she's doing up here?" Jeff asked

"I have no idea, but I guess we'd better find out. She looks a little rough."

"Well. You look peaked yourself." Jeff stated. "Are you sure you don't want to just drive on by her? Someone else will stop."

"No. If she's broken down or hurt, Angie would never forgive me." Kevin said. "At least we can make a call for her."

Lisa was just standing by the side of the road, hands on her hips, staring at them. Not making any gestures or motions. Only staring. The same as in the dream. After a few seconds of this stare-down, she stepped off the gravel and sat on the ground. Her head was bowed as in defeat.

"Might as well," Kevin said more to himself, easing the truck up beside her.

"Hey," Jeff spoke out the window.

"Hey yourself," Lisa replied, eyes never leaving the dirt. "You might want to turn around and go home."

"What do you mean by that?" Jeff inquired.

"Get your wives, pack some clothes, and get out of town for a while." She continued. "Things are about to go all to Hell around here until I can fix something."

CHAPTER TWELVE:

JOINING THE MADNESS

At this statement, the two men looked at each other with puzzled expressions on their faces, Both shrugging their shoulders in unison. Coming to a hasty decision, Kevin opened his door and exited the truck. Jeff followed suit. He walked around to stand in front of Lisa, facing her in silence, waiting for her to explain herself.

When she raised her head to look up at him, he could see tears flowing over her cheeks. All the confusion and curiosity acquired these past minutes was replaced with concern. He noticed the cuts and bruises on her face and neck. He glanced over her clothing, noting the streaks of dried blood. She appeared to still be bleeding from along her ribcage.

When his eyes rested on the tear in her blue jeans, the images from the dream came back to him with a vengeance. The blood streaks, the tear in her Levi's, they were in the exact same places. He was overwhelmed for a moment, finally able to regain control of his senses.

Gentle but forceful, he reached down, taking her by the arm. Getting her to her feet, he and Jeff examined her to make sure she wasn't hurt or bleeding anywhere else. Lisa glared at him when he reached into his back pocket, removing a handkerchief. This he wet with water from his bottle and began wiping the dirt and blood from her face.

"What happened?" Kevin asked.

"Nothing that I can't handle. I don't need you." She said, her voice rising. "Just take me to my truck, get the hell out of town for a few days, and leave me alone!"

"What have I done to you?" Jeff chimed in. "Hell, I hardly even know you. Haven't talked to you since High School, and all you've got to say is for me to leave town? What the Fuck?"

"No. You don't understand, and you'd better pray to God you never do." She came back at him.

"Just tell me what happened up here." Kevin persisted.

"Look, if what I've caused becomes so far out of control I can't stop it, You'll be dead. And there's not a Damn thing you can do about it." She stated with conviction.

"Jeff. Get her a cold bottle of water, would you? Now," Kevin looked her eye to eye, "You're going to explain this whole situation to me. So help me God, if you don't, I'm going to get the Game Warden and the Sheriff's office up here, and you can explain it to them."

If looks could kill, he wouldn't have to wait on what she was talking about. He'd drop dead right then and there. But he kept pushing.

"Well, which one's it going to be?" He asked.

Taking a sip of the water Jeff had handed her, she glared rebelliously at Kevin. For a minute, he thought she was going to charge him. She shuddered, took in a long, deep breath, and slumped her shoulders in defeat.

Surprising both men, she buried her head in his chest and began weeping heavily, shaking from head to toe. As Jeff stood watching in bewilderment, Kevin looked at him and, standing still, let Lisa cry until she started to calm down. He took her face in his hands and led her to look at him.

"Are you okay now?" He asked. "Can you tell us why you're here alone, bruised and bleeding?"

"Yes. Take me to my truck, and I'll fill you in on everything. Then maybe the three of us can figure out what to do about this predicament." She said.

"I still don't understand," Kevin said.

"It's not only my troubles. It's the situation I've put all of us in. Especially you two. And Angie." Lisa told him.

"Start explaining," Kevin ordered as he and Jeff led her to the truck.

＊＊＊＊＊＊＊＊＊＊＊＊＊＊＊＊

A few minutes later, the three of them were standing around the bed of Lisa's F-150. Both men were shaking their heads in disbelief at the tale they had just been told. As promised, Lisa had started at

130

the very beginning, starting with the hunt that ended in the accidental death of her brother, how that had grown into a hatred for her childhood friends and everyone with them.

Why she couldn't accept the fact that it had been an accident or why her feelings had grown out of control, she couldn't explain. She then went into detail about how she and Becky had become close. Both women had gone through a tumultuous time, and they had connected.

"Why would you go to such an extreme, though? You could've just written me out of your life instead of letting it consume you." Kevin asked her.

"I don't know. It's like I was drawn to it. After a while, all the research and time spent with Becky had become enjoyable. Plus, I was learning new things about my ancestors." Was the only answer Lisa came up with.

In all truthfulness, deep down, she hadn't believed such a thing could work. She had read and heard the legends. But that's all they were. Legends and old wives' tales to keep people in line. Never in her wildest dreams did she think that she herself could wield any true magic.

"Truth be told," she explained, "I thought Becky and I would have the ceremony, and nothing would come of it except a little disappointment and a girl's night on the mountain."

"So, you're trying to tell us that this happened?" Jeff asked.

"Yes. Both the legends *AND* the magic are real. So is the death that came with it." She answered.

"Tell me about the deaths," Kevin said. "Are you positive they aren't only injured?"

"I watched them die. Except for Neil, he ran. But I heard his screams of pain." She said. "He's somewhere along the lower half of the Flint Mill. Rick was gutted, and Becky was savagely raped and killed. Both happened right in front of me." Lisa continued.

"What did you call this thing again?" Jeff asked.

"A Daemon. His name is Chivas, and he's risen from the Netherworld. The Cherokee version of Hell." She answered. "And now he's on the loose."

The two men stared at one another for a brief moment, each knowing the other's thoughts. Agreeing upon a course of action in silence. At least the beginning of doing something, as unpleasant as this first part, might turn out to be.

"Well," Kevin spoke up, "I guess we need to hike in there and find the bodies to verify what you've told us."

"Fuck you," Lisa said.

"You did say that you were smoking pot and drinking some. I'm not implying that you're imagining things. But you have to admit it sounds a bit outlandish." Kevin stated.

She stood there glaring at him a moment longer, then turned to look up the trail she had entered the afternoon before.

"If we find them, and they're either hurt or dead as you claim, we can call the authorities then," Kevin said.

"Fine. Get your gear together, and come on. Time's wasting. That thing could be anywhere by now." Lisa replied.

Both men went back to the Chevrolet and retrieved their backpacks. They then got their handguns from the cab compartments, loaded them, and slid them into their respective holsters. Sliding into the packs, the three of them walked to the trailhead and entered the woods, Lisa in the lead. They had only hiked fifty yards in when the strong odor of iron filled their nostrils.

"Blood," Jeff stated.

Motioning for the group to let him in the front, Kevin withdrew his forty-millimeter, chambering a round. Jeff did the same with his .380 caliber. They approached the upcoming blind curve with caution, Jeff in the rear keeping an eye out behind them while Lisa watched the sides.

As the threesome emerged from the bend onto a straight stretch, Kevin held up his hand to halt progress, indicating that the two should move forward to join him. Looking straight ahead, he pointed out a huge rock at the edge of the trail. It appeared to be covered in blood, with small pools of it on the surrounding ground.

With a gesture, he let Jeff know to stand guard while he and Lisa searched the area for Neil. He hoped that his friend was only injured. If all of this blood was his, though, there wasn't much chance of finding him alive.

Drip. Drip. Something wet hit Lisa on her face. Wiping her jaw with the palm of her hand, she saw red. When she looked up, her legs gave out, taking her to the forest floor, where she began screaming. Both men instantly turned their heads upward. There was Neil.

IIis arms were stretched tight, tied to sizable limbs, with his legs and feet bound in a similar fashion. He was hanging about fifteen feet in the air, spread eagle, facing the ground. It appeared he had been sliced open from breastbone to pelvis. His ribs were broken away from his spine and spread apart. Intestines had been wrapped around his arms up to encircle his throat.

He had been tied up there with his own bootlaces.

"Oh God! Oh God! Oh God!" Jeff repeated.

Lisa had crawled to the side of the trail, where she was vomiting up everything in her. It was all Kevin could do to catch his breath. His mind was reeling. He had never seen anything like this in his life and didn't want to again. But he knew that if Rick and Becky were in the same shape, then he had better keep his shit together. Someone had to think with a clear head.

Pulling out his cell phone, he dialed 911 and informed the dispatcher that they had found a body with the appearance of a murder. After he gave them their location, he agreed to have Jeff meet them at the gravel road to lead them in.

With that taken care of, he looked at Lisa and asked if she was going to be okay. Getting a thumbs up even in the middle of puking, he turned his attention to Jeff. Having to shake him some to bring his thoughts back into focus, he finally got the other man to meet him eye to eye.

"Hey, come on. Hold it together. You have to go back to the road and wait on the sheriff's department, game Wardens, whomever shows up first. Then you're going to have to guide them back here." Kevin told him.

"Where are you going to be?" Jeff asked.

"I'm taking her to show me where Becky and Rick are. You might as well send some people on up the trail as well."

Lisa groaned and rolled her eyes at this last statement. Then she bent over and commenced throwing up again.

He grabbed the woman by the arm, dragging her to a standing position.

"Let's go. It shouldn't take them long to get here."

****

Mark Canter and Jake Ellis had been on the mountain all night, ever since passing the two women yesterday afternoon. They had met some friends at the pull-off below the split that took you to the campground, walked to the lake, and partied the night away.

Everyone else had wimped out in the wee hours of the morning and had gone on home. Not them. Hell no. They were the masters of the party, so they claimed. In reality, what had happened was the two had drunk themselves sober. After a good sleep, they'd have one heck of a hangover.

Standing by Mark's jeep, drinking what alcohol they had left, they were bickering about what to do with the rest of the day. Being the friendly type, they waved the stranger over as they spotted him walking alone. Jake began a conversation with his usual question.

"You want a cold beer, man?"

Chivas believed the 'beer' that was referred to was some sort of ale. The type served in the bars and saloons in the last days he walked this Earth. He accepted and began asking questions of his own about the area and the people residing in it.

It didn't take long for Chivas to realize just how much things had changed with time. He was looking over this horseless carriage these boys called a jeep as he listened to them talk. And that was something both liked to do. Talk. He heard about everything from bars to apartments, mustangs, Jeeps, and towns named Johnson City and Bristol. He was surprised when he took his first drink of the Bud Light.

"How did you keep this ale so cold?" He asked.

"The cooler, fill it with ice, and it keeps anything cold for a long time. How else did you think?" Mark inquired.

"My people used to keep things in a stream to stay cool," Chivas replied.

"Where are you from?" Jake asked. "Way back in the Boonies?"

"I'm from a different place. A friend that lives in Piney Flats, I think that's how he pronounced it, is letting me stay there." Chivas said, remembering the location of the Miller sacrifice. "Can you show me how to get there?"

"I can do you better than that," Mark said, laughing. "I can drive you there. We're going home that way anyhow."

"Yeah. When we get to the crossroads, take a left, and we'll come out on 19-E. Take a little longer, but we can drink more," Jake chimed in.

"As long as I get there," Chivas said.

They climbed into the Jeep, Jake settling into the back seat, giving the front to the Daemon. Neither young man had any idea of what they were riding with. Starting the engine and making a U-turn, Mark drove the vehicle in the direction Chivas had just come from.

As they passed the entrance to the Flint Mill trail, they noticed Lisa's truck still parked there. Joining it, however, was a Z-71, several sheriff's vehicles, a couple of troopers, and a crash truck. The boys could hear an ambulance coming from down the road. Chivas did not know what to think of this new experience. He guessed it best to follow Mark's actions.

"I wonder if anything happened to Lisa and Becky last night? Her truck was still there," He asked Jake.

"I don't know. I hope not." Came the reply.

Chivas sat staring out the windshield.

As the Jeep approached the crossroads, they discovered a blockade had been set up. This was being manned by both county and State officers. One of the Sullivan County deputies directed them to pull over to the side. Two advanced on the Jeep.

"What's your business up here this morning?" one asked Mark.

"We camped out with some friends by the lake last night and just decided to take this route home." He replied.

"All three of you?" The officer asked.

Looking at Chivas, who seemed out of place, Mark answered quickly.

"Yes. All of us were there from around two yesterday afternoon until a little while ago. We are the last ones to leave."

"did you happen to notice or hear anything out of place in the vicinity of the Flint Mill Trail late last night or early this morning?" The second deputy asked.

"No. Like I told you, we were way on the other side at the lake. Past Little Oak Campground. All night." Mark stated.

"Yeah. All three of you smell like you threw a good drunk. If this wasn't a priority, I'd take you in for DUI and your friends for public intoxication." The officer said.

"What did happen up here?" Jake questioned.

"Nothing. Just go home and sleep it off. I'm sure you'll hear about it on the news tomorrow." The first Deputy said as he stepped away from the Jeep.

If the two had been halfway sober or even paying attention, both would have seen the Daemon's eyes begin to shine with a bright silver tint. As Chivas was smiling at the thought of the new world that awaited him, he noticed that feeling growing in him again. Soon. Soon, he would appease by taking another soul. He joined the conversation once more.

****

"So. What made you think of something like this Daemon Legend? I don't get it." Kevin asked as they hiked the steep trail.

"I don't know. I had tried to hire a hitman, but they were too expensive." Lisa said.

"You're kidding."

"Nope." She answered. "I really did. But, without that kind of money, my next option was to turn to my heritage. I knew there were Cherokee Legends of spirits that would do someone's bidding for a price other than money."

"Why couldn't you accept the fact that Lee's death was an accident? It was nobody's fault?" Kevin asked.

"He was my baby brother. How did you expect me to feel? Plus, at that time, before the accident, I mean, I was sort of in love with you." She said.

"So, at that age, it hit you as if the person you loved killed the sibling that you loved more. Am I right?"

"Yes. You could put it that way. It didn't matter. You went ahead and took him hunting even though I told you not to, and he ended up dead. So, I left. But the anger and hatred continued to grow." Lisa replied.

"And when you came back, you felt as though Angie had betrayed you as well by marrying me. Correct?"

"That about sums it up." She said

"This summoning some kind of devil thing…"

"Daemon." She interrupted.

"Okay. This Daemon. But, bringing it to life to kill us? Come on. That's taking things too far. Wouldn't you think?" Kevin said.

"Yeah. I can't explain why I went to those extremes. Saying sorry won't help now. I just have to deal with it and find a way to send it back." Lisa stated.

"I believe we ALL need to find a way to stop it. Hell, I don't even know what kind of criminal charges they could bring against you, if any." He said. "I don't know anyone who would believe this shit anyway."

"I'm not worried about that." She replied.

"You better start worrying about something. Whatever it was that killed our friends may come after you. I still don't know what I believe." Kevin told her.

"It's a Daemon, Chivas. And it doesn't matter what you believe now. You'll believe it soon enough. Remember, he's also coming for you." Lisa stated.

"That's what you say. I'm still not so sure that if you were drinking and smoking weed, it wasn't a bear or something. Maybe a mountain Lion?"

Lisa only stared at him with a hateful expression.

As they continued in silence, both lost in thought, Kevin observed the woods had an unnatural quietness about them. This time of the morning, the birds should be singing, squirrels playing, and the forest would be alive.

Now, it seemed as if everything was afraid to move. Waiting. There was a feeling of electricity in the air itself, as though this ridge had been invaded by something unholy. This alone was enough to get him wondering if there might be something to what she claimed had happened.

As she came upon the same spot where she and Becky had last rested on the way up yesterday, Lisa sat on the same rock. She glanced around the area and then lowered her head. Kevin could see that her hands were shaking.

"Are you alright?" He asked.

"Can we just sit a minute and let me catch my breath? I've had a long, rough night, and it looks like it's going to be one hell of a day as well." She said.

"Sure. Take five. What do I expect to find up here anyway? Is it as bad as Neil? As it is, I won't get a good night's sleep for months." Kevin replied.

"Steel your nerves. I've seen it already. It's as bad or worse." Lisa answered.

"Not meaning anything bad by it but how did you become close friends with Becky? She was always so quiet and withdrawn in school?" He asked.

"I really couldn't tell you. I was sitting on the park bench one day, griping and complaining to myself, and she was there listening. After that, we just started hanging out. I think she only helped research those legends to make me happy." She replied.

"Yeah. Maybe she didn't think it would work. She was just doing something to make you feel better. That way, even if it failed, you could say you tried."

"And for that, she paid with her life," Lisa said with sadness.

"Well," He said, changing the subject, "Let's go on and have a look. It shouldn't be too long before emergency personnel arrives." Kevin stated.

The two of them made their way around the last bend, entering the clearing at the top of the ridge. The scent of blood was so overpowering that it drowned out any other smell at all. The scene that was laid out before him reminded him of a slaughterhouse. It was all he could do to keep from becoming ill.

Too late for Lisa. She was back on her hands and knees, puking out anything that might have been left in her system. She was moaning and crying at the same time. He felt sorry for her until he realized that whatever had happened was, for the most part, her fault. She did this.

Walking over to inspect Rick's body, he glanced over and did a quick once-over of Becky lying in a drying pool of blood. He would go to her in a minute. He knelt beside Rick, making a mental note of the damage done to his employee, his friend. Abdomen opened up, shattered arm, broken neck. He closed the man's eyes.

Taking a deep breath and saying a silent prayer, he stood and went to Becky's inert form. Listing to himself the various injuries and mutilations that had been bestowed upon the woman, he almost lost his breakfast himself. He knew, beyond a doubt, there wasn't any man or animal that could have achieved this much damage as quickly as Lisa claimed.

"Lisa. Come here," he ordered. "Did you touch her before leaving? I know she didn't die with her eyes closed and hands folded across her chest."

"Yes. I did. I just couldn't leave her in the position she was in. She was my best friend." Lisa answered.

"I understand. Let's not disturb anything else before the police get here, though. Okay?" Kevin said.

"Okay. I'm sorry. She looked so pitiful, though."

"Show me the exact spot where this so-called ceremony took place." He told her.

She guided him over to the remains of the fire, pointing out what was scattered and left of her belongings. It wasn't, but a few seconds later, they heard the helicopter approaching, flying low. When the chopper passed overhead, Kevin waved his arms and shouted to get the pilot's attention.

He noticed the logo on the side stated that it was a county search and rescue team. He knew they had been sighted when the pilot gave them the thumbs up. The aircraft banked down over the ridgeline in the direction of the gravel road. He should be able to land there.

"What are we going to tell the police?" Lisa asked.

"Certainly not your story." Came the reply.

CHAPTER THIRTEEN:

THE DETECTIVES

Detective Stan Becker was the lead on this call, and at this moment, he was wondering why he had chosen this line of work. He should have become a doctor like his father. He looked around the crime scene and realized that even the best trauma team in the world could not have saved these victims.

Stan had known Kevin and Jeff for years. They had built both his and his older brothers' houses. Had done a good job, too. The two men had excellent reputations, and though he knew they had a cold beer or two and partook in a little marijuana every once in a while, neither had been in any legal trouble. They had actually done quite a bit of charity work in the area.

When first arriving and learning these two were involved somehow, he couldn't figure it out. Then, he found out that both male victims had been employed by them. They had also been the unfortunate ones to stumble upon the gruesome scenes while scouting for deer.

Lisa Smallwood was another issue, however. She had been in a few scrapes with law enforcement throughout the years. Stan himself had arrested her a couple of times before making detective while still a patrolman. Nothing serious. The charges had all been misdemeanors. Fighting, possession of marijuana (a single bowl full), and a DUI.

The possession charge was what she referred to as a 'peace pipe' in her glove compartment. And well... she was a full-blood Cherokee, and it was legal on the reservation. That charge was dismissed in court.

When he had first arrived at the staging point of the investigation, the entrance to the Flint Mill had already been blocked off. It had been manned by two State Troopers and a TVA policeman. By the time he had produced his Identification and had made it to the first crime scene, techs were combing the area and bagging anything that might be considered evidence. Things were moving quickly.

Since he didn't see Calvin Jenkins anywhere, he guessed that the coroner's office was running a little behind. The medical examiner would be here when he got here, he told himself. Stan began looking around to decide where he wanted to start. He noticed that both Jeff and Lisa were talking to a couple of other deputies. He assumed they were giving their statements. They would have to do so again.

On the other side of the area, Kevin Miller was on his phone, presumably talking to his wife from the animated conversation it appeared to be. At that time, Henry Barber walked up beside him Henry was an old acquaintance and also one of the county deputies assigned to this case.

"What have you got, Henry?" Stan asked.

"We've got a mess, is what? There's one body here. Male, Caucasian… approximate age forty. Identification says he's Neil Baines, former Air Force, Hickory Tree address." The deputy answered.

"I knew him, and I've been informed of the two victims on top of the ridge. I was acquainted with both Miss Combs and Mr. Harris as well." The detective stated.

"Then you've heard that all three bodies were basically ripped apart."

"I was told that they were cut up pretty good. It was also mentioned the Combs woman may have been sexually assaulted." Detective Becker said.

"That's what I was told as well," Henry said.

"Make sure forensics knows to check on that. If so, I want a rape kit ordered. And go ahead and get word to her parents. She still resided with them." Becker commanded.

"What about the other two?"

"Notify Mr. Harris' wife. I don't believe Baines had any relatives that we know of. Check on that also as well," was the reply.

"You know the news crews will be here shortly. What about them?" The deputy asked.

"You know the drill. Basic statement. No names of victims or witnesses released until I give the okay." The detective said.

"You got it," Henry replied.

"And get Miller off the damn phone and over here now. I need to get his statement from him myself." Becker said.

"Right away." The deputy shook his head.

"By the way, if they haven't moved it, where's Baines' body? I thought it was right here." He asked.

Henry Barber just raised his head upward, and Stan followed his gaze. It took a minute for him to comprehend what he was seeing. Until the day he died, Detective Becker never forgot the sight of Neil's butchered body strung up between the tree limbs.

"Holy shit!" He exclaimed. "Will somebody please cut that man's body down? The M.E. can examine him on the ground just as well. Have some fucking decency."

Turning his vision away from that gruesome sight, he noticed Kevin was now off the phone. He motioned for him to come over. Watching him walk towards him, Becker thought that Miller looked mentally and physically drained. Didn't matter. He could recoup later. Right now, Stan needed to talk to him.

As Kevin approached, he also noted that the other two were finished talking to the deputy. They were watching him with pained expressions. He would have passed it off as grieving for the loss of their friend if it hadn't been for the way Miller was eyeballing them back.

Gathering from the looks that had just happened between the three of them, he had the impression that he would not get the full truth of what really went on here. It was as if an unspoken agreement had been made. He didn't like it one bit.

"You wanted to see me, Detective Becker?" Kevin asked.

"I wanted to get a statement from you. Yes. And I want every fucking detail of how you and Bishop happened to be here. And the truth about what you know of the events that transpired here." Came the answer.

"Well, Jeff and I were going to the Josiah Trail to do some scouting….."

"Long way from the Josiah, son. And it doesn't tell me how you ended up here with her." Becker interrupted, pointing at Lisa.

"Like I said, we were on our way to the Josiah when we saw Lisa walking along the road towards her truck." Kevin went on.

"So, you just stopped to say hello then."

"She looked like she had blood on her shirt. We thought she had been injured, so we stopped to see if she needed medical attention."

"Continue on," Becker said.

"She told us she had been hiking this morning and heard some gunshots come from this direction. When she arrived, she found Neil injured but alive." Kevin stated.

"MmmHmmm."

"Well, she said he told her that Rick and Rebecca were up top badly injured themselves. She raced up there and found them as they are now. Mangled." Kevin stammered through it.

"Is that correct, Miss Smallwood?" The Detective asked Lisa as she walked up.

"Yeah. That sounds about right. I was panicked. So, I ran back down here, and Neil was gone. I assumed he had made his way back to the road to flag down some help." She said.

"He was badly injured when first you arrived, yet an hour later, you assumed he was well enough to make it back down," Becker questioned.

"Yes. That's all I could think of. Like I said, I was in a panic. Anyway, my phone was in the truck, so I went to get it to call 911 when I saw these two coming up along the road." She stated.

"After she told us what had happened, and there was no sign of Neil, we hiked back here. That's when we finally saw him up in the tree as you see him now." Jeff added.

"I then called 911. Then she and I went up so I could see if there was anything that might possibly be done for them. She was stressed enough that I thought maybe she was wrong about them being deceased." Kevin continued.

"But she wasn't," Becker said.

"No. It was too late for them also. They were already turning cold." Kevin stated.

Detective Becker was trying to decide just how much of this story was fact and how much was made up. He was about to conclude that most of it was total bullshit with a smidgeon of truth thrown in for good measure. At that time, a young deputy ran to him and told him he needed to talk to him for a minute.

"Do you think he believed any of it?" Jeff asked in a hushed tone as Stan walked away.

"Not a word. But he has no choice as long as all three of our statements match. We were here, and he was not. He'd have us all committed if we told him what Lisa said happened." Kevin said.

"It happened. Are you calling me a liar, or are you saying I'm crazy, you bastard? Why would I make something that insane up?" Lisa snapped.

"All I know, from what I've seen, is that your story has to hold some truth. I don't see how else they could have died like that. And a woman your size couldn't have taken Rick alone, much less Neil." Kevin told her.

"And Becky. Don't forget her. Why would I do that to my best friend?" She added.

The Detective walked back to the group, shaking his head. He stared at them for a few seconds before speaking. Lisa was the only one to look him eye to eye. He bowed his head, sighing heavily.

"Dispatch just received a call from a motorist on the road going out towards 119-E. Does one of you know a couple of fellows who might be running around in a 1998 Jeep Wrangler? Navy Blue in color?"

"Sounds like Mark Canter and Jake Ellis to me," Lisa spoke up.

"Well, they were found on the side of the road, parked in a pull-off, still in the vehicle. One in the driver's seat the other in the back. Both mutilated like your friends here. Looks like our killer's a fast mover, huh?" The Detective said.

"Just those two alone? No one passed anybody walking?" Jeff asked.

"Statesman at the blockade says it sounds like the one that went through earlier. Except there were three people in it. So, tell me again, exactly how long have you three been up here?" Becker inquired.

"Look," Kevin said. "We've told you all that we know. It sounds as if you guys have your hands full. Can we go now?"

"You're free to go for now. Don't leave town or I'll have a warrant out on you. I'll be in touch." Becker said as he turned to speak to another deputy.

The threesome headed back down to the road, not saying a word as they worked their way through the police, crime scene techs, and EMTs. When they reached Kevin's Z-71, all three slid into the front seat, leaving the windows up so they wouldn't be heard.

Deciding to leave Lisa's truck here, staying together for safety, Kevin pulled out, driving only as far as what's called Cinder Pile. It was close to the opposite end but not quite. Either way, this place was miles from the Detective.

"Can you get ahold of that Indian witch that gave you that summoning spell or whatever it was?" He asked.

"I don't know, maybe." She said.

If not, there might be someone on that reservation who could let us know how bad this really is. They could put us in touch with some-one that knows these legends." Kevin stated.

"I'll try." She replied, pulling out her cell phone.

"Angie's going to get a substitute to teach the rest of her classes. She said she would meet us at The Tavern as soon as she can." He continued.

"Why the Tavern?" Jeff asked.

"Because from what I saw back there, and with Lisa saying you and I are high on this Daemon's to-do list…"

"You are." She interjected.

"Well, then we need to stay as much in public as possible. We can't let this thing keep us isolated. He may not make any moves with other people around." Kevin finished.

"We're screwed," Jeff concluded.

★★★★★★★★★★★★★★★★★

CHAPTER FOURTEEN:

BEGINNING THE HUNT

Chivas had left the two men in the Jeep, not caring if they were found or not. No one knew that he was here other than the young woman who had rebirthed him into this world. He had figured out quickly that in this day and time if she told anyone, they would not believe her.

He couldn't imagine when or why people had lost their faith in the spirits and the old ways. They were too trusting, too complacent. And they depended too much on their machines. He, however, was in constant touch in some way or the other with the Death Spirits who had made the way for him to exist in this world again.

He had assignments from them to be completed, but the sacrifices given him by the woman would be of great help. They would aid in the number of souls he was to obtain as well as create chaos and confusion, thus assisting in covering his movements. It seemed to him that these people had never been hunted by such as he had before. They would not know how to react. This was going to be easy.

Although he had to slow it down a bit, Chivas had been given a specific task with a certain number of souls. So many in this area, so many in the next, and so on. The excess he had accumulated at his summoning was unexpected, and therefore, he counted them as bonuses.

He had not been forewarned of the extra humans. The one trying to attack him from behind or the beautiful female ripe for the taking. He had enjoyed the chase and final fight given him by the one that had bravery enough to face him down.

Chivas had only been told of the lone squaw that was to raise him up. She had been chosen by the elders for him to take first. The spirits had not confronted him in the matter of letting her live for now. He planned on making her the last life force collected before leaving for the next area to pursue new conquests.

The Daemon traveled as though he were pushed by the wind. Quick and silent. Aided by a vision sent to him from the Netherworld, he found the way to Kevin Miller's home with ease. This one was the main target, and he would take care of this man next.

Chivas cut through the Allison Timbers subdivision, entering the woods at the end of a cul-de-sac to stay as concealed as possible. Too many people had already seen him, although they did not know the beast that he truly was. Walking straight through the wooded patch, the trees thinned out until he came upon a barbed wire fence.

Crossing the wire, he walked among the cattle, hiding his movement from the houses below. The other side of the field held another patch of woods, which he entered and changed his path, heading downhill. Another fence brought him to a halt. This one had a few feet of tree line beyond it. But that's not what drew his attention.

Looking at the two-story dwelling surrounded by a couple of outbuildings and a barn set a little further back, he knew that he had arrived at his destination. Sitting with his back against a large tree trunk, Chivas decided he would observe this area for a bit. He drew himself a mental map of the yard buildings and was patiently waiting to see who might appear. These he might have to take care of as well as the main occupant of the home. He did not want any more surprises such as those already encountered.

At this point, he did not see one of the machines termed as a vehicle on the property. This led him to believe that no one was in the house. He stood up and began easing towards the entrance. He figured that having a look around and then determining where to wait until his target arrived wouldn't hurt. He wanted to have the added advantage of surprise.

The Daemon presumed that these humans couldn't have been informed of his presence in this world yet. They would not believe it if they had been told. Humans, especially the white man, were a skeptical lot. Most only believed what could be seen with their own eyes.

As he neared the entryway, due to his connection with his wolf persona, he caught the scent of a canine. Be it a common dog, coyote, or another wolf in the vicinity, he couldn't tell in his human form, but it was definitely some sort of mongrel. Whichever it was, it would be able to smell him as well.

Testing the door and finding it locked, he began searching the perimeter for another way in. An open or unlocked window. Something he could force his way without leaving any noticeable damage.

He didn't have to worry about being spotted by any passerby. The landscape and distance to the road hid the property well. Someone would have to be looking through the trees awful hard to get a glimpse of him moving around the yard. He stayed within mere feet of the dwelling also making a view of him near impossible.

When he came to the far side of the home, there was a second door. This one was unlocked. Taking his boots off, so he wouldn't leave any prints to be found. These he sat to the side of the small wooden porch within easy reach in the case of a hasty exit.

Chivas opened the entry inch by inch until he was able to squeeze his body into the house. As he walked into what looked to be a cooking section, the sound of thumping came from overhead. It moved across above the next room and down a set of steps. He made himself ready for a skirmish.

A moment before the large black dog rounded the corner, he both smelled it and felt the vibrations of a deep growl resonating from it. The animal stopped four feet from him. Token was visibly angered by this stranger's intrusion. The black Labrador, having smelled the beast in Chivas as well, bared its teeth, viciously snapping and barking at him.

The Daemon took a step back, preparing himself for the inevitable attack. His eyes began to glow a bright silver while only transforming his hands into razor-edged claws. The Lab struck him, biting down on his forearm. He placed his other hand on the rear of the dog's head, giving it a hard jerk. There came a loud popping noise from Token's neck, then silence.

Dropping the dogs' carcass, he went through the rest of the downstairs, looking for any other animal or traps set for those unwelcome here. Finding none, he went up the steps to search the remainder of the home. He hoped to find either Kevin or his mate in hiding.

After a thorough search of every room and closet, behind and under all furniture, he determined he was alone. Going back to the kitchen, he retrieved the dog's body and carried it up the stairs. He took it to the largest sleeping room and stuffed it under the bed so it wouldn't be discovered right away.

The Daemon then retraced his steps to the first level and to the access he first entered the home through, making sure nothing had been disturbed. He quickly made his exit, closing the door behind him. Snatching his boots off the porch, he made his way to one of the outbuildings, sat behind it, and put them back on.

He looked over the property close to the house until he found a suitable place to hide in anticipation of his target arriving home. Being cautious, he stayed as low to the ground as possible as she moved to a thick group of bushes at the rear corner of another building. From here, he could see the entire driveway and front yard.

Chivas settled into the branches covered in leaves. He began waiting… and watching.

****

On the way to the Tavern, Kevin, Jeff, and Lisa were discussing possible strategies on how to track the Daemon. Lisa kept telling them all that needed to be done was watch one of the homes of the 'sacrifices' she had listed in the ceremony. That would only pertain to their two places, Anson's and the Combs' residence.

"And how are the three of us supposed to watch four places at once?" Kevin asked.

"We split up and warn one of them to leave until I call them," Lisa replied.

"There's two problems with that scenario," Kevin said. "One, we don't need to split up. By ourselves, we're as good as dead."

"Stay in the public eye as much as we can," Jeff added.

"When you put it that way, I agree. So what's the second thing?" she asked.

"Two, if we were to find it, how do we kill it? I haven't any idea, do you?" Kevin inquired.

"No, I don't," Lisa said. "The old man gave me a hex bag to throw up on another fire at that exact spot. But I also would have to lure it there."

"Do you trust that?" Jeff asked her.

"After instructing me wrong on the summoning? Hell no. Besides, it couldn't be that simple, could it?" She answered.

"This has got to be the most stupid-ass stunt anyone has ever pulled. What were you thinking?" Kevin raised his voice.

"Fighting isn't going to solve our problems now. So, let's just go in, get a table and a beer, and rationally discuss this." Jeff said as they pulled into the parking lot.

"You're right. Sorry, Lisa. Shew, I guess the first thing to do is try and get ahold of that old Cherokee Witch. He'll either laugh or try to help." Kevin said.

As the three of them exited the truck, a green Dodge Ram pulled up beside them. The driver yelled for them to wait a minute. They recognized him immediately, causing Jeff to roll his eyes and elicit a groan from Kevin. It was Bobby Turner.

He was a 'good ole boy' from the holler. One that had orchestrated his own accident on a freshly mopped floor at a local Gas-n-Sip. He sued the store's insurance, the flooring manufacturer, and anyone else his shady lawyer could think of. That lawsuit set him up for life financially, ending with the local store owner closing its doors permanently. Kevin hated pieces of shit like that.

"Hey," Bobby began, "I see you're wearing camo. Been up on the mountain? I heard a bunch of stuff on the scanner. Do you know what's going on?"

"No. The police aren't letting anyone past the crossroads, so I don't know." Kevin stated.

"Well, hey… where'd you get her? I thought you two hated each other." Bobby pressed.

"Car trouble. Goodbye, Bobby," Kevin said as he went into the bar, closing the door in Turner's face.

It took a minute for his eyes to adjust from the bright sunlight to the dimness of the lounge. As it did, he noticed that several people must have taken the day off. There were a lot more tables than usual occupied this time of day.

"Scooter," saying the bartender's name as he walked over. "Has Angie come in yet? She's supposed to meet us for lunch."

"Haven't seen her since you guys left last night." The bartender replied.

"Give us three Bud Lights and a burger apiece. We're going to grab a table." Kevin told him.

"wait a minute, Kev. There was a gentleman who came in a few minutes ago asking for you. Any one of you, and he named Lisa specifically." Scooter told them.

"Who was it? Did he leave a name or number where he could be reached? Did he say what it was about?" Kevin asked.

"Ask him yourself. He's the older man in the back. He has long white hair. Indian, I believe. Anyway, you can't miss him."

Puzzled, they picked up the beers and turned around, heading towards the back of the room. Passing the pool tables, they spotted the old Cherokee sitting by himself in the darkness of the corner.

Lisa took off running to the man, leaving the two men wondering what the hell. As they approached the table, Lisa was engaged in an animated conversation with him. She turned to them and grinned.

"I don't have to call the reservation at all. Meet Thomas Keeler."

"How. What are you doing here?" Jeff asked.

"Let's just say I know things are very wrong right now," Keeler said. "Sit. We have much to discuss and little time to take action, or all will be lost."

Each one pulled a chair from the table and sat as told, not knowing where to begin. They were also filled with numerous questions that none of the three knew quite how to ask. Looking the old man over, Kevin didn't see any similarity to how he had thought a witch would appear. Of course, he also had never seen a real mage before to compare with.

The aged man was tall, medium built with waist-length hair as white as snow. He seemed to carry himself well for his age, which was hard to pinpoint. If you looked at him one way, he seemed ancient. Another way and, he gave the impression of someone who was timeless.

Thomas sat there taking time to look each of them over as well. He was making a mental profile of each by the way they held themselves and whether they committed to eye contact either directly or halting. Though they didn't know it, he also reached with his mind and glimpsed at the animal spirit hovering over their souls like a guardian.

Lisa's shown herself as a cougar. Swift, aggressive, yet cunning as he had seen when she had visited him. For the men, Kevin Miller's appeared in the form of a bear. Slow to think, fast to act, full of strength and courage. His partners emerged as a wild Boar. Attacking without thought or provocation, charging into the unknown, sometimes taken down with ease.

With this insight into their personalities and underlying abilities, he could now figure out the most effective way to use each of them. But first, he knew that the Daemon would have to be lured or herded back to the sacred ground. It might find that being free in this world was too invigorating to take a chance on getting sent back to the Netherworld.

Then again, he knew Chivas had a reputation for believing himself invincible, thinking he was protected by the Death spirits completely. To an extent, he was. But even those that rule the Lower Earth have certain weaknesses, and you just have to dig deep enough to find them.

"The spell you gave me worked. The Daemon arose from the flames as you said it would." Lisa began. "But I had no control over it. Chivas told me that you had instructed me wrong on purpose. Did you?"

"Yes, I did," was all she got in the form of an answer.

"Why would you do that? Hell, why even give someone a way to resurrect something that could do that kind of damage, to begin with?" Kevin asked.

"You would not understand the way of the Indian of old. I doubt the younger generations of Native Americans do either." Keeler stated.

"Then explain it to us. Help us understand so we can send the thing back to Hell or wherever." Kevin kept on.

"To ones like myself, who still study and follow our ancestors' ways, there are things of this world you could not begin to fathom." The old man said. "I only did as I was told."

"Told by whom?" Jeff asked.

"To those of us that work with the supernatural arts, when the spirit world gives you a vision or task, you do it or suffer dire consequences," Keeler explained. "When you are the chosen one to deliver a message or told how to affect the outcome of a spell, you obey."

"So, you're telling us that the Spirit world is real?" Kevin inquired.

"Very much so. Have you not witnessed some of its outcomes this morning?" Keeler answered with a question.

Thinking back over the things he had seen earlier and what Lisa had claimed to have happened, he was starting to believe. There was no denying that Lisa had been through a rough night. No skirting the fact that their friends had been brutally murdered. From what he remembered of Lisa, she had been a straight shooter, not one to tell a lie in any capacity.

"Okay," Jeff chimed in, "Why do these spirits want some beast like this unleashed?"

"First, you must not confuse the two spirit realms," Thomas stated. "The Life spirits work for the greater good. They are emissaries of the Great Spirit. God as you call him."

"And the other?"

"Death spirits reside in the Netherworld, a place of torture, pain, and wanting. Your religion refers to this place as Hell." Keeler continued. "They demand a certain amount of chaos and turmoil. In their eyes, the Life spirits have held the advantage far too long."

"But, why here? Why Lisa?" Kevin asked.

"They, by the laws of nature, could not free Chivas themselves. The spirits had to have someone to channel or summon him." The old man went on. "They recognized the hurt and anger in Lisa. Combined with the relentless drive of her personality, she was perfect."

"But that still doesn't tell me why it was something that I could not let go of," Lisa said.

"They multiplied your pain and anger a hundredfold. Then, it was just a matter of dropping hints in your searches that led you to me." Keller informed her.

"Are you here to stop it? Or, to make sure nothing gets in its way?" Kevin asked.

"The Daemon cannot be stopped or destroyed. He can only be bound, vanquished, and imprisoned in the Netherworld if it is possible to accomplish this day and age." Keeler answered.

"What do you mean, if it is possible?" Jeff asked.

"When Chief Pathkiller did it two hundred years ago, it took four witches. Three black robes and one white, and twenty-one seasoned warriors to put him there, and very few survived."

"What about the National Guard?" Jeff pursued.

"Will they believe you or lock you up? Right now, there are only four of us. I have called Charlie Redwing asking for his assistance." Thomas stated.

"Who's Charlie Redwing?"

"A Black witch that I have known and dealt with all of my life. If he is willing, he should already be on his way here." Keeler said.

CHAPTER FIFTEEN:

ANGIE'S NIGHTMARE

Just what in the fucking hell is going on?" Angie asked with a hateful glare at her sister as she walked up. "You're supposed to be deer scouting, and the next thing I know, you call about some crap about Neil, Rick, and some other woman dead."

"Angie. Honey. Sit down." Kevin said.

"Hell no. Then after that fucked up phone call, I walk in here to meet you and find you with my sister, whom we haven't heard from in years. You've got some major explaining to do." Angie said, still glaring at Lisa.

"Let's go get a booth, and I'll tell you everything. We don't have a lot of time." Kevin said as he took his wife by the arm, leading her across the room.

Lisa sat watching them walk to the corner booth, a cloud of disgust and anger in her eyes. It seemed as if Angie would have at least spoken to her. Something other than that hateful look. Turning back to the old man, she saw him raise his eyebrows.

"My sister Angie. One of the sacrifices." Lisa explained.

"Oh. That's the one, is she? Well, I guess we'll have to try and save her, too, don't we?" Keeler said with a grin.

"Yeah, I reckon," she replied, laughing a little. "So now what?"

"Mr. Bishop," Thomas turned to Jeff, "you need to get your wife away from this. Even though she wasn't one of the chosen she could still be harmed."

"Why would this thing harm her?" Jeff asked.

"As one upon the list, Chivas might punish those close to you for added effect. Call your wife now and have her leave town as soon as possible." Keeler told him.

At this, Jeff rose, pulling his phone out as he walked to the other side of the room, dialing Casey. Sitting at the bar, he ordered another beer, trying not to sound too crazy as to why she had to leave town now. Kevin and Angie came back to the table during this time. They sat. Angie had a calm but puzzled expression on her face.

"Mrs. Miller," Thomas began, "I don't see that you can be of any help in the matter at hand other than get yourself killed."

She turned red in the face at this blunt statement. He continued.

"The best I can recommend for you would be to go home and pack as fast as you can. You can either go with Mr. Bishop's wife or just go many miles from here. Your husband will call you when it is safe." The old man finished.

"I don't even know you, sir. Who are you to tell me what is best for me? And you," she said, pointing at Lisa, "you caused all of this, you little bitch. I hope you get what you deserve.'

"Quickly now," Keeler said in a tone that let her know he meant business.

Angie stood, looked at Kevin with tears in her eyes, and turned, stomping towards the door. She gave him one more glance before leaving. "I love you," she said, waving goodbye.

"Kevin," Thomas continued, "You and Mr. Bishop must go to one of your construction sites and gather any explosive materials you might have."

"Why explosives? I thought this thing was supernatural." Kevin asked.

"They won't do any damage to Chivas, but maybe we can use them to steer him in the direction we want him to go. I hope to lure him back to the sacred site on the mountain." Keeler answered.

"Now, Miss Smallwood," Keeler said to Lisa, "The way I see this, we could also use the help of a medicine man of the white man's God. After all, the Great Spirit of the Cherokee and that of the Christian are the same."

"I don't know any. Not true holy men anointed by God." She replied.

"Surely there is one. He must be full of the Holy Spirit, unwavering in his beliefs. One who knows there is a spirit world, not just life here on Earth. For it is quite a story you have to tell them." Keeler finished.

"Father Ellis. I know he will believe me. And he is strong in his faith. Plus, now he has an ulterior motive." Lisa said to Kevin.

"What kind of motive are you talking about?" He asked.

"Remember before we left the mountain. The call to Becker about the Blue Jeep? His son Jake was in that Jeep. Father Ellis will be out for his child's killer." She informed Kevin.

"If you can convince him of the truth and that it wasn't just a random act of violence." He told her.

"I can, she said as she got up to leave. "I'll call you when I get him and bring him back here."

"How are you going to get there?" Kevin asked. "We left your truck parked on the mountain, remember?"

"She can take mine," Keeler said, tossing her the keys. "Second gears a bitch to get into, but she'll go."

Nodding her head, Lisa headed for the parking lot. Jeff was now off the phone and was walking back to the table. They looked at him as he sat and stared at the floor for a few seconds. He looked up and shook his head.

"I got accused of everything from tripping on acid to having a side chick lined up for the weekend." He said.

"Is she leaving to go somewhere safe, though?" Thomas asked.

"Yeah, Casey's packing a suitcase now. Said she was going to get up with Angie and go to her brothers' condo in Atlantic Beach. He doesn't have it rented out for the next two weeks." Jeff said.

"That should be far enough away," Kevin said. "Come on. You and I have to go to the storage shed at the office. I'll tell you why on the way. What are you going to be doing, Mr. Keeler?"

"Why, I'll be right here waiting on Charlie Redwing, trying to devise a workable course of action." The old man said with a smile.

With that being said, the men left to run their errands. Thomas leaned back in his chair and motioned for the waitress to bring him another beer.

****

Angie Miller left The Tavern less angry than when she had arrived. Still a little pissed, but that was now mixed with confusion and fear. How could something like this be happening? At first, she had deemed it a wild tale. Recalling her heritage and the old stories her grandfather used to tell, she knew it was possible.

She had laughed at some of the Legends and tales the old ones used to tell the children. Looking back, she seemed to have heard the story of a Daemon that had once protected the Cherokee. It had gone rogue and had to be banished. This couldn't be it. Could it? What Kevin had told her seemed awful close to the old Myth.

Five people were dead. There was no disputing that. Turning onto Bluff City Highway, she retrieved her phone from the console and dialed her parent's house. If anyone would know about the tales, it would be her father. He needed to know that his other daughter was back anyway.

No answer. Shit, it was Friday, she remembered. Her mother and father usually spent the day on the reservation helping clean and do any kind of upkeep to the school. This her father considered penance for moving to town. As soon as she pressed the call-end button, the phone rang.

"Hello."

"Hey Ang. It's Casey. I just got the most frantic call from Jeff. He told me to pack a bag and go somewhere for a few days. Have you heard from Kevin? What have those two got planned?"

"I had a similar talk with Kevin. And somehow, that damn sister of mine is right in the middle of it," Angie answered.

"All I was told was that there was something bad happening around town right now. And that a few people had been killed, and he didn't want me near it."

"He didn't tell you that Neil and Rick were two that had been murdered on the mountain?" She asked.

"No! He didn't say anything about murder either. No wonder he wants me away. That hits too close to home." Casey said.

"There was a third. The woman that Lisa has been close to these past few years. From what I understand, it was brutal." Angie stated. "He sounded and looked so afraid, I'm going to do as he asks and leave for a little while."

"Well, you can go with me. My brother's condo is empty, so what the hell. Let's you and I take some beach time while they sort this out. It's probably just some crazed druggie running around anyway." Casey said.

"Yes. I'll go with you then. Give me two hours to make work arrangements for next week and to pack a suitcase. How about picking me up at the house around three?" Angie asked.

"That's fine with me. See you then."

After hanging up the phone, she stopped by the drug store to grab a few things, picked up a late lunch at a drive-thru, and then headed home. A few minutes later, she pulled up the driveway. Something didn't seem right. She sat in the Blazer a minute, then shrugged it off as being the circumstances that brought her home early.

Angie got out of the vehicle, gathering the bags from the drugstore. She was puzzled when she wasn't greeted by Token at the door with his usual excited barks and leaping face kisses. She whistled and hollered for the dog as she walked into the kitchen. Nothing. That was strange.

✳✳✳✳✳✳✳✳✳✳✳✳✳✳✳✳✳

Chivas had been lying back in the bushes by the garage, waiting patiently, when he heard a vehicle coming up the path to the house. Remaining hidden, he shifted position in order to have a better view of what approached. It took only a second or two for the grey Blazer to appear over the top of the small hill. It came to a stop in front of the entrance to the home.

He watched silently and with interest as a petite, black-haired woman got out, retrieving some bags from the back seat. Watched as she dug through her purse, removed a set of keys, unlocked the door, and entered the dwelling.

This must be the wife, he realized. She was on his list as well. Too bad they both weren't here together, it would save him some waiting time. But he could be patient when it came to killing when he had to be.

He decided to give her a few minutes to get comfortable and settle in. She would not be expecting anything to happen. Then, he would slip in the entry he had used earlier. The woman would never know what hit her. Quick, but not painless.

A few seconds later, he heard her whistling and calling for someone. Ah, it must be the dog. Chivas stood and eased around behind the building, moving along the wall until he came to the opposite corner. He peered around it to make sure the woman wasn't looking out of a window.

She was not in view, so he jogged across the open yard to the back of the house. As he scooted next to a window, he could hear her talking to someone. This confused him, for he had not witnessed anyone arrive before or with her. She should be alone.

"I'm telling you, Token is not here," he heard her voice.

Silence then.

"No, he didn't follow me out this morning, and I didn't leave the fucking door open. But he's still gone."

Silence again. "Who the hell is she talking to, and where are they?" Chivas wondered.

"Okay. I'll hurry and then ask Casey to come earlier. I'll leave within the next hour. Call me when we're on the road. Love you." She said to someone.

He heard a noise of something solid being laid down, then footsteps going through the house and up the stairs. Quietly moving around to the back porch, he leaned against the wall next to the door. He looked in to make sure no one was in sight.

Seeing the coast was clear, he once again removed his footwear to ensure he wouldn't be heard by her until it was too late. Chivas grasp the knob, opening the door barely enough to squeeze in, shutting it silently behind him. He proceeded to make his way to the next room with caution, then on to the next. He was at the stairs.

Standing still, listening to the sounds coming from above, he could hear her rummaging around. She was opening and closing drawers, walking back and forth across the room. He took the steps two at a time until he reached the top landing. Making slow advancing movements, he heard her speaking to someone again. He stopped by the entry to the bedroom.

He looked in the room and saw that she had her back to him with an object cradled against her head. She was telling whomever she was speaking to that she would be ready in a half-hour. To come get her as soon as possible. She must be going somewhere. Not now, he thought.

He stepped into the open doorway and stood. Watched her put some clothes in a bag until she said goodbye to whom she had been speaking to. The moment she laid the device on the bed, he came upon her swiftly, grabbing her by the arm and spinning her around to face him. She screamed.

Angie's reaction caught him off-guard as she both kneed him in the groin and punched him in his windpipe at the same time. Surprised more than hurt, he let go for a minute. She tried to run past him towards the open door. Before she had gotten two steps, however, Chivas had her by the throat.

With his free hand, he swept the suitcase and its contents onto the floor, clearing off the bed and slamming her down on it. She tried to knee him again, but this time, he blocked it, retaliating with a single punch to the head,

leaving her in a semi-conscious state.

He stood there for a few seconds gazing down upon her. The Daemon could smell the pure Cherokee blood coursing through her veins. This aroused him considerably. From the way she had conversed with the person she had been talking to on the device, he had time for a little enjoyment. A half-hour, in fact.

****

Angie's mind was reeling. She was trying to grasp what was happening. She recalled hanging up with Casey when she felt the hair rise on the back of her neck. As soon as she was grabbed, she saw the black-haired man, and her defense mechanism took over.

She couldn't remember after that. Time had escaped. Her vision was blurred, ears were ringing, and she wasn't thinking straight. It was as if she were drunk and out of control. She knew the man was still there. She closed her eyes, then opened them again, hoping to clear them enough to see what kind of position she was in.

Trying to focus on the intruder standing before her, all she could tell was that he wasn't moving. Just standing there looking at her as if he were deciding what to do now that he had her. She tried to move her head to see if her phone was near enough to grab. Maybe she could hit 911 before he attacked again.

Her neck was numb. With the limited movement she mustered, it seemed as if the blow to the head had paralyzed her. She knew it was temporary, though, because she could still feel her hands and feet. Nothing felt broken, either.

She began to wonder if this was the man, the supposed beast, that Lisa had sworn to Kevin she had raised from the Netherworld or wherever. The one they claimed to have murdered Rick, Neil, and the others. To Angie, as her vision came back to her somewhat, he appeared to be an ordinary man. Native American, rather large, but a man.

This train of thought vanished as he reached over her, and she witnessed his fingers and nails elongating into razor-sharp talons. With these, he cut away her blouse. The realization of what was happening and the intentions this man or beast had sent jolts of horrified energy through her. Her senses became fully awake now.

She regained use of her arms, hitting him repeatedly in the ribcage and on his chest, trying to get at his face. He still held her by the throat with one hand, continuing to slice away her clothes. By this time, he was moving through the waistband of her blue jeans, cutting off the rest of her garments.

"No, no, no, no," over and over, she screamed.

The beast took his free hand and cut gashes along her side from armpit to waist. Not too deep, just enough to start the blood flowing and hurt. He didn't want her to bleed out. At this point, Angie had all but given up. The only thing she could do was hope Casey would arrive, see what was happening, and call for help.

Or, a better scenario would be that Kevin and Jeff came by to check on her and put a stop to this. She knew that neither was going to happen, though. Casey would just get herself into the same mess, and the boys would probably end up dead. Any hope at all was lost as she felt him move up between her legs.

A second after his hand was removed from her throat, she felt her legs being violently spread apart. Something in her lower back ripped. Moaning in anguish, she was racked by intense pain as the flesh parted on the insides of her thighs. He had cut her to the knees.

As he moved his body forward, she was aware of him entering her. His manhood was as cold as the dead. She begged him to stop. Angie didn't know how much blood she had lost. The sheets were red. Tears ran unchecked, and she closed her eyes. The last thing she heard was his laughter as she mercifully lost

consciousness.

CHAPTER SIXTEEN:

TERROR ON THE LOOSE/ THE

PREACHER

Chivas was angered when the Black-haired beauty passed out on him. Infuriated, he cut her face and arms up more, even though he knew that she couldn't feel it. She would when she woke up. And she *would* awaken. He had decided to leave her alive, sending a message to the others that he was coming for them. It would also serve to throw them off emotionally.

That was a human problem. They became attached to other people, things, and even animals. Where he came from, there was no such thing as caring. It was either dominate, kill, or be destroyed. There were no friends or family.

When he had finished with her, he decided to add insult to injury. An extra warning. He knelt at the foot of the bed and reached under it, grabbing the dog's corpse by the leg. He pulled the animal out and dragged it just outside the doorway into the hall.

Bending low, with the hand still equipped with the talons, he tore the dog's underside open, spilling its intestines onto the floor. Standing back to look at his handiwork, he thought this sight would make for a homecoming no one would ever forget.

His keen hearing picked up the sounds of another vehicle turning up the drive from the road below. He eased the curtains back to see if it happened to be Kevin, the main target he had originally come after. It was not.

Seeing that it was another female and knowing that his number of bodies and souls was accumulating fast, he decided to let this on off with only a scare. He still had souls on his list to gather and this one was not on it. The Death Spirits would not take it too well if he surpassed their commanded numbers. He would search for his next target elsewhere.

Dropping to all fours, he drew deep within himself, calling to the wolf. Muscle and tendon tore only to reassemble. Joints dislocated and re-aligned. His forehead receded while his jawline and nose elongated into a wicked snout. Long, sharp teeth dripping saliva.

Feeling the full power of the realm of death, he raised his head and cut loose a blood-curdling howl. Taking the entire staircase in a single leap, he ran through the house, bursting out the front door onto the closed-in porch. Tearing out the door frame and part of the wall with it as he came through, he jumped onto the hood of Casey's car.

For a moment, the wolf stood there looking down through the windshield at her. He hooked his claws into the metal, found purchase, and pulled himself back to the ground, digging trenches as he went.

The beast paused and kicked the fender with both hind legs, producing enough force to jar the vehicle off the driveway into the grass. Chivas turned and swiftly ran up the hill, disappearing into the trees.

Casey could only sit in stunned awe when the wolf landed on her car and stared at her. As soon as it kicked into the lawn, however, she fired the vehicle back up. She smacked the shifter into reverse and backed down the hill, grabbing her phone at the same time.

She immediately called 911, then Kevin's cell telling him to get home. Locking both doors on the Camaro, she began dialing Angie's number, knowing there would be no answer. She waited.

****

It had taken Lisa a few minutes to get used to driving the old Dodge. It had its quirks. Hell, the thing was older than she was. One thing Mr. Keeler was right about, second gear was a bitch. And you had to "feather" the gas pedal when pulling out.

Instead of going up the Volunteer Parkway, she turned onto White Top Road, following it until she came out on the Weaver Pike. This way seemed to be the fastest route to take on a Friday afternoon so close to workers' shift changes and quitting time. Less traffic.

From here, she'd go the back way through town, eventually ending up on the Virginia side. A few minutes later, she pulled up in front of the church on Mary Street. Sitting there a moment to get her thoughts in order, she wondered if the police had informed Father Ellis of his son's murder yet.

If they hadn't, she did not want to be the one to tell him. Better it comes from the authorities. But that also connected to the reason she had come here to begin with. So, if he wasn't aware of the situation yet, how could she broach this supernatural subject?

Lisa took a deep breath and exited the truck, taking her time walking up the sidewalk. Time to think of the best way to start a conversation such as this. If he was here, if he had been notified of his son's death, he would be gone to handle that. She presumed the sheriff's office would be the first place they would have him go, and she did not want to discuss this there.

They had all three lied in their earlier statements, knowing that there could be no other explanation. She can't go there now with a different tale. She'd be held for more questioning if not arrested on the spot.

Arriving at the double doors, she turned the knob on the right and found it unlocked. Lisa stepped in and stood there for a minute, letting her eyes adjust to the dimmer light. She looked in the sanctuary. Seeing no one at the altar, podium, or in the pews, she went left, down the hall towards the administrative section, searching for the pastor's office.

She heard a voice coming from the next-to-last doorway on the right. When she got to the office entrance, she saw Ellis on the telephone. He held up a finger to indicate that he would be with her soon.

As she viewed his workplace, she spied a wall-to-wall bookcase that held hundreds of books. She could make out some of the titles, seeing that they dealt with everything from ancient religious lore to modern-day practices. To her, this meant that he had somewhat of an open mind. Good.

Father Ellis regarded her with some interest as he hung up the phone.

"I know you, don't I."

"You might. My name is Lisa Smallwood, and I know your son Jake." She said.

"Okay, Lisa. What may I help you with today?"

"Have you heard about what happened on south Holston Mountain this morning?" She asked, figuring honesty with this man went a long way.

"No. Should I have?"

"There were some murders there earlier. Five to be exact," she told him.

"Oh no. That's terrible. But unless they or their family were members of this church, I don't see what that has to do with me." He stated. "But if this congregation or myself can be of any help, we'd be glad to."

"How do you feel about the supernatural? You know. Demons, witches, Indian ceremonies, and spirits?" She felt like she was pushing it now.

"I believe that there is something to them. The Bible tells of Jesus casting out Demons. And, I know there are practicing witches or those that claim to be." Father Ellis responded.

"What about the Cherokee religion and beliefs?" She asked.

"The Native American religion has spirits, and those are akin to angels and demons." The Pastor continued. "Their Great Spirit can be taken in the understanding that he and God, our God, are one and the same."

Lisa sat there in silence, deciding how much further she could take this without getting into the murder of his son. This conversation was going to be harder than she had at first thought. As she sat there deliberating, he asked a simple question that led to where she was going with the discussion.

"I feel sorry for the victims and their families. But, how do these questions pertain to the murders this morning?"

"Okay. There was an old Cherokee Indian ritual performed. Jake was there." She stated.

"What about Jake? Is he alright?" Father Ellis asked in an excited tone.

"I'll tell you everything, but you'll have to promise to listen with an open mind," she said.

"Yes. Yes, of course. Now tell me about my son."

Lisa told him all from the beginning, trying to shorten some parts of it for expediency. Father Ellis listened with attention, not interrupting, although he did get up and pace the floor a couple of times. By the time she got to the part about Detective Becker getting the call on the Blue Jeep, he was back at his desk, head in hands, sobbing uncontrollably.

Finished with her story, she sat there in silence, waiting to see how he would react. He continued crying into his hands, looking at the ceiling after a few minutes, lips moving, praying without sound. He stood then and went to the doorway, motioning her to follow.

He led them into the sanctuary, where he turned and locked the doors behind them. Making his way to the altar, he knelt in front of the life-size crucifix and indicated she should do the same. He bowed his head in prayer while she could only stare at him and wonder what was going through his mind.

"What do you want of me?" He asked.

"I just thought that you, being a man of faith, along with the murder of your son by the hands of this Daemon, would want to help stop it." She stated.

"How can I stop this thing? If it even exists. How do I know that you're telling the truth? Maybe you and your friends used him as a sacrifice in your ritual." He said.

"How can you say that?" Lisa said, appalled. "If nothing else, you could ask your God to help us or, at the least, give us the assistance of one of his angels."

Reaching onto the communion table on his left, Father Ellis took the knife used to cut the bread out from underneath a cloth.

Laying it on the altar rail between them, he turned and glared at her with a contorted look of hatred on his face.

"You have dealt with realms not favorable to the Father in Heaven and have caused the death of my son, among others. Yet now you come to me to speak to him on your behalf?"

"I just thought……"

"God will not provide you with any comfort or aid. God will not help you. You raised up an abomination. You will depart this house of the Lord and leave me to my grief, lest I change my mind and take an eye for an eye." Father Ellis said with a stern expression.

Not another word was spoken as Lisa stood up and walked to the door, letting herself out. She made it back to Keeler's Dodge and stuck the key in the ignition. Sitting there in silence, she leaned her head against the steering wheel and let the dam of tears that had built up loose.

After the outburst had subsided, she turned to look at the church once more. Father Ellis was standing on the stoop, staring at her. It gave her an ill feeling. She started the vehicle and pulled onto the road, headed back to The Tavern. The phone began to ring, but she ignored it.

Even after she made the first turn, out of sight of the church, Lisa could still feel his eyes burning into the back of her head. And she heard his last words yelled as she had driven off.

"God has turned his back on you. He damns you for what you have done!"

****

CHAPTER SEVENTEEN:

RISING BODY COUNT

The detective knew the address of the last 911 call. After the dispatcher had radioed him, he thought that it sounded as if it could be connected to this morning's incidents on South Holston. He had suspected the story given to him by Kevin and crew at the last crime scene was false.

There was no way in hell Miller and the other two had stumbled onto the bodies there. Then, a few hours later, there happened to be an emergency call of a possible homicide reported at his home address. No. They were lying to him. Why, he didn't know as he was sure none of them had part in the actual murders.

Also added to the mix now was Bishop's wife, who, by coincidence, had been the one who had placed the emergency call. How and when had she entered the damn picture? Of course, the Millers and Bishops owned a business together, and the wives hung out a lot. That part was the only one that made sense.

Hitting his siren as he tried to get through the afternoon traffic, he decided it would be faster just to drive the emergency lane. The caller had said possible homicide. Hadn't she checked to see if her friend was alive or not? Something must have scared her good.

"Shit, if I were still patrolling, I'd write half of these idiots a ticket," he said aloud, even though he was alone in the car.

As Becker pulled up the private drive, he noticed that Miller was already there. His Z-71 was parked among the ambulance, police cars, and a state vehicle. Coasting over in the grass, he put the Crown Victoria in the park, shutting it off. After climbing out of the car, he stood there for a moment, surveying the scene to get an idea of the layout.

Yellow tape had been stretched around the house and sections of the yard and driveway. Pulling the pack of Pall Malls out of his pocket, he shook out a cigarette and lit it. He inhaled deeply and let the smoke out slowly. This he did to try and keep calm before confronting this new twist in the case. There had to be a connection to this morning.

He knew the two cases had to be related. Same group of people, or some of them anyway. Miss Smallwood wasn't present. But from what he gathered, the same type of brutality, probably the same suspect, same old shit. This time, he was going to get the truth out of the two men, even if he had to beat it out of them.

For a few more minutes, he just stood there observing. He was trying to see which officers were present and if he was well acquainted with any of them. Both from the county sheriff's office and those with the state or FBI. The latter had been called in because they were dealing with multiple homicides this morning. They had been notified of this incident because of the similarities, and some of the same parties were involved.

Another plainclothes walked up to stand beside him quietly. Detective Hamby. Recently promoted and transferred to work under him. From what Stan had been able to tell the past few months working with the younger man, he was a fine detective.

"Where's Miller?" Becker asked.

"In the house. Upstairs," Hamby replied.

"Is he the victim or a witness?"

"Neither. His wife, Angela Smallwood Miller, she's the victim."

"Anyone else here when it happened?" Detective Becker inquired.

"Mrs. Casey Bishop arrived as the assailant was leaving," Hamby answered. "We haven't been able to get her account yet. She's emotionally distraught at the moment."

"Is Mrs. Miller dead?"

"No. She was sexually assaulted. She's cut up badly and lost a lot of blood. Whomever the perp is, he also killed the dog." Hamby told him.

"What!" Becker asked as he jerked his head around to look the other detective in the face.

"The dog. A full-grown Black Labrador was found in the doorway of the bedroom in which Mrs. Miller was accosted. It was probably trying to protect her. The animal was also gutted." Hamby stated.

Shaking his head in disbelief, Becker walked up to the back of the ambulance with the other detective. A commotion was coming from the house, just inside the doorway. People were moving and being moved out of the way as the EMTs guided a gurney through the opening with a female strapped on it. Oxygen mask on, Iv in her arm, as well as a brace around her neck.

Halting them for a second, Becker gazed upon her visible wounds. Noting that the numerous cuts and gashes were similar, if not identical, he would say that it had been the same attacker here as the one in the earlier murders. Indicating that they should proceed, he turned and grabbed Kevin by the arm.

"You go on, be with your wife. But I'll be at the hospital soon, and you are going to give me the truth. Period." The Detective told him as he pointed at Jeff and Casey. "You two are staying and talking to me now."

That being said, he let go of Kevin's arm and stepped back out of the way so the ambulance could get turned around. Becker then ushered the Bishops into the house, steering them towards the kitchen table. He motioned for Hamby to join them. The two detectives sat in silence for a moment, both observing and assessing the couple's body language.

"Ma'am," he said to Casey, "You were the first on the scene, so let's start with you."

"Okay."

"What did you see, and why were you here at that time of day? Mrs. Miller would normally be at work. Would she not?" Becker asked.

"Yes, she usually would have. But as you well know, this has not been a normal day by far." She said.

"Casey," Jeff began.

"As I told your partner before he left, I'm getting the truth this time. Don't hinder her statement, or I'll lock you up until I do. Understand?" He said to Jeff.

"Yes, sir."

"Now. Go on, Casey. Don't leave anything out, no matter how little it may seem." Hamby directed her.

"Well, Jeff had called earlier. He was upset and insisted that I leave town for a few days. Kevin had told Angie the same, so she and I planned to go to my brother's place at Atlantic Beach." Casey told them.

"Continue."

"When I pulled into the driveway to pick her up, this huge wolf, bigger than any I could have imagined, burst through the porch door and wall. It landed on my hood and stared at me." She said.

The two detectives looked at one another, each wondering where this wild tale was going. Becker figured that he was getting snowballed again, but he aimed to hear her out. "Go on," he said.

"It leaped off, tearing my hood in the process, then kicked the front of the car so hard it knocked it onto the front lawn. I backed down the drive. Called 911 and then Kevin right after. Other than that, I was still locked in my Camaro when the first officer arrived." Casey stated.

"You're telling me that a huge wolf raped Angela Miller, killed the dog, and did all that damage to your vehicle without attacking you as well?" Detective Becker asked.

"That's exactly what happened." She looked him in the eye.

"Answer me this then. Just how much have you had to drink today, or what kind of drugs are you on? That was one hell of a hallucination you had." Becker asked, irritated.

"I'm telling you, it's the truth!" She yelled.

"Officer Barber. Take these two down to the jail and lock them up on whatever charge you can come up with. Interfering with an ongoing investigation will hold them." The Detective said.

As Jeff and Casey were being led out in handcuffs and placed in separate cruisers, Becker led Hamby out to the back porch. Here, he could say whatever he wanted without being overheard. Some of the press had arrived and were now gathered out in front.

"What do you think?" He asked.

"I think it's total horseshit if you ask me." Hamby said. "there's no way a wolf did all this."

"Why don't you go to the station? Give those two an hour or so to rethink telling us the truth. Then take them into separate interrogation rooms and see if they come clean.?"

"What are you going to do?" Hamby asked.

"I'm going to look around here some and see what I can find. Then I'll go to the hospital and see what Kevin Millers got to say." Becker told him.

As the other Detective departed, Stan Becker made his way upstairs to view the actual crime scene. The master bedroom. The first thing he saw was the dog lying at the doorway, belly sliced open, head twisted almost completely backward. The blood trail from the foot of the bed told him this wasn't the location where the Lab was killed.

He spoke with a few of the technicians and then left the room. He picked his way back down the steps, eyeing the floor and railing closely to see if he could pick up anything the attacker may have left on his way out. Nothing on the stairs themselves.

Reaching the landing, however, he noticed deep scratch marks on the hardwood flooring. Bending to get a better look, he saw that the same type of marks had been gouged into the sheetrock at the bottom of the wall. He placed his hand over them to get a size comparison. Gauging from the dimensions, he knew the dog had not made them. They were much wider and longer than his own hand.

Beginning to get curious now, he went to the screened-in porch and looked over every inch of the hole left where the door and surrounding wall had been torn out. Finding no evidence that stood out, he proceeded to Casey Bishop's Camaro.

From twenty feet away, the gouge marks in the hood stood out like a sore thumb. Whatever had split the metal had to have been extremely sharp. The edges were not ripped or torn but folded back and curled under. Eight long cuts evenly spaced apart. Four began near the windshield, four halfway down the hood, both sets running to the grill.

He made a mental note that the width and spacing between the marks were a match to those on the landing. Walking to the side of the drive, he began to pay closer attention to the ground. He hadn't gone far when he spotted an indentation in the dirt. He knelt down and perceived what appeared to him to be a large paw-like print.

This newfound item opened his mind a little and led him to several different possibilities as he continued following the tracks towards the tree line. A terrifying thought came to his mind. "What if it was a person with control over an enormous wolf?"

****

When Casey had phoned him about the incident at his home, Kevin and Jeff had been at the storage shed loading up a couple of cases of Thermax. It's an industrial explosive of some kin to dynamite, mainly used to blow apart rock when digging on a job site.

The news of the attack sent him into such a state of panic that he jumped in the passenger side of his truck, having Jeff drive. He didn't trust himself to drive right now. Neither man noticed they had left the door to the building standing wide open.

Arriving at the house, he rushed through the door and up the stairs, ignoring the shouted commands by officers to stop. Walking upon the sight of Token, his beloved Lab, and then seeing Angie on the bed surrounded by emergency workers sent him beyond his mental capacity for a few minutes.

He dropped to his knees as one of the EMTs took ahold of him by the shoulder to steady him. Kevin stared at his wife of fifteen years, and the same words kept repeating themselves in his mind. "So much Blood."

And there was. Blood all around her, running off to the pool on the floor. It splattered the walls both beside and behind the bed. Hell, it was all over the place. There was nothing in the room that didn't have at least a drop on it.

The emergency crew had blood up their arms and all over their shirts as they tried to staunch the flow of numerous wounds. It seemed to him as if there wasn't a single area on her body that had not been sliced open. Her face was so cut up and had already swelled bad enough that he hardly recognized her.

He felt another hand on his arm, and then Jeff was gently pulling him up and leading him to a chair that had been placed in the hallway, out of the melee. Here, he could stay and watch as medical aid was given to her without being in the way himself.

A gurney was brought up, which she then was placed upon with care. Angie was momentarily whisked away to the waiting ambulance for transportation to Bristol Memorial. The staff at the hospital had been alerted to her condition and had the trauma team standing by.

Kevin barely heard the Detective as he stepped into the back of the transport vehicle with his wife and an EMT. He did notice Becker stop Jeff and point back to the house. His guess was to get a statement from the couple that the police still had their jobs to do.

How this occurrence could be covered up after everything else that had happened in the last ten hours, he didn't know. What he did know was that Casey was still much in the dark as to what was happening. She wouldn't know better than to tell the absolute truth of that which she had witnessed.

What that had been, he could only imagine. He assumed the authorities would think her mentally unstable, therefore disbelieving anything she said. While the ambulance was en route to the hospital, he tried to reach Lisa to let her know about her sister. She didn't answer until the third try, saying she was just leaving the church and would meet him at the emergency room.

CHAPTER EIGHTEEN:

THE HOSPITAL/ TRUTH

Flatline on the heart monitor. He was pushed to the side, and Paramedic grabbed the paddles to shock her heart. Kevin felt as if he were in an illusion. Time slowed, sights and sounds became a blur, and he fought to catch his own breath. Then it snapped back to full speed. "Clear," he heard. The paddles were applied to her chest. Electricity lifted her body inches off the gurney.

Once, twice a third, and fourth occasions. Finally, the monitor began making its steady, semi-rhythmic beeping, and all calmed once again. It wasn't long after that the doors were thrown open, surrounded by emergency staff. They retrieved the gurney and rushed his wife through the sliding doors to the awaiting trauma team.

Kevin was instructed to a family waiting room and told that he would be kept up to date on the progress and condition of his spouse. Lisa walked in about five minutes later and took a seat next to him, tears flowing. She now had another casualty of her actions to face. Only this time, it wasn't one of her friends. It was her sister, her own flesh and blood.

Even though the years had passed, and she had placed the blame for her separation from family on Kevin, sitting here, in this situation, she realized that it all really boiled down to her. It was all her fault. From beginning to end, her actions or reactions to events caused all of this. That knowledge hit her like a ton of bricks.

"How is she?" Lisa eventually asked.

"Cut up real bad. She's lost a lot of blood. Her heart stopped on the way here, but they got it started again. She's in surgery now." Kevin told her.

"Kev, I don't know what to say. I'm sorry. I know this whole thing is on me, and I would take it back if I could." She said.

"You're damn right. It's all your fault. You should have left everything alone. I know what the old man said about the spirits multiplying your feelings or some shit to set this in motion. But it was a fucking accident! Shit!" He yelled.

"I know. Just help me stop this, and I'll disappear out of everyone's life. Okay?" Lisa said.

"You do know that beast, Daemon, or whatever raped her, don't you?" Kevin asked quietly.

Silence.

Kevin got up and moved to a chair on the other side of the room where he could look out of the window, shutting the rest of the world out. Lisa sat staring at the door, anxious for some news from the operating room, all the while contemplating her next move.

An hour later, Dr. Sommers strolled into the waiting room, asking for Kevin. They both stood and approached him, noticing the lack of expression on his face. Neither could tell if he had good or bad news for them.

"How is she?" Kevin began.

"Truthfully, I don't see how she lived to make it here. We had to give her six units of blood during surgery. She's got over two hundred stitches and staples holding her together, and her heart stopped twice." The Dr. stated.

"Is she going to make it, though?" Lisa asked.

"She's in as stable a condition as possible, given the trauma her body has been through. I'd say that if she makes it the next forty-eight hours, she has a good chance of surviving." Dr. Sommers stated.

"Did you know that she was sexually assaulted?" Kevin inquired.

"Yes. There was some tearing in both her vagina and rectum and bruising to the insides of the thighs that were not caused by the main assault. We did find some seminal fluid which has been sent for DNA testing. The police may have a match on file." Came the answer.

"Can I see her now?"

"That's not possible. Your wife is in a precarious position at this time, and I don't want her disturbed for those crucial next forty-eight hours. You need to get some rest yourself. And leave your numbers with the desk so we can get in touch with you." The Dr. ended the conversation.

As Dr. Sommers walked away, they both looked at the floor, then back up at each other. Each knew what was going through the other's mind. Kevin moved back to the chair by the window as Lisa followed and sat next to him. She didn't care if he liked it or not.

"I'm sorry for yelling at you earlier. If you had only come and talked to us years ago, none of this would be happening." Kevin said.

"No. You have every right to be pissed. Hell, I'm pissed off, humiliated, and ashamed of myself all at once." She replied. "We can fix this. At least Angie's alive. Maybe if we act fast enough, no one else will get hurt."

"Yeah," he said. "I can't see her for a couple of days anyway. Let's get back with Jeff and see if old man Keeler has come up with anything."

As they stood to leave, Detective Becker strode in through the door. Holding his hands up to stop them, he blocked the way out with his body. They stared at each other for a few seconds, and then he motioned that they should sit back down.

"You two aren't going anywhere," he stated.

Seeing that Stan Becker hare more than just a determined look on his face, both sat back down. Knowing that this Detective was one who made things happen and took care of business, Kevin admitted to himself that he was going to have to tell to this man.

Becker would hound them until he was satisfied with the information and evidence they gave him.

He could believe them or not. Fuck it. Maybe telling the truth would get them some help. Maybe it would be a one-way ticket to a mental ward. Who knew? The one thing he did know for sure was that this Daemon, this thing, had to be stopped before more innocent people were killed. If they were locked up, or if they couldn't get Becker to give them a chance, it was over.

Stan stood there looking from one to the other with a hard expression on his face until, pausing on Kevin, he dropped his gaze to the floor for a brief second. When he raised his head back up, his countenance had seemed to soften. He sighed and sat down across from them both.

"Any word yet on your wife?" He asked Kevin.

"Yes. She's out of surgery. As stable as the doctor can get her, and she can't have any visitors right now, so there's no point in trying to ask her any questions." Kevin informed him.

"I doubt she's regained consciousness at this point anyway. Maybe not for a few days. I hadn't planned on bothering her until the Dr. says she's up to it. Now, how are you holding up?" Becker asked.

"Mentally, I'm a wreck. I'm tired, and yet I know there's a long way to go."

"I heard you two talking about stopping something. Yes, I was eavesdropping a little before making my presence known. You mind telling me what you meant by that?" The Detective asked. "And not that bullshit story you fed me this morning."

"You won't believe us. I still don't know if I believe us." Kevin said.

The room became silent once again at this. Stan was trying to contemplate what was meant by that revelation. And Kevin was right. If he didn't believe it himself, how could he expect a man such as the Detective, who dealt in hard physical evidence, to believe him? He knew it wasn't going to be easy, but Becker was willing to listen.

"I promise I'll have an open mind, especially after what I've seen today. I heard Mrs. Bishop's story, and I must admit, I thought she was on something." The detective told him.

"How much did you trust what she told you, and what did you say to her?" Kevin inquired.

"None of it, and I had them both locked up," Becker said, as a matter of fact. "But after they were taken to the county lockup, I did a little extra searching and found some unexpected evidence. It matched parts of her story in an odd way. So, try me."

"She knows more than I do," Kevin said, turning to Lisa. "Let her tell you."

"Detective," she began. "What do you know about Cherokee Legends and their connections to nature and animals such as the wolf?"

"Indian legends, huh? Wolves. Sounds like something that might catch my interest. Educate me."

And so, Lisa told her story, the real one, from the beginning. And Stan Becker leaned forward in his chair, his attention on every word spoken. Seldom did he interrupt, never did he laugh, not once did he look away.

As the tale progressed, he couldn't hide his emotions. They announced themselves across his face. From the sadness at the death of her brother, then impressed with the dedication to research. This was followed by awe and a horrified look as she arrived at the part where Rick had been torn open and Becky was raped and mutilated.

"That's it, the absolute truth. After Chivas, as he calls himself, took off following Neil, I haven't seen him. I don't know the details of his killing, nor did I know that he ran into Mark and Jake," Lisa finished.

At this point, Detective Becker stood and walked to the other side of the room. He gazed out of the window, arms folded across his chest as if in deep thought. Kevin and Lisa glanced at each other, not knowing whether he had believed or not. He gave no indication either way. Shaking his head, Stan made his way back to his seat, looked at them both, and leaned back in the chair.

"I'm not saying that you're lying now. I believe that you believe in what you are saying. I'm inclined to give you the benefit of the doubt." Becker said. "This is based on Mrs. Bishop's account and what I found at the scene myself. In some ways, they tie in together."

"So, you're saying that you'll help us?" Lisa asked.

"If this is really what's happening, then I'll try. But this goes beyond all reason and logic. I've never heard of anything like this outside of fantasy books and movies before." The detective said.

"What happens now?" Lisa inquired.

"There *are* crimes here committed by you. But in this case, I can't charge you with murder for hire. No payment exchanged hands."

"What other crimes?" She asked.

"And I can't charge you with aiding and abetting someone that has no birth record, social security number, or anything that ties him to this country. For now, you're free of any of those." Becker replied.

"Tell me," Kevin chimed in, "What did you find at my house?"

"Mrs. Bishop claimed that what exited the home and tore her car up was a rather large wolf. White glowing silver eyes to beat it all." Becker said. "I found claw marks in the house on the landing and huge prints outside. They were not made by a dog."

"So, what do we do now?" Lisa asked.

"You two go meet this Keeler fellow you told me about. I'm going to call Detective Hamby and tell him to release Mr. and Mrs. Bishop. He and I will meet you at the Tavern but I think it's best if Mrs. Bishop goes ahead and leaves town." Becker stated.

"Okay," Kevin said. "You have my cell number."

The three of them departed the waiting room, letting the nurse at the duty station know they were leaving. Also making sure she had the numbers to get in touch with them should anything happen.

"I'll be in touch soon," the Detective told them.

"I'll follow you," Lisa said as she got into Keeler's old Dodge truck.

****

Chivas had stopped when he was well into the cover of the trees. Reverting back to his human form, he eased to the edge, staying out of sight from any people below. He had a clear view of the event now transpiring around the chaos he had left. He chuckled to himself as he recalled the terrified look on the woman's face in the vehicle.

The way she reacted, backing down the path. He could have caught and punished her easily enough. He wished now that he would have. At least he would have left her alive, but not in any shape to alert any others. Now, they would begin to learn what he was. It didn't matter; they could do nothing to him.

The Daemon watched with amusement at the comings and goings of these puny humans, always acting as if they could overcome any obstacle in their way. He observed the vehicles with flashing lights arrive, men in different uniforms, and some in everyday clothes. Some went into the dwelling, others searching the outside of the house.

His guess was that they were trying to track him. He was sure that he had left nothing to find, not anything these people in this day and time would pick up on anyway. These humans had given up and retreated from nature and had lost most of their inherent abilities. Or, so he had thought.

Chivas' anticipation rose when his spiritual guide informed him of the man Kevin Miller's arrival, his main target for now. He watched as the white truck pulled in and parked in the grass. Two men got out and went inside the house. Miller on the run, the other stopping to speak to a uniformed man.

He then realized that both men were his targets. The one that had stopped was the second on his list the woman had emblazoned in the ceremonial fire. Thinking that this would be the best chance at catching the two together, he at once began to morph into an alternate form. Deciding on the dragon, as there were many men. The dragon would also cause the most damage.

Halfway through the transformation, the voice of reason entered his mind. He realized that to re-enter the scene would require a vast amount of killings just to reach the two men. This would far exceed his limited number of souls granted him by the Death Spirits.

It could also cause a great upheaval in the community. By doing so, he would have every able-bodied man and woman, including soldiers and lawmen tracking him. He was not worried about being injured; there wasn't a weapon the humans had that could mortally wound him. He had been born of magic, and only the most powerful sorcerer or spirit could cause him death.

What he was concerned about was his not completing the task assigned by the masters. To fail them meant eternal torment. Returning to full human form, he would have to be satisfied with monitoring the actions of the men and women in this situation. Then, he could determine the best way to go about completing his mission.

Chivas then noticed the woman he had just had his way with being brought out and put inside one of the conveyances with the flashing lights. The man, Miller, entered with her and two others. The doors were closed, and the vehicle left the scene. He would catch up to Miller later. For now, he would continue watching.

A bit later, the second targeted man and the woman from the car were being led out of the house, wrists bound together, and placed in separate vehicles to be taken away as well. He began to rise from his hiding place to leave in search of his next victim when Chivas noticed a lone man.

He wasn't wearing a uniform like the others. This man also was searching separately from everyone else. He watched as the man observed the marks left in the hood of the car the woman had been driving, kneeling to place his hand on the ground beside it. This human was paying attention to what little evidence was left behind.

The man scoured the soil, following Chivas' path by the outbuilding, past the place where he had originally waited for the Miller woman to arrive home. On occasion, he would pause and stoop to look closer at the soft dirt, taking his time to study his findings. This one was succeeding in tracking him.

As the newcomer continued to follow the obscure trail up the slope, he was getting closer to the tree line and coming straight at the Daemon's hiding place. Chivas decided that this one had to die here and now. This human was different from the others, and that made him a threat to his task.

He had crouched on all fours, preparing to take the form of the wolf, when someone from below called to the man tracking him. He relaxed as the human turned and answered, walking back towards the dwelling once again. This man, he concluded, would need to be taken care of before leaving this territory.

He could continue his search at a later time, discover the truth, and alert the surrounding towns and settlements before the Daemon could complete his tasks in each one. With this in mind, he got up and went in search of his next victim, putting this annoyance out of his thoughts. He relished the anticipation of the fun yet to come.

****

After receiving a call from Becker, Detective Hamby released both Bishops and drove them back to the last crime scene to retrieve her vehicle. This was not normal practice, but he was going there to meet back up with Stan anyway. Something about some evidence that was known only to himself. Why he hadn't shared this with the other investigators was puzzling.

When he arrived back at the Miller home, almost everyone else had finished their jobs and left. Becker had just made it back and was exiting his Crown-Vic. Hamby joined him as Stan waved Jeff off and turned to converse with the other detective, ignoring the Bishops.

Casey's Camaro had been towed in for examination for further evidence. Kevin had left the keys in his Z-71, so they removed her suitcases from the trunk of the car and deposited them in the truck. Jeff drove his wife home and helped her re-pack her luggage into their spare car, a Dodge Stratus. He then followed he to Interstate 81 to make sure she was safely on her way.

He phoned Kevin and joined him and Lisa back at the storage trailer. There, they finished loading up the explosives and anything else that might be of use. When finished with that task, they locked the door this time, and the three of them headed back to The Tavern to meet up once again with Thomas Keeler. Detective Becker would join them there as soon as he could.

With Kevin and the Z-71 in the lead, Jeff was following in Keeler's Dodge. Halfway there, he noticed Lisa had been staring at the side-view mirror for some time. She occasionally glanced out of the rear window.

"Something wrong? I mean, besides the obvious." Kevin asked her.

"I think we've got a tail." She replied.

"Are you sure? Which car is it?"

"The gray Expedition, five cars behind Jeff. He was behind me on the way to the hospital, and I'm sure it's the same one that followed us from there to the storage trailer." She stated."

"Ever seen it before?"

"Not to my recollection. I have no idea who it is. But he's tailing us alright." She said.

"Keep an eye on him. Let's see where he goes when we pull into the bar." Kevin told her.

She rode the rest of the way with her eyes glued to the mirror, keeping watch on the tag-along. It had her wondering if this could be another threat to get in the way. She quickly jumped out of the passenger side as Kevin parked the truck, staring the SUV down as it passed. It didn't slow any.

"I don't know who it was, but the same vehicle followed me to the hospital, then tailed us from the storage trailer," she said, shrugging her shoulders.

The threesome entered The Tavern, stopping at the bar to order a beer and a dinner plate apiece. They then made their way to the table the group had occupied before seeing that Keeler was still sitting there, only now there was a new face with him. Evidently not one for small talk, Thomas got down to business the moment they were seated.

"This is Charlie Redwing, the Black Witch I was telling you might join us. He is twenty-sixth generation and well trained in the dark arts." Keeler stated. "Lisa, did you find a Holy man?"

"I found the only one I knew. He will not be of any help." She replied.

"Then we will have to make do. You three will have to serve as both bait and warriors while Redwing and I will do the work of four mages. We will be lucky to survive." Keeler said.

"Thomas, I called your nephew Jacob. He is bringing an object. He will help as well." Redwing informed Keeler, who only rolled his eyes.

"Do you think that we can get rid of this Daemon?" Jeff asked.

"It will be hard, the hardest thing you've had to do. But it can be done acceptable enough, I think." Keeler answered.

"Acceptable enough? What do you mean by that?"

"Here comes your food," Keeler said. "Eat, take nourishment. It may be the last meal you have together. We will plan when you are finished."

Giving each other a concerned look, they began to dig in. Kevin was biting into his cheeseburger when Lisa elbowed him in the ribs. She leaned her head towards the middle of the room, indicating he should take a look. Father Ellis was settling into a booth. He glanced back at her with eyebrows raised. An unspoken question to which she nodded and mouthed, "Yes."

Without saying a word, she stood and walked to the door, easing out into the parking lot. Two minutes later, she was back at the table. Jeff started to say something, but she held up her finger indicating for them to give her a few moments. She continued to eat her dinner. Kevin and Jeff looked at each other, puzzled, while the two Native Americans watched in amusement.

As he was finishing up his plate, Kevin's phone rang. He walked away from the group, standing as far away from the crowd noise as possible without going outside. He talked for a few minutes, shaking his head a lot while staring at the others. After the conversation ended, he made his way back to the group and filled them in.

"That was Detective Becker. He and Hamby found something at the house that led them to believe at least part of our story. They're on the way here to meet with us. He said they would explain when they got here." He said.

"Who is this Becker?" Keeler asked.

"One of the policemen that is investigating the murders. He and the other Detective may be of tremendous help to us." Kevin told them.

"I wonder what they could have found," Thomas asked. "Chivas moves as fast as the wind when he wants. He never leaves a trace or any way that someone could track him – unless his imprisonment has made him careless."

"What do you need us to do to help send this Daemon back to the Netherworld where he belongs?" Lisa inquired.

"We need to wait until your friends arrive, so Thomas and I will only have to say it once," Redwing answered. "We don't have the luxury of time to repeat ourselves over and over."

"That man over there," Lisa said to the others, "That's Father Ellis. He had to have been the one following us. Since he's come in, that Grey Expedition is parked at the lower end of the lot."

"Your Holy man." Said Keeler. "What did he say to you? If he's not going to help, why is he following you?"

"The police hadn't told him about his son's murder yet, so I had to tell him. Along with the whole story of what this Daemon was and where it came from." Lisa answered.

"But he did not believe you," Keeler stated.

"I don't know, he just got weird acting and said that God would not help me, that I was damned. Then he obviously followed us here. Why, I don't know." She said.

"It may not be for any good purpose, little one. We will have to watch him."

What was left of the daylight shone in the door as it opened. Several men entered with Becker in the lead. Four county officers and Detective Hamby had accompanied him. They rapidly approached the table and pulled some chairs around the perimeter. This created a gathering that was two rows deep and doubled in number.

Stan reached out his hand, introducing himself as well as the others to the two Natives. The rest of them nodded their heads in greeting. As he looked around the group, they could tell he had come to a decision. After a minute of silence, the Detective confirmed his participation.

"By the number of us, I'd say that we all leave and re-group in the briefing room at the station. Any objections?"

****

CHAPTER NINETEEN:

CHIVAS AND LEONARD COMBS

Chivas now had a specific target of his own – The tracker. That meant there were still a few around who had some warrior blood coursing through their veins; this man was one. Few people would have been able to discern the true nature of the marks he had left in his wolf form.

They called him Becker; I will draw him out later, he thought to himself.

Brightening up his spirits as he contemplated his next kill, he let the winds carry him in the direction of the fourth name he had been given. Unknowingly to him, it was the father of the first woman he had ravaged at his summoning. Her soul was already in the Netherworld, being toyed with and tortured.

The man he was searching for was Leonard Combs. He made his way along the river, back towards the settlement of Hickory Tree. As he traveled, he was deciding which kind of attack he wanted to make. He was here for a purpose, yes. But why not have some fun with it while executing his duties?

Then again, he was still getting used to the growth of this land since he was here two hundred years ago. The population had increased, dwellings had become closer together, plus now, there were the armed guardians that came rushing in with their flashing lights and fast, horseless wagons. They seemed to be at every turn in one way or the other.

Breaking off at the river, he cut across an open field with only the waning daylight to left to mark his passage. He avoided the two farm houses set off to themselves, even though they would have made for some easy pickings to whet his appetite for blood. He had an unquenchable thirst for battle.

Crossing a smaller paved route, he found solace in entering a new, longer stretch of woods that would conceal his travels better. There had been a time when he could destroy entire villages, roaring through in Dragon form, and leave no trace. It had been as if those small communities had never existed.

In those times, the villages had been spread out far apart. He could linger in one spot for days, having his way with the women, listening to them scream and beg as he killed them slowly. Each one had been a new experiment in the art of keeping one alive longer than the last. It would then be weeks or even months before someone came along to find nothing but a burned-out swath of land.

These images of the past were still lingering in his mind as he realized that he had arrived at his destination. He was standing at the edge of a pasture, looking at the dwelling of his target from atop a small hill. He sat in the damp evening grass, leaned against a fence post, and began searching for the path he would take.

The ground was open between here and the home. He would have to walk first among cattle, then through some goats without getting them stirred up, thus alerting those in the house of something out here. The dogs in the yard would be the tedious part. Those he would have to dispatch off quickly as they would be able to smell the wolf in him.

While Chivas waited with impatience to make sure the right one was inside, he noticed a middle-aged woman talking to a teenage girl. It appeared as though she was cooking. He'd had his fill of sexual conquests for a while, so if these two got in the way, he would dispose of them in a quick fashion.

A short time later, he saw two sets of lights coming up the driveway. A smaller vehicle followed by what he had heard referred to as a truck. Another woman remained in the car as a man, this one he sensed as his target, climbed out of the truck carrying a bag in one hand and a bottle of whiskey in the other.

The man, Leonard, appeared to have already been in the bottle as he was staggering noticeably. He stopped by the side of the car and glared in at the woman operating it, then yelled at the house for someone named Sherry. Ah... it was the teenager. One less body to deal with, he told himself as the girl left in the vehicle.

He gave the man a few minutes to settle in for the evening, then rose and stretched. Chivas looked around to get his bearings and decide which direction he would leave in after completing this task. He discerned that the logical course would be the way he came.

He would go back across to the river using the same stretch of woods to cover his departure as well as it did his arrival. He would let the spirits take over as a guide from there, leading him to the location of the main target – Miller. Or maybe it would be the man that had and could track him. That one had to go.

Making his move, he eased down the knoll and crossed the fence into the cow pasture, slicing the animals' throats with his elongated, talon-tipped hand as he went. This was done for no reason other than the smell of blood brought him pleasure.

Treating the goats in the same fashion, he then slipped behind the barn, making his steady way towards the dog lot. As he jumped the six-foot fence, the canines leapt into action, barking, gnashing, and biting at him. This situation was resolved with a few slashes of his hands, dispatching the animals in less than ten seconds.

The Daemon dropped to the ground on his stomach just as the back door was thrown open. The man stepped out onto the porch, shotgun in hand. He peered around the backyard for a minute in his half-drunken state before he realized that his dogs were all lying down. His inebriated mind told him they should have been up running to and fro, yelping and barking.

The woman joined him on the deck, inquiring if something was wrong. Leonard didn't hesitate as he swung around, back-handing her across the face, drawing blood. He then shoved the woman back into the home.

"So," Chivas thought, "this one is already living in her own torment."

As the man stepped off the porch with caution and took a stride towards the still dogs, Chivas instantaneously transformed into a wolf. He sprang up over the fence closest to the house, crashing into the man with enough impact to send them both flying through the doorway back into the kitchen.

Leaving Leonard lying for a moment, moving around the table, he spied the woman crouching behind a shelf as if to hide. Figuring her to be stationary for the time being, he turned his attention back to the man. He had risen to his feet and was fleeing into the next room towards a gun rack.

Hurdling into the room, he inserted himself between the man and the firearms, lurching back and forth. Toying with his prey, herding Leonard back into the kitchen. He laughed, as much as a wolf could, as he watched the stain of urine spreading down the front of the man's pants.

Having nowhere to run, the male picked up a chair and began jabbing it at the wolf, who swiped both the man and chair to the side with one swing. With his front paws, the Daemon pinned Leonard to the floor and just hovered over him, snarling in his face.

The smell of death and decay washed over the man; hot saliva dripped on his cheeks. Chivas morphed back to human form with the exception of his clawed hands. He enjoyed the smell of fear. This one was emanating much.

Holding the male down, watching the knowledge of impending death sink in, he was filled with amusement as this puny human shit himself to match the flood already in his jeans. He sunk his talons into the sternum at the top of the ribcage, ripping the man open from neck to waist, ending him.

The Daemon stood, looked at the woman, still cowering behind the shelf and shook his head. He turned and walked out of the house. He didn't need the numbers adding up that quickly. Colleen Combs breathed a sigh of relief and passed out.

****

CHAPTER TWENTY:

THE UNCONVENTIONAL MEETING

Kevin was amazed as he looked around the room. It surprised him how a little faith in each other could draw people together as a community. Not as a whole in this particular matter, they were all still sworn to secrecy as far as the press went. They didn't want a county or city-wide panic.

Some people would take things to the extreme and start crying Armageddon and that type of stuff. More innocents could be harmed than saved. Of course, the way most media put their own spin on things, not factoring the whole truth, it could and would hinder their efforts at stopping the Daemon.

Between Detectives Becker and Hamby, those two had brought in five county deputies who were loyal to them. Two were Cherokee themselves and knew about the legends of old; all five had military experience.

Charlie Redwing had summoned two young bucks from his tribe, and Keeler had called his nephew in. The nephew was an apprentice white witch of some renown himself. He was on his way, bringing with him some spiritual and enchanted artifacts.

Kevin had also made a few calls himself, mostly to friends who were hunters and knew the mountains as well as they knew their backyards. One call he had made, though, he hadn't been too sure about, was from Larry Black. He had the reputation of being a partier who loved the ladies and the nightlife.

Years ago, however, he had served in the Air Force with Neil and was said to have been one of the best munitions men as well as trackers around. His misgivings were set at ease when Larry had shown up fully dressed in his camouflage, sporting his old 30-30 rifle. This appearance was topped off by the dual semi-automatic nine-millimeters strapped in shoulder holsters, complete with spare clips and boxes of ammo.

All the men Kevin had called in were ready to go to war when they heard about Neil, Rick, and the other murders. They still hadn't been told that they would be going up against a Cherokee Legend come to life. As far as any of them knew, it was a man-hunt for a serial killer who had disappeared into the mountain.

We would see just how much of an open mind these people had when Becker took to the podium with the truth in a few minutes. Some may laugh, some may leave, and others, he hoped most, would at least listen to the evidence.

While waiting to get the meeting underway, Jeff and Lisa were in the corner of the room, talking quietly between themselves. Feeling out of the loop, Kevin joined them. They were trying to get an idea of where to even begin to find the Daemon and how to attempt to lure it back to the sacred site.

So far, the only route they knew Chivas had taken was straight down the ridge at the Flint Mill, where they had found Neil, to Kevin's house to attack Angie. Other than that, they hadn't a clue as to where something like it would go besides the other targets' homes, and there had been no notification of that.

The door to the briefing room opened noisily and Detective Becker strode in, motioning for everybody to take their seats. He went to the podium at the front of the room. Reaching overhead against the rear wall, he grasped a handle, pulling down a screen. It burst to life as Hamby activated a laptop wired into a projector. "The two of them had been busy," Jeff thought.

Crime scene pictures of each victim so far appeared on the screen, showing the horrendous wounds left by the beast. Kevin cringed as the photographs of his wife were shown. Every man in the room was paying the utmost attention, not a sound was made.

Becker then used a laser pointer to identify each wound and the similarities between them, estimating the lengths of the non-serrated blades used to make them. He had left Angie for last, acknowledging that she had been the only one left alive, and that was touch and go at best.

The Detective stated that she should awaken soon, at least enough to give a description of her attacker, which he presumed was the same one that committed the other atrocities. He noted that there had been one eyewitness to the departure of the assailant and that she had been interviewed, then advised to leave town until contacted.

"At this point," he stated, "We do have a very good theory as to not whom, but what it is committing these killings. Most of you will find it unbelievable, as I had trouble comprehending it myself."

"Just what in the hell is it then?" One of the men questioned from the back of the room.

"Those of you with Native American backgrounds will come closer to an understanding," Becker continued. "That is if you believe the tales of your heritage and the legends."

This declaration brought about quite a few questions about the meaning implied in the last statement. Holding his hands up for silence, he then hit the remote, bringing up pictures of the gouges in the hood of Casey's Camaro. The next slide showed an extensive paw print in the dirt beside it.

These led to a series of photos showcasing the prints as they trailed through Kevin's backyard, bypassing the garage and up into the woods. He had captured their full attention once again. At this revelation, both Jeff and Lisa turned in their seats to look at Kevin, who only shrugged and mouthed, "I didn't know either."

"What are you saying?" one of the men asked. "That a big dog or wolf did all this?"

"To grasp the thought of what I'm indicating, we believe the culprit to be. You need to listen with an open mind to the complete story," Becker told them. "These two have been involved since the beginning. Lisa Smallwood, Thomas Keeler. Would you come up here and explain the best you can?"

Both made their way to the podium as Becker stepped away and was approached by a young dispatcher. He motioned for Detective Hamby to stay and beckoned Kevin to accompany him outside the room. Giving a puzzled look, Lisa began speaking as the door closed behind them.

"To really understand what is happening right now, we must take you back in time with a small history lesson. Mr. Keeler will begin with that."

Lisa stepped aside as Thomas commenced speaking. Looking at the men sitting, they were listening to the old man attentively and with respect, but also with a curiosity that held them in awe. She couldn't tell if they were giving Keeler time to talk out of politeness or if they were considering what he was telling them.

Gazing across the room at Jeff, she realized that for all she had been through, she didn't know if she believed all of it. If these men laughed it off, if they didn't give them the benefit of the doubt, then they were right back where they started from – Alone, except for the two Detectives.

She wondered if the twists to this situation hadn't just gotten their help out of desperation to find this killer in any way possible. Thomas had finished with his part of the story. Seeing that the men were still paying close attention, not fidgeting or looking for an excuse to leave, she gathered her courage and resumed her place at the podium.

"Gentlemen," she began, "this would not be happening if I hadn't made a terrible mistake searching for a sense of revenge…"

And with that, ending for better or worse, Lisa told her tale.

****

After leaving the Comb's dwelling, Chivas made his way back to the crest of the knoll he had been at earlier, once again observing the house as to the comings and goings that surely would take place. He didn't know why he had left the woman unmarred by his hands, only that it occurred to him that his number of allowed souls was closing in. He wanted to have a room for a little extra activity should the mood hit.

The Daemon leaned his head back against the fence post and wondered if the tracker would show up here. He closed his eyes lest the silver that was shown during communication with the spirits draw attention. As soon as he reached out to them from the depths of his mind, they answered.

The death spirits informed him not of the next task or location but with a warning. Men were gathered at that precise moment, led by the one who had summoned him and the witch who had instructed her to do so upon their command. The White Witch had turned his back on them and would pay for eternity.

His masters told him of the manhunt that would soon ensue and bade him to proceed with caution. He was to linger at this place a while longer, giving them time to be led in this direction. While occupied at this location, Chivas was to depart to another location, thus throwing them off his trail for a bit. He was to take care of the next target, to which the location would be provided at the needed time.

The communication with his bondsmen ended. He opened his eyes and waited for the sign to leave the area. In the next half-hour, he witnessed no movement inside the home or vehicles pulling onto the property. This led him to believe that the woman was still out cold. The thought had crossed his mind to go back and have his way with her and add to the number of souls anyway.

Chivas dismissed that notion in an instant as he saw the lights of an automobile moving slowly up the driveway. It was the same car that had left earlier with the young girl. He rose to a full sitting position, watching the pair intently. Both the older woman and the girl exited the vehicle and walked to the porch, stopping when they saw the door hanging off of its hinges.

"Daddy," the girl yelled.

No answer.

"Daddy, Momma," a little louder.

Silence.

The older woman gestured for the girl to stay put as she eased up on the porch and peered into the open doorway. She took a step inside. It took about five seconds before Chivas heard a loud scream of terror as the woman had lain eyes upon the gore of what had been a living man.

She ran back outside and cradled the girl into her arms, quieting herself down in the process. She walked back to her car and retrieved her phone. He heard her informing someone of the findings at the residence. She had apparently not checked on the Comb's woman. If so, she would have known that the woman had been left alive and intact. Any marks on her had been made by the man. Not him.

Still not feeling any guidance to leave the area yet, he continued to sit and watch as both the older woman and the girl climbed into the car and locked the doors. He assumed they were waiting for the men with the flashing lights to arrive. They did not have to wait long.

He moved further back into the treeline so the silver of his eyes would not be detected or, if it were, it would be mistaken for an animal. He watched as the emergency vehicles came, both carrying the medicine men (he assumed that's what they were) and the smaller ones that brought the armed guardians.

"A lot of good those firearms will do you," he thought with a chuckle.

The Daemon noticed the scene played out as it had at the Miller residence. They brought the man out on a wheeled bed, only this time there was no rush. He was draped in a white shroud covering from head to toe. They did have a woman he had spared up, awake, and walking her to the second of these vehicles. She was placed inside with the doors closed behind her. This one left a little faster.

Just as he had decided to go ahead and leave, Chivas spotted two more conveyances advancing up the drive to the house. One was the truck driven by the main target, Miller, at the other event. They parked in the yard, out of the way. He waited with anticipation to find out who these latest arrivals were.

His patience was rewarded with the sight of not just one but all four of his objectives together, including the tracker. Settling back into place, he surveyed the scene, expecting that, at some point, they would separate from the rest of the crowd. Then, he would make his move.

****

CHAPTER TWENTY-ONE: LEARNING THE DAEMON

Stan Becker was communicating with other officers as they arrived at the Comb's residence. When the 911 call first came in, the dispatcher thought it was going to be a domestic dispute, but they received one for that address at least once a month.

It usually turned out to be Leonard drunk and yelling obscenities. Every once in a while, there were bruises on either the mother, teenage daughter, or both. Neither would press charges, so all Mr. Combs ended up with was a drunk and disorderly charge for a few hours in the county jail.

Kevin stood listening to the conversation between Becker and the officer en route, having a heavy feeling in the pit of his gut. He knew. Just as sure as he was standing there, he knew the Daemon had found his way to Becky's parents' house, bringing death and destruction to another home. He prayed that the little girl, Shelly, was alright.

Within seconds of announcing his arrival, the officer informed Stan via radio that of the three family members, only Leonard had been attacked and killed. Trying to describe the scene as he was viewing it, the deputy grew silent, and then the sounds of vomiting came over the airwaves. He had not been able to look much closer.

Becker handed the mic back to the dispatcher and instructed him to let those at the scene know he would be there soon. Leaving the dispatch office, the two men headed back to the briefing room. They slipped in quietly as Lisa finished up her version of what was happening and how it came to be.

Kevin noted that some men had slight grins, some a look of astonishment, while others carried a thoughtful expression. The two officers, who were of Cherokee descent, had apparently listened to their elders as children. Both wore hints of anger on their faces.

Motioning for Detective Hamby to move to the farthest corner of the room with them, Becker told him of the call from the Comb's residence, giving him the details of the crime that he knew, including that it must have been bad for the officer to have gotten sick.

He then informed the other detective of his plans to visit that scene, taking Kevin with him to locate some of the odd kind of evidence he was looking for. In essence, he said that he was hoping to find prints like those at the Miller home and maybe get an idea of the direction where the beast was headed.

In the meantime, Hamby was to take as many men as would join, along with some national guard friends of Larry Blacks that had just volunteered to the mountain. They were to rig explosives, traps, and whatever else the two old Witches deemed necessary. He stressed that this meant the entire area from the Flint Mill trailhead across the ridge, encompassing Holston Mountain Trail.

He would need to take the explosives supplied by Miller, along with incendiaries and whatever heavy firepower he could gather from the armory. Hamby would also get together anything Keeler and Redwing required, no matter how useless or ridiculous it may sound.

Becker, himself, would contact the Feds and the TVA, as well as the Fish and Wildlife services, to inform them of an emergency. This would get them to clear all civilians from Camp Tom Howard Road and evacuate Little Oak Campground. The road was then to be blocked at both entrances, allowing only his team in or out.

The excuse that he would give Fish and Wildlife and the TVA that an anonymous call indicating a terrorist or biological attack. That ought to get them the proper clearance and, at the same time, keep those not in the know out of the way. It would also cover his ass legally as well.

The men were to set up a base of operations in the soon-to-be empty campground. They would take shifts riddling the trails with traps if for nothing else but to herd the beast in the direction the old Indians needed. Once set up and these tasks begin, Keeler and Redwing will be in charge.

When not on watch or working under Keeler, the men and women were to rest until alerted to take positions. When that call came, Becker, Miller, Smallwood, and Bishop would either have the Daemon on the run, or they would be pursued by it, thereby leading it straight at them. Hopefully, the situation will be the former. He would much rather be chasing the thing than have it chasing him.

When Hamby moved back to the podium, taking the meeting back from Lisa, Stan went to confer with the two old witches in private.

Kevin beckoned Lisa and Jeff to join him out in the hall, where he explained their part of the plan as he understood it at this point. He informed them of what was happening at Comb's place and added details he could share. At this news, Lisa backed away, shaking, tears coming to her eyes once again.

"Will this nightmare ever end?" She asked herself.

Just as Becker entered the hallway, she had an overwhelming insight.

"I know where he's going next. I know exactly where the damned thing is going to be."

"Where do you think it's going?" Becker asked.

"I don't fucking think, I *know*," she replied with confidence. "Listen, the Daemon has an order, a pattern if you will. One that he is following even though he doesn't realize it. Why didn't I think of it before?"

"I don't understand," the Detective said.

"Do you remember me telling you that I gave Chivas a list of persons I wanted sacrificed for my revenge?" She asked excitedly.

"Yes. I recall you saying something about it. I thought you were hysterical, though." Kevin returned.

"No. The names of these were dropped in the fire one by one, in order. In a way, it gave him a list. Your name was first. That's why he went straight to your house. Being that you weren't there, he attacked Angie." She declared.

"But what was his reasoning behind that? If he had a list, shouldn't he have stuck to it?" Kevin inquired.

"I don't know. Anyway, he was probably going to wait until you got home, but Casey's arrival spoiled that for him." Lisa theorized.

"Okay. Go on." Becker said.

"I have no idea why he didn't kill Casey, but I'd bet that he hid. Still waiting on you but couldn't do anything with all the police and such there. It would draw too much attention to himself."

"I'll buy that. Whose house was next, Leonard's?" Kevin asked.

"You left in the ambulance. So, he's got to wait on you. Jeff's house should have been next; he was the second name on the list. But Chivas saw him and Casey carted off in the police cars." She stated.

"Thanks a lot, bitch. What did I ever do to you?" Jeff snapped.

"Nothing. Other than the fact you're his best friend, and I wanted to hurt him in any way possible. Sorry. I don't mean any of it now." Lisa looked at the floor.

"Don't do much good now, does it?" Jeff said.

"Anyway, the next one was Anson, Kevin's brother. You know, an eye for an eye and all that. But the last name on the list was Leonard's, and it happened to be on the way." She informed them.

"So, where is he going next? My brother's?" Kevin pled as he asked.

"Yes. The only other name left until he can catch up with you two, he'll be heading straight to Anson's," she stated.

"He's not there, thank God. He's staying with a friend over on Iron Mountain this weekend. I'll call and warn him, though." Kevin said as he pulled out his phone.

"We can go stake out Anson's house and see if this Daemon shows up. We might be able to lure it to the mountain from there." Becker said.

Kevin rejoined the group as they exited the sheriff's office and entered the parking lot. As they walked towards his pickup, he noticed the gray expedition belonging to Father Ellis sitting at the end of the last row in the back. It was as if he had tried to keep it out of view.

"Look," he said. "Is he still following us, or did they call him over his son's death?"

Becker radioed the front desk, from which he received an answer he didn't like at all. "Nobody's been able to get in touch with Father Ellis. He's not supposed to be in there."

✳✳✳✳✳✳✳✳✳✳✳✳✳✳✳✳✳

After Detective Becker and the others had departed the room, Hamby went to the front of the room. He was trying to listen to the hushed conversations between the men. He was determining which ones, if any, had believed the story they had been given by Keeler and Smallwood.

It seemed, from what he could hear, that the odds were in their favor, if for nothing else, out of curiosity. He knew for a fact that the five officers hand-picked by Stan and himself were loyal to them no matter the circumstances. The others, well, he was fixing to find out. Stepping behind the podium once more, he held up his hands for silence.

"Men. We've all listened to this incredible account. Though it's overwhelming, we need to come up with a quick decision. With the evidence Stan and I have seen, combined with the speed this killer moves great distances and strikes, I believe it's the only feasible explanation." Hamby said. "How many of you agree with me, and how many want to go home and keep this to themselves?"

All but two raised their hands, agreeing with the Detective that this, at least, warranted enough to take some sort of action. The two hold outs were surprisingly Keeler and Charlie Redwing. Seeing the look of confusion on Hamby's face, Thomas stood and spoke to the crowd.

"I say to you. This is not the most feasible explanation. It is the only one. I am the one who instructed Lisa on how to summon and raise this Daemon. I have conferred with the Death spirits. There are also Life spirits. These are very much a part of this world as the air we breathe."

Hands were raised to question.

"Hear me out." Thomas ignored them. "This Daemon can and will rape, maim, murder, and destroy as much as he possibly can. He is a product of chaos. His name, Chivas, means 'Soul Harvester.' He takes both wolf and dragon form. This is to be taken seriously. Your life and those around you hang in the balance."

Taking Redwing by the arm, the two old witches made their exit to wait in the hallway and let the men decide for themselves. Hamby, clearing his throat for attention, asked the question once again. This time in a simpler form.

"How many?"

All hands were raised again.

"Okay then. All of you." the detective started issuing orders. "You six, go with Officer Frasier, get all the ammo and explosives loaded. I'm going to take Jensen and Blair to take the old men where they feel like they need to be."

"What are the rest of us to do?" He was asked.

"Larry, you're in charge of base camp," Hamby told him. "Take the rest of the men, join up with the few National Guard members you called, and set everything up at Little Oak."

Feeling somewhat satisfied that things were now in motion, Hamby sighed. The three teams moved out.

✳✳✳✳✳✳✳✳✳✳✳✳✳✳✳✳✳✳

Deciding that it would be better to stick close together, Kevin and Lisa followed Detective Becker and Jeff in the Z-71. The first

238

ambulance they passed didn't have lights or sirens on. The next one did. Becker figured the first one held Leonard's corpse.

Parking in the yard, the group exited the vehicles and joined the deputies who were in the kitchen. From the way things first appeared, it had been nothing but a pure massacre. It was hard to find a spot that didn't have blood splatter on it.

Kevin nudged the detective to the side, nodding his head towards the flooring at the door. Becker looked at the boot prints leading outside. They followed the tracks onto the porch and into the backyard, where they disappeared as if the wearer had vanished.

"Shit," Becker said, looking at the others, "Any ideas?"

"Not much of one. We know from the lore that Chivas can change into either a wolf or a dragon. I suggest we get some flashlights and search the area for prints." Kevin stated.

"That seems to be our only option right now," The detective agreed. "You three start looking around, I'm going back inside and see what I might dig up."

Jeff went to the Z-71 and retrieved two lights and a third from the unmarked Crown-Vic. AS he walked back up the yard, watching the other two engaged in conversation, his mind was filled with questions. He had never believed in the supernatural, witchcraft, or magic. He always had thought of it as bullshit for someone to make money off others' gullibility. Now, it was smacking him in the face.

Handing each a flashlight, he looked at Kevin questioningly, always following the others' lead. Jeff would do whatever it took to accomplish something. He just needed someone to take over and get him started.

"It's obvious we begin here at the deck, then split about ten yards apart and ease towards the smokehouse," Kevin said. "What we're searching for is prints much larger than what Leonard's old dogs would leave."

"What then?" Jeff asked.

"Alert the other two, and together, we'll follow them." Came the answer.

Lisa moved ten or twelve yards to the right, Jeff did likewise to the left. Sweeping the lights back and forth, each scoured the ground in front of them as they advanced. Fifteen feet from the dog pen, Kevin spotted the first set of large prints. He whistled at the others, motioning them to join him.

He dropped to one knee, brushing the area around it clear of leaves and gravel. It was a wolf's print, for sure. He had never seen one so huge, though. From one side to the other, it was much wider than any man's hand, at least fourteen inches from one digit to the other. Just as he fully comprehended the size the animal had to be, he heard a sharp intake of breath escaping Jeff at his first view of it.

"I guess that answers the question of how big this thing is," Kevin said. "Size and viciousness. We're in trouble."

"And it's up to us to stop it," Lisa added. "I'll go get Becker."

By the time she had returned with the detective, the two men had followed the tracks through the pen, out the other side, and were headed up the hill. They had traveled to within fifty yards of the tree line by the time Lisa and Becker had reached them, far from the residence.

"Hey guys, wait a minute," Becker said as he approached. "Let's think about this for a second before we get too far away from everybody else."

"Think about what?" Jeff asked.

"Listen. Aren't the woods ahead a little too quiet? Don't the air itself feel a tad bit heavier as if it's pressing down on us?" Becker stated.

"Now that you mentioned it," Kevin observed as he looked at the other man, "I've got the feeling as if we're being watched. Have ever since we arrived."

"That's what Miss Smallwood and I were discussing earlier. Maybe it's paranoia, but I've had years of experience. Military and police training, not to mention plenty of time in the woods coon hunting. I know when something's watching me." The detective stated.

"What are you suggesting we do?" Jeff asked.

"Our best bet is to stick to the plan. We'll go to your brother's place. Wait it out there, or lead it directly to the mountain and Keeler." Becker said.

All four agreed. They turned and began making their way back to the vehicles, unaware of how close they had just come to being slaughtered.

****

Chivas's anticipation grew as he observed the foursome exit the dwelling. Three of them produced lights and were trying to track him, while the fourth went back into the home. If they did pick up his trail and follow it close enough to the wooded area, he would take the opportunity to get rid of them. He would send their souls on to the Netherworld to be tormented for eternity.

He was more excited than he had been in centuries.

"Ahh, they have found it," he said to himself as the first print was uncovered. "And now the mice come to the snake."

He noticed the female conferring with the men, then turned to go back into the home. With his keen eyesight, he observed every move the two men made as they shadowed his trail through and over the dog pen.

The one named Miller was a good tracker. This he could tell by the way once the trail had been established, the haste with which he pursued it increased to almost a normal walking speed. At this rate, they would be within striking distance in the next sixty seconds.

Just as he moved himself into a crouching position, the most comfortable one in which to obtain the wolfen form, he felt a hand on his shoulder. Smelling the scents of the dead, he did not have any doubts as to whom the presence belonged to, one of the Death Spirits.

As Chivas moved his head to see which master had chosen to be by him at a moment of triumph, he felt, more than heard, another move up on his other side. Both confused and humbled by this unusual honor, he looked to his right to see Raven, Master of War, in human form. To his left, Tuloc, Master of Witches, had appeared cloaked as a bear.

"Not yet, my son; others draw near. Wait and watch," Raven's voice came directly to his mind.

Relaxing his stance, Chivas only then noticed the woman and the other male emerge from the dwelling. They quickly caught up to his original prey, yelling for them to stop. He witnesses the hurried conversation that ended with the group descending back towards the house and other humans.

Oh, he could take on his dragon persona and wipe every one of them out with ease. Only, it would cause a great disturbance and, in time, give warning to the surrounding settlements before his arrival. Maybe, just maybe, giving those in the cities time to find a way to defeat him as they learned more about him.

"We can hear your thoughts,' the bear began, "And you are wise to let your logic go in this direction. We do not need to take any more souls than was decreed by the council."

"I will get my chance," Chivas said.

"The time for you to take these humans will make itself known to you. It is not far into the future." Tuloc finished.

"During my time in this world, in my mortal life, I was a leader to vast armies," Raven continued. "My most successful battles came not only from straightforward attacks but employed the strategy of patience."

"I believe that you have another one to seek. Go take that sacrifice, and these will come, giving you yet another opportunity," the image of the bear said as the two Masters departed, once again leaving Chivas to his quest.

The Daemon knelt there long enough to watch his enemies converse with a few other humans, once more disappearing into the dwelling. They finally emerged and split up between the two vehicles they had arrived in. He then stood and turned to proceed with the next stage of his assignment, pausing briefly to watch the car and truck vanish down the driveway.

Normally, he fought and killed without any emotion, so it came as a surprise to be filled with such intense rage. It also felt akin to ecstasy, and he liked it. If any involved in the scene below had glanced into the tree line, they would have seen two bright silver orbs glowing for a moment, then moving away.

Instead, the investigators were so consumed with their work at home the sounds of the Daemons' traveling song being whistled were carried away on the breeze. Completely unheard.

****

CHAPTER TWENTY-TWO:
SETTING UP BASE CAMP ON THE MOUNTAIN

While Larry Black had part of his crew hooking up to RVs and travel and Storage trailers, the rest were loading up communications equipment, listening devices, and portable video monitors. The other officers not attached to this endeavor, observed the activity with wonder.

As far as the general department, all the remaining deputies knew was that the two senior detectives had ordered those not tied to this mission to stand aside. They were not to ask any questions or leak anything to the media. They assumed this had something to do with the five murders on the mountain and the one in Hickory Tree.

The loading procedure took an hour to complete, ending with two dozen pick-ups pulling their loads out of the county storage lot. Larry was the last one through, towing the trailer that contained most of the weapons and ammunition. The explosives he carried were stacked above the bed of his truck, strapped down.

His mind wandered as he drove up Highway 394, back to the times he had spent with Neil, growing up hunting and fishing together. They had both joined the military together, surviving basic training as well as special ops training, leaning on each other for support. Had been stationed together overseas.

Larry had been the best man at his wedding, was there when Neil's children were born, and gave him a boost when his family was killed by a drunk driver. But, even after all that, somehow, their friendship had become distant. They now only spoke four or five times a year and on holidays and special occasions. Now, he was dead. The only thing Larry had his sights on was revenge, no matter the cost.

He was brought back to reality as the radio came to life. Kyle, who was driving the lead truck, wanted to know if the whole convoy should pull into the store on 421 and get fuel, including propane or should only he stop since his vehicle carried the tanks.

"No, just you and I," Larry replied. "The rest of you go on to Little Oak and start setting up base camp. It should already have been evacuated."

When they reached the store, he followed Kyle into the parking lot, pulling right up to the propane tanks. Now, he had to come up with an explanation why he wanted every bit of propane they had and charge it to the county. He radioed Detective Hamby for an authorization code and went in to sign for everything.

After all was confirmed by the sheriff's dept, he helped load the fifty-plus tanks onto the flatbed. These were secured with ratchet straps and rope. The two hurriedly exited the convenience store's lot and drove to Camp Tom Howard Road.

Forty-five minutes later, they pulled into the campground amid a flurry of activity. RVs were being set up and leveled, and miniature satellites were in the process of being mounted high in the trees for the best reception.

While some participated in these tasks, others busied themselves running the electric and telecommunications cables to what would become the heart of the operation. Video cameras were placed in strategic areas to view the entire area surrounding them.

Larry looked around and was satisfied that so far, everyone here was taking this seriously. They worked well as a team. He chose the sight next to the command center to back the ammunition trailer into, swiftly setting it up in a convenient location.

Taking a moment to catch his breath, he then went to help the others with the campers in which they would sleep in shifts. With every man and woman working steadily, it wasn't long before the recreational campground took on the appearance of a portable military base.

All video and audio feeds were working perfectly and he had instructed a couple of the men to distribute weapons and ammunition equally between the participants. He, himself, was stationed at the radios getting ready to contact Hamby with a progress report.

He took a sip of the coffee someone had set beside him and picked up the microphone, hoping he was on the right frequency. They had decided it better to use a seldom utilized channel for privacy to avoid as much public knowledge as possible. This undertaking would be handled under the radar unless it became an imminent danger to the general public.

So far, with the exception of Carter and Ellis, who just happened to be in the wrong place at the wrong time, there was a specific hit list he was told. The perpetrator should stick to this, they hoped. If that were to change, then the media would be alerted in order to inform the community. Then, he supposed, all of law enforcement and the National Guard would be deployed.

"Hamby, this is Black. Do you read me?"

"Loud and clear. How's everything going up there?" came the reply.

"Set-up is almost complete. I'm fixing to assign sentries around the perimeter and send the rest to get some sleep." Larry told him. "We'll rotate every two hours in order to keep the men fresh and alert."

"That's the way to do it," Hamby said. "You're falling back into your military routine. It never leaves you, does it?"

"No, sir, I guess it doesn't."

"Hell, I always knew that party boy life you were trying to push was bull. You're trying to bury something. Seen some rough times over seas, didn't you?" Hamby observed.

"Yes, sir. Several times, I wouldn't have made it if it weren't for Neil." Larry acknowledged.

"Well, things are going smoothly so far. Lay down and get some rest yourself. I want you one hundred percent when the shit hits the fan." The detective said.

"When might you be joining us?"

"I'm back at the Tavern with Keeler and Redwing. His nephew is meeting us here with some sort of ancient instrument or weapon they say can be used against this daemon." Hamby informed him. "I'll get back to you in a couple of hours."

"Sounds good. Talk with you then." Larry ended the conversation.

Giving instructions to the sentries and those monitoring the radios, he retreated to a camper close by and took one of the beds. Sleep fast took him over.

****

Father Ellis had been in the county Sheriff's office trying to get a report on the death of his son. The only version he had heard so far was the troubling account that Miss Smallwood had related to him earlier. That story was so perverted and distorted that he thought it to be the ramblings of a mentally ill person.

The way she had portrayed herself as the true cause of the killing, even though claiming not to have been involved in the actual murder, made him wonder if she hadn't lost touch with reality. Surely the girl had to be living in a fantasy world to have acted out some ritual on South Holston to begin with. It had angered him to hear such blasphemy believing in more than one God. And to speak of it in his church at that!

On the way to the jail offices, he passed a briefing room filled with people. Odd for this time of night, he figured that it was possible the meeting had to do with the murders that had taken place earlier. He might find out something about his son. So, he slid into a small offset in the wall to eavesdrop for a minute or two.

With caution, he peered in the window and took note of a couple of dozen officers and other individuals he had seen around. He noticed the two old Native Americans seeming out of place, as well as the contractors that had done some repairs for the church, Miller and Bishop. Then, to his dismay, he saw Lisa Smallwood standing next to a detective at the podium.

"Oh no," he thought, "She's got them listening to her outlandish tales. Maybe when she's finished speaking, they'll send her to a nice hospital to get some help."

Though he had already heard her craziness, he stayed to listen to her go through it again, waiting to see what kind of response she received from this crowd. When she stepped down, to his surprise, there was no outrage, no shaking of heads or laughing. The Detective was inviting one of the old men to speak of what he knew.

Staying long enough to hear most of what the old Indian had to say, he determined that if all these officials halfway believed them, maybe there was something to this version of events. It was at least enough to get his curiosity aroused. He decided to follow Miss Smallwood when she left.

The priest made his way back out to the parking lot and concealed himself behind a hedgerow that allowed him a clear view of Miller's Chevrolet, guessing that she had been accompanying him. Less than thirty minutes later, she and the two builders exited the building accompanied by a Detective.

He saw the girl recognize his vehicle. She and the officer went back into the Sheriff's office. No doubt they were searching for him. They came back out within ten minutes, talked among themselves for a few seconds, and then split up between the two vehicles. They both turned left out of the lot in the direction of Bluff City.

Hurrying back to his Expedition, he pulled out in the same direction, not far behind. He would stay with the truck she was riding in. By the time they had cut down River Road towards Webb bridge, he guessed they were going into Hickory Tree. Crossing the bridge, he spotted the flashing lights of police cruisers and ambulances illuminating the landscape of an old farmhouse.

Ellis pulled off the pavement where he had a good view of the comings and goings of the residence without being too noticeable. An hour later, the two vehicles he had been following came out of the driveway and turned in his direction. As they passed, he backed into the field enough to turn around and continued behind them.

CHAPTER TWENTY-THREE:

A MAGICAL PLAN

D etective Hamby, along with officers Jensen and Blair, had brought the two old Indian Shamans back to The Tavern to await Keeler's nephews' arrival. The artifact he brought with him was referred to as a 'Locking Staff.'

This, according to both, would not destroy the Daemon, but would at least imprison it back to the Netherworld, unable to re-enter long as the staff remained undisturbed. To ensure this, when all was finished, the top of the rod would be driven at least a foot below the surface and covered back with dirt and rocks.

As they entered the bar and grill, noticing that the place was now filled almost to capacity, Hamby approached the bar. He showed his badge and asked that the large back table be cleared for an official meeting. He knew that his request could be denied, but he was ready for that contingency.

He figured the hassle of moving a few customers shouldn't be too much trouble as he could put a damper on the atmosphere by conducting a few ID checks and random searches. A busy place like this, well, you could always find something.

"Hey, Scooter," he said as he leaned against the bar. "I've got a party of five. Expect it to grow a little. I need that big table in the rear corner. Can you handle that?"

"Awww, man, come on. It's Friday night, Soul Collision's playing, and you know that means soon it's going to be standing room only," The bartender whined. "Can't you go somewhere else?"

"No, we can't and won't go anyplace else. Our guest is on his way, and I can't reach him to change plans," Hamby stated.

"Police being around is going to make everybody nervous, you know. It'll take the fun out of the night."

"I'll tell you what," Hamby said, "I won't harass or mess with your customers as long as you oblige me. How many under-age drinkers do you think are in here right now?"

"Shit, come on." Came the reply as Scooter wiped his hands on a towel. "Tony, watch the bar for me a minute."

The hefty bartender came around and led the group to the furthermost table in the rear. Then, he informed the college-age-looking people that they would have to find another table for the evening. Although there was some hesitation at first, they grudgingly stood and left as soon as they noticed the uniforms.

"I appreciate it, Scooter. You're a fine man," Hamby told him as the five took their seats.

"Yeah, fuck you too. That bunch won't be spending any money in here tonight," he replied as he watched them make for the exit.

"Can I get you something to drink, or are you just going to cost me money?"

"Seeing as how you're losing profits because of us, yes, bring us a round of Bud Lights," Hamby said with a laugh.

"Make mine a Coors," Jensen added.

Scooter motioned for a waitress to fill the order and went back to tend his customers at the bar. The five of them sat in silence, observing the crowd mingling and dancing as they waited for the band to start.

Not long after the beers were brought to the table, the DJ stopped his music and announced the Soul Collision as the band took the stage with a loud roar from the party goers. The Detective noted the two old men conferring with each other in hushed tones and watched as the two young officers stared as if trying to figure out what was being discussed.

"Guys, unless you speak Cherokee, I don't think you're going to make hide nor hair out of that conversation," Hamby told them.

"I understand that, sir," Blair said. "It's just that we only know what they say is the cause of this ordeal. We're trying to figure out if they have a plan."

"Yeah," Jensen added. "We feel like we're left in the dark about the important part and being asked to trust someone we just met. If we don't know the end-game, we could get killed ourselves."

"That is correct, young man," Keeler said, hearing the officer's remarks. "As a matter of fact, you will be told every aspect of the strategy as it becomes clearer to us. You will be instructed of every move to make."

"Yes, sir. I didn't mean any disrespect," Jensen said.

"Understood," Keeler continued. "In the end, most of those who participate will suffer injuries. Some severe, some to the point of death. That is sadly unavoidable."

Hamby, perceiving the troubled expressions on the men's faces, turned to Keeler and asked, "They do have a point. When are we going to lay out a plan of attack, or are all of us going in blind?"

"We do not expect anyone to enter into this ignorant of the actions to be taken," Redwing interjected. "But we, ourselves, do not have a strategy completely devised yet."

"How do you go about planning to fight a Demon?" Blair asked

"*Daemon,* not Demon," Redwing continued, "It really comes down to your detective friend and the three with him. How they lure Chivas to the mountain and the reaction of the Daemon to their moves determines what we do."

"So, for now, we're at the mercy of events that haven't unfolded yet," Blair stated.

"That is correct, my young friend. As the white man says, sucks to be us right now," Keeler chuckled.

"There is your nephew," Redwing stated as a man in his mid to upper twenties approached the table.

The detective moved to look as the man stepped up to the table. He appeared to be more of an athlete than an apprentice witch with his build. The younger Cherokee stood around six and a half feet tall with broad shoulders, muscular chest, and biceps as thick as corded steel.

All this tapered into a "V" shape to his waist, which rested on legs that were carried by thighs the girth of small tree trunks. Long, Black hair flowed over the top of a flannel shirt to his belt loops. Herman Survivor's hiking boots completed his appearance.

"Hello, Uncle," the newcomer said. "I can only guess by the instrument you asked of me and the speed it was needed that you've gotten yourself and this territory into some real trouble."

Motioning for the waitress to bring another round of drinks plus one, Keeler indicated the young man should take a seat. As he sat, the young Indian looked around, taking mental notes. After taking in the crowd and staring each one at the table in the eyes for a few seconds, he retrieved a beer for himself as the drinks were delivered.

"Gentlemen," Keeler began, "This is my nephew Jacob Ryder from the Northern tribe. Although still under apprenticeship, he is a formidable sorcerer on his own. He will be of enormous help."

"I still do not know what you want of the Locking Staff or of me," the young man replied.

"Join the crowd, Jake," Hamby said as he turned up his Bud Light.

"The name's Jacob," he said with a firm tone. "Not Jake."

****

Kevin could feel her eyes on him as he drove towards Anson's homestead on Graybeal road. Glancing in the rearview mirror to make sure Stan was keeping up, he reached for the radio, turning it down to almost a whisper.

"You know, Leeland's death was an accident. I would never have let that happen on purpose." He said.

"Yes, I realize that now," Lisa replied.

"Then why do you keep staring at me like that? Still trying to figure out a way to get rid of me?" Kevin asked. "That's as good as done after we clean up this damn mess you've gotten us into."

"No, I'm telling myself how stupid I was to carry a grudge like this all these years. You're right to be angry over this," She stated. I should've been happy for you and Angie. I felt as if she abandoned me, too. Now, this disaster is all because of my unwillingness to forgive."

"It's not only a disaster, it's crazy. Six people we know are dead. Murdered by something that shouldn't be in this world, to begin with, and we've got what a few policemen on our side?" He said.

"This *thing,* as you refer to it, has a name, Chivas. And according to Keeler and Mr. Redwing, he can be banished from this plane of existence as he was once before." Lisa replied.

"If we can trust the word of two old witches that supposedly talk to the spirit world. One of them told you wrong how to summon this Daemon without a way to control it," Kevin said. "Listen to me. I sound as if I belong in an asylum."

"Trust me, I myself feel like we're walking in a nightmare, wondering if I'm ever going to wake up." She said.

"Lisa, there's no point in disbelief now. All we can do is try to send this monster back to hell or wherever you dragged it from. Then maybe we can go on with our lives. What there is left of them." Kevin said turning the radio back up, letting her know this conversation was over.

Riding alongside the moonlit river, he let his mind run through the chain of events from when he and Jeff had driven up on Lisa walking up the mountain road early this morning up to this minute. It took him a few seconds to realize that all of this mayhem had occurred in less than eighteen hours. Mind-Blowing.

His train of thought drifted from memories of Neil and Rick pulling pranks at work to having a cold beer together at The Tavern after a long day to wondering about Angie. The hospital said they would call if anything about her condition changed, but so far, he hadn't heard a word. He would call and check after they were set up at Anson's.

In a way, he was eager to face the Daemon head-on and take his anger out on that which deserved it. Then again, Kevin knew that he had no idea of what it really was, what it was capable of, or how to defeat it. He had never heard of a beast such as this before. How could you begin to possess the skills to fight something not of this world?

He looked in the mirror to see Becker's car ease to a stop behind him as he braked for the red-light at the Bluff City bridge. Turning left, he reached into his pocket for a cigarette, looked over at Lisa, and gave a painful grin.

"You know, a swift kick in the balls would have been sufficient," He said half-jokingly.

At this, she turned away from him and burst into tears.

"Women."

****

The ride to Kevin's brother's house had been accomplished mostly in silence. Both Jeff and the Detective were lost in their own thoughts. Jeff was wondering if Casey had made it safe to Atlantis Beach, far from the reaches of this situation. He hadn't heard from her.

He was also pondering the few details he did know for certain pertaining to the task they were about to undertake. There wasn't much he was assured of other than the fact that it would be lucky if any one of them survived it.

CHAPTER TWENTY-FOUR:

A SHORT REST

Stan, on the other hand, was thinking back to his three tours of duty in Iraq, comparing the bloodshed he had witnessed there to the gruesome sights seen today. It was these images that filled his head as he followed the Z-71 through the gate at the end of Graybeal Road. They drove down the driveway that led to a two-story home set on the river. The nearest neighbor was thirty-some acres away.

He and Jeff exited the Crown-Vic warily, eyes searching the surrounding landscape for any signs of danger. The other two climbed from the Chevy truck and made their way to the front porch. Knowing where his brother kept the spare key, Kevin retrieved it from the top of an exposed rafter and unlocked the set of French doors.

Having observed nothing out of the ordinary, the two followed Kevin and Lisa into the house, locking both the door and the deadbolt behind them. He surveyed the rooms that he could see from his current position.

Kevin had just begun to do a walk-through to see if the Daemon had beaten them there when Becker grabbed him by the arm. Stan shook his head no, and held up two fingers to indicate that no one was to go anywhere alone. Picking up on the meaning, Jeff motioned that he would go as well, stepping beside his business partner.

After watching the two creep up the staircase, he commenced searching the lower level with Lisa on his heels. They each took stances on the sides of the doorways, peering into the rooms with caution before entering.

The first floor consisted of a kitchen that led to a 'mud room' before exiting onto a large deck surrounding a swimming pool and changing rooms. These he would leave alone as the entire area was completely enclosed by a six-foot privacy fence. There would be no surveillance of the back yard and bordering field from this level.

The door to the right of the cooking-dining area entered into an oversized bedroom, enhanced by a twenty by twenty walk-in closet. It had its own private bath with a separate shower and a make-up/dressing table for any female visitors.

Hearing a sharp intake of breath, he turned to see Lisa admiring the bath with a grin. He realized they each needed to take turns freshening up, maybe getting a small amount of sleep in shifts if allowed. Short naps and even shorter shower times as the others kept watch.

The next entrance descended two steps down into an entertainment room filled with a variety of amusements. On one wall was mounted a seventy-inch flat screen, in front of which sat a huge couch with recliners on each side.

To the left, there was a regulation pool table with a wet bar and stools behind it. Far-right of this sat a second set of recliners in front of another flat screen into which PlayStation Three and Four and an X-box were wired.

"Damn, I'm in the wrong line of work," Becker said.

"Nah, all this isn't from construction work. Anson designs new game proto-types in his spare time and sells them to the highest bidder," Lisa stated. These are just perks. He was always smart like that."

Still shaking his head in wonder, Stan noticed the sliding glass door. He promptly checked it to make sure it was locked tight, drawing the curtains closed. The pair entered the living room once again by the opposite opening of the one originally used.

They found that the other two had returned. Jeff was sitting by the window observing the side yard and driveway. Kevin also was keeping a watchful eye out the other window which gave him a clear view of the front on the opposite side leading to the pool area gate, which was always secured from the inside.

The Detective opted to kick back in the lazy-bot for the moment, arranging his thoughts.

"Miss Smallwood," he began, "I saw the way you were slobbering over that shower. Why don't you go ahead and make use of it? It might refresh you some."

"You don't have to tell me twice," she replied with a grin, turning back in the direction of the private bath.

After she had been gone for a minute, he got both men's attention with a wave of his hand. He obviously had something to say for their ears only.

"I wanted her occupied for a while to let her calm down some. She may act like she's made of steel, but she's held it together so far. I'll give her credit for that. But, out of the four of us, I believe that one will be the first to break," Becker told them.

"Maybe," Kevin responded, "What do we do in the meantime, just watch and hope that we're right about this being next on the Daemon's agenda?"

Stan rose to his feet, moved across the room and reached into the next one, and flipped the switch that lit up the kitchen. He then strode through the living room, switching on the lamps. Grabbing the remote, he turned on the television, turning the volume up to a normal level.

"Nope," he said, "we make it appear as if your brother's home entertaining a couple of guests and wait."

Kevin resumed looking out of the corner of the window.

"Shit."

****

CHAPTER TWENTY-FIVE:

LENA AND HEATHER/ RUNNING

INTO THE ENEMY

Chivas had swiftly moved through the small patch of woods and across the fields, slowing some as he stepped onto the road. His senses, or maybe it was the masters, were leading in the direction of the younger Miller's home. Moments later, headlights rounded the curve. The vehicle they belonged to came to a stop alongside him. Two women occupied the car.

"Hey, handsome," a young sandy-blonde woman asked. "What are you walking out here in the dark all by yourself?"

"I have a task I must perform," Chivas answered, leaning on the passenger door.

"Well, a good-looking man like you doesn't need to be in such a hurry on a Friday night. You should be out having some fun," The brunette added, taking a long pull from a whiskey bottle.

He thought for a minute how easy it would be to have his way with both females, leaving their corpses behind when finished while sending their souls to the Netherworld. Suddenly, the voice of one of the masters spoke to him in his mind.

"Why don't you go with them, get a viewpoint of how people congregate in this time and place? We may return in the future to collect a few more souls. The information would be good to have."

Grunting approval in his own head, Chivas asked the women, "Where is this place you're going to have fun at?"

"A bar and Grill named The Tavern. You mean you've never heard of it?" The brunette asked.

"They've got a great band playing tonight, Soul Collision," the driver added.

"No, I haven't been in this area long, so I do not know of this Tavern," Chivas said.

"Hell, climb in if you want to go with us; there's no cover charge tonight. We'll make sure you get where you're going when the parties are over," The Blonde stated.

After the brunette moved to the back seat, the Daemon climbed in the front, barely getting the door shut before they were rolling. His senses and desires grew, becoming a rollercoaster inside of him. He didn't notice the one in the back seat had asked his name twice until she tapped him on the shoulder.

"Chivas," he replied.

"As in the liquor? That's neat. I'm Lena," then motioning to the driver, "and that's Heather."

The Daemon sat back in the seat, only speaking when necessary in order to mask his true nature. A nature of forced sex, pain, and murder that was begging to be cut loose in the presence of these two females. He controlled it, however, and before long, the car was one parked among many in a gravel lot.

The name of the place was boldly lit in bright blue letters above an entrance from which overpowering musical beats radiated. Watching the people lined up for entry, he didn't know if he could trust himself in a brash crowd such as this one.

"Here we are," Heather proclaimed. "Let's go party."

Chivas had never, since his creation, seen or heard of a place like this. His mind was riddled with the sights and sounds of the nightspot as they entered. He spied an empty stool at the bar and decided that would be a good place to observe. He started in that direction when the blonde tapped him on the shoulder.

"Hey, aren't you going to come sit with us?" She asked.

"Oh, yes. I just wanted to go ask those men about the hunting around here. I may stay in town a while," he told her.

"Suit yourself. Lena and I will be on the dance floor or by the stage when you get ready to join us," She replied while walking away.

Taking the empty seat at the bar, he felt an otherworldly presence in the place. As he surveyed the crowd, trying to pinpoint where it was emanating from, the hair on the back of his neck began to rise. His vision sharpened immensely.

Chivas could feel the energy crackling in the air with a spiritual and magical manifestation almost equal to his own. He started looking deeper into the corners of the room searching for the source of this power, scanning the crowd or people gyrating to the pulse of the music.

As his gaze shifted to the right-rear corner, the cluster of humans parted for a minute, enabling him to spot two old and one young Cherokee. They were sitting with a couple of the ones in the uniforms he recognized from the places he had taken sacrifices from earlier.

In that instant, one of the old ones turned his head in the Daemon's direction, eyes locking like vices. Recognition immediately came to both, even though Chivas had averted his gaze in a second. He knew it was too late.

The old one had identified him, as he had known in an instant that the one staring at him was known to his masters as Keeler. They had conferred with him across the thresholds of the spirit world on many occasions.

But what was he doing here? Certainly, the old man would not interfere with the Master's conquest, and he was the one in this realm who had helped set this chain of events in motion. What confused him more was that he felt a power equal to his own emanating from both the old wizards as well as the young one.

The difference was that these two had the intensity of Life Spirits surrounding them whether they knew it or not. Rising from the bar stool, he decided to confront them about their gathering together with the humans. Here and now.

****

Deputy Jensen gave Hamby a tap on the elbow as he nodded towards Keeler. The Cherokee Witch had become motionless, staring at something across the room. He noticed the old man lay his hand on Redwing's forearm. The other one also stiffened up as his gaze followed that of his friend to the other side of the room.

At this point, both Blair and Jacob, who had been in an animated conversation, became silent as they turned in to see what the others did. Their focus was immediately drawn to that of the tall Native American advancing towards them with a curious but determined expression on his face. Pushing his way through the crowd, Chivas continued his steady approach.

"Is that who or what? I think it is?" Detective Hamby asked with concern.

"It certainly is," replied Keeler. "That, my friends, is the Daemon Chivas."

"Shouldn't we get the hell out of here?" Blair asked.

"I know we do not have a complete plan of action," Redwing said, "But I do not believe that even one such as he would show his hand in a crowd of this size."

"If he does, we're fucked," Hamby muttered under his breath as the adversary closed in on the table.

The six of them watched as the Daemon strode across the dance floor with a purpose. He came straight to their table, only stopping when his thighs hit the wood. The air surrounding them became thick and noxious, half smothering them while the large entity stood in silence. He stared upon them one by one until his gaze fell to rest long and hard on Thomas.

"Chivas, it is surprising to find you here. Why don't you sit down before you draw unwanted attention to yourself," Keeler said, gesturing to and empty chair.

"I don't think it's as much of a surprise as you let on," the Daemon answered as he pulled up the chair. He reached over, took Jacob's beer, and downed it in one long drink.

"As a matter of fact," Chivas continued, "I believe that you knew I was here in this town. You instructed the girl, after all. And you have gathered your little band of warriors here to plot against me."

"Yes, I knew you were in this area. I was referring to the fact that it threw me off guard to find you in this place. This bar, at this moment." Keeler answered him.

"But you are planning to try and stop me, aren't you?" he said as he flicked the bottle lid across the table at the young deputies, "Why else would you be here with another Witch, a Black Witch at that, and an apprentice."

"You tell me," Keeler came back at him.

"These weak humans won't be of any help to you against me. You must be using them as fodder to keep my attention focused away from what you three are doing. It won't work. I'm too strong for this few in number and power. You know that." Chivas stated.

"There are ways of removing you from this world, and you must understand that," Redwing said. "The balance must be restored. Only your masters are trying to tip it too far in their favor."

"Does it matter? I was given a task, and I will complete it." The Daemon said.

"Go do what you feel you must. But remember, we will be there, and I will see to it that you encounter a force that even your masters cannot overcome," Keeler stated.

"We will see," Chivas replied as he stood to leave. "Know this: I will give each of you the most painful death imaginable if you get in my way."

With that statement made, he turned and strode back across the room and out the door, leaving the six watching the exit long after his departure. The men could only sit in silence, thinking of how close they had sat to death.

****

As Lisa was drying off after the soothing shower, she heard the ringtone of Detective Becker's phone chime. She finished toweling herself off and then began brushing her hair out, taking the time to observe the cuts, scrapes, and bruises over her body.

"Son-of-a-Bitch," she heard Becker exclaim from the other room. A quick conversation followed in hushed tones that weren't as easy to make out.

Lisa cut her primping short, quickly dressing in a pair of jeans and a shirt that belonged to one of Anson's girlfriends. They fit well enough, not perfect, but they would do. She finished brushing out her hair, pulled her hiking boots on, and went back to the living room. Here, she joined Jeff and Kevin as they stared in silence at Stan as he completed his discussion.

Ending the call, Becker laid his phone on the end table. He held his finger up, indicating they should give him a minute before any questions were asked. He ran his hands over his face and through his hair, finally looking up at the three of them.

"Well, shit,"

"Shit what?" Kevin asked, puzzled.

"That was Hamby on the other end of that call. It seems our Daemon had a sit down with the six of them at the Tavern. He even partook in a Bud Light with them while carrying on a conversation." Becker told them.

"You're kidding. Right?"

"Afraid not. He said our Native American friends got chilled looks on their faces, and all of a sudden, this huge Cherokee buck approached from across the room and pulled up a chair with them." Becker said.

"So, no violence or anything went on, I take it?" Jeff asked.

"No, David, I mean Detective Hamby said it more like a couple of adversaries sizing up one another's strengths and weaknesses."

"But does Chivas now know our plans? And, is everything ruined now?" Lisa inquired.

"Hell, I don't even know what our plans are. Do you?" Becker shot back. "Because if you have any more knowledge of how to stop this thing than I do, Miss Smallwood, I suggest you speak up and save us a lot of worry."

Lisa walked to the opposite side of the room and sat on the couch, shaking her head.

"A little harsh there, weren't you, Stan?" Kevin said.

"I didn't mean to sound like an ass, but I haven't got a clue as to what your witch friends have up their sleeves. Or if he can even pull off what needs to be done." Becker replied.

"I met them at the same time you did, so I wouldn't exactly call them my friends."

"All I know is that we've got a murderous beast on the loose that's a danger to anyone or anything that crosses its path. And, apparently, it's not from this world either, which is mind-boggling in itself," The Detective stated.

"Well," Lisa spoke up, "Thomas is a very powerful witch, and from what I understand of Charlie Redwing, he is the most adept sorcerer in his tribal conglomerate. As far as Keeler's nephew, I don't know a thing about him other than he is ranked high enough to have access to ancient artifacts."

"Hey, what do you hear?" Jeff asked as Kevin had moved back to the window.

Making a circling motion with his hand, indicating they needed to keep the conversation going, he slid against the wall. He heard them chattering on, but his attention was now on the door as he eased towards it.

"Okay, let's recap the facts we do know," Becker continued on, catching on to Miller's hand signals.

"Fine," Lisa said as all eyes now followed Kevin's movements. "We have definite knowledge that this thing is a cruel, cold-blooded killer."

"If it has blood running through its veins at all," Jeff added.

"Second, it can obviously assume other forms, at least that of a wolf that we know."

"Huge at that," Stan Becker chimed in.

Kevin had reached the door.

"Three, because of me," Lisa said, as a tear ran down her cheek, "My friends are dead, and my sister is in a coma."

At this, she dropped off the couch onto the floor, sobbing uncontrollably. Kevin jerked the door open, grabbing and dragging a man into the house, throwing him to the hardwood floor. Becker drew his 380 Smith and Wesson, shoving the barrel against the man's head.

"What the hell are you doing here? Show your face!" The Detective commanded.

AS the man elevated his gaze upward to look at them, Lisa let out a gasp.

"Father Ellis?"

"I've followed you, and I saw the last crime scene. I believe you now and want vengeance for my son's murder. So, I and my faith in God are yours, I am here to offer what help I can."

****

CHAPTER TWENTY-SIX:

LARRY/ THE GIRLS MEET CHIVAS'

BLOODLUST

Larry could only sleep for a couple of hours. It was more like laying there dozing in and out. He was restless, ready to get things underway. When something was set in his mind as firm as this, he hadn't the patience to sit and wait. He had to be moving, doing something to get events in motion.

When he could no longer lay there, he rose and put his boots on, deciding that it was at least his turn to watch. He would relieve one of the others so they could get some rest as well. He was lacing up his Zamberlans, a premier boot, when his phone rang. Seeing that the caller ID showed David Hamby, he answered.

"Yeah, what's up?"

He listened to the Detective re-live the conversation with the Daemon at the bar and grill and was informed that the object they had been waiting for had arrived. He was told that the group was now departing to join him and the rest of the crew at the campground.

Larry exited the camper with renewed vigor and a new direction to vent his energy. He practically bounced off the steps of the RV and headed for the Southeast Sentries. This position offered the widest and furthest view from which something could come upon them. Officers Clarence Dietz and Joyce Caldwell turned with eyebrows raised in question upon his advance.

"Any movement?" Larry asked.

"Nothing out of the ordinary. Some wildlife was moving in the bottom," Dietz replied.

"Their probably curious, keeping a wide berth to forage for food. I received a call from Hamby."

"What did he say?" Caldwell inquired.

"Just that he and the others are coming to us now. We need to switch off for a bit so you guys can catch at least an hour's rest," Larry said. "Go tell the other sentries on post and send the replacements out."

As soon as the two officers left, Larry turned and faced the darkness below the ridge. Staring into the night, he couldn't help but wonder what was waiting for them in the near future. Was it pain? Torture, death, the loss of more friends?

He had no idea what they were up against or where it came from. HE did not know the chaos it could bring or, most important, how the hell they were supposed to defeat it. All he could do was trust that what Lisa and the two old men had told them was true.

Now, the crazy stories were backed up by reputable police officers, so what choice did he have? Larry had stopped by the morgue and looked upon the terrible wounds inflicted upon both Neil and Rick's broken bodies. He had never seen an animal do that to a human, at least not in that capacity. So, believe he did until proven otherwise.

If this beast could move like the wind, as they said, and inflicted that king of damage, he couldn't see them defeating it with explosives and traps. Hamby had better hope the object the old Cherokees now possessed, combined with their Native magic, had a lot more go juice than imaginable.

Thinking back to Neil, his lifelong friend, his eyes roamed over the side of the opposite slope. He took in the ghostly silhouettes of the trees they had passed many times while hiking this side of the mountain. They had only been allowed to come within so many yards of the campground, but the deer had been abundant along the fringes of the park. Trails ran down to the water, around the lake, and over to the net hollow.

His memories were interrupted by the approach of two men arriving to take over the watch from this position. Silently, he walked back to his camper and his makeshift bed.

"Those motherfuckers better bring an army of wizards," was the last thought that crossed his mind before he drifted off into a restless slumber.

****

Chivas had gone only as far as the edge of the outside lights when he exited. He decided to wait for his adversaries to leave. He crouched behind a dumpster at the end of the parking lot, giving himself a clear view of the entrance of the establishment.

He elected to remain until the group had left, then re-enter the building to question their waitress as to what of their conversations she had overheard. Curiosity tickled at the forefront of his thoughts. The old witches must think they had something of use, or they wouldn't chance facing him.

The Daemon had not heard any warnings from his Masters. Therefore, he didn't think they felt this small affront was anything to worry about. However, his better senses told him the old sorcerer and his allies at least believed that they had a chance. That led him to assume the group had something up their sleeves.

Whatever it was, he needed to find out and take the surprise out of it. If he expected anything, then Chivas would be better prepared for an ambush and could counter it without any problems.

Finally, the rag-tag group of six came strolling out the doors, stopping to converse a few moments more. They were splitting up, he concluded. "Hell, they don't have any idea where I'm going. All they have is guesswork," he muttered to himself.

Not realizing the older witches' levels of power and downplaying the young apprentice's abilities, Chivas was putting himself in a more vulnerable position than he should have. Overconfident and brash, he left the safety of the trash bin and chanced, easing up to the side of the building.

Making it to the front corner undetected, he took another risk by peering around the edge, watching the men from a distance of only fifteen feet away. If any of them happened to glance in his direction, he would stick out like a sore thumb.

It seemed to him that the only person doing any speaking was the one they had called a detective, although he couldn't make out what was being said. To him, it looked as if orders were being given to and agreed with by the others. Why was this human giving the orders? He knew nothing of the Netherworld or of magic.

After a couple of minutes, the ensemble separated and split into three different vehicles. Chivas watched as they pulled out onto the roadway, one going in the opposite direction of the others. This confused him somewhat. He assumed they would be traveling together to set up whatever lame ambush that had been dreamt up.

It didn't matter anyway. There was nothing to his knowledge that this small group of men could do to cause him any serious damage. Shaking his head in wonderment, he re-entered the building. Spying the young woman who had served Keeler's table, he started walking towards her casually so he wouldn't draw extra attention.

"Hey," one of the women he had ridden there with waved at him. The blonde, what was her name? He couldn't remember but went to see what she wanted to keep her from making a scene.

"I thought you were going to party with Lena and me? Instead, you went and sat with those weird-looking men," she said in a slurred voice.

Lena – that was her name, he recalled.

"Ah, Lena. I had some business with those men and just needed to confirm a meeting in the near future," Chivas told her.

"Oh? What kind of business are you in, honey? Because that one was a cop, he arrested me once," she said.

"A cop? What do you mean by cop?" He still hadn't learned the terminology of things in this day and time.

"You know," Lena replied. "Johnny Law, the police."

"You mean a keeper of the peace. A Sheriff." Chivas was beginning to understand the suited and the uniformed men's involvement. "No, my business with them is turning into a more personal nature, it would seem."

"Well. Do you have anything else to take care of tonight, or can you hang out with us for a while? I'd love to find out how a handsome buck like you could make a girl feel."

"Just one more thing. I need to speak with the woman who was waiting on them for a moment," He told her.

"It won't take long, will it?' Lena asked.

"No. If you want to get your friend, we can get away from this crowd, and I'll show you how I can make the two of you feel," he said.

As he rose from the bar stool and strode across the room, her eyes followed him.

"You don't know what you're in for, honey," she muttered to herself.

After Chivas was convinced the waitress had almost no information for him than he already had, he rejoined the two waiting women. They rode merrily back to Heather's home on the river.

Two hours later found him walking the road. He was pleased with himself for the way he had remodeled the girl's house so fast. Chivas had left it with a complete color change from Beige to Blood red.

****

CHAPTER TWENTY-SEVEN:
THE WHITE WITCHES PLAN

Officer Blair took Redwing the circuitous route to the mountain in order to stop and pick up some extra munitions. Hamby and Keeler went on to join Larry at the mobile command center at the campground. In the meantime, Deputy Jensen and Jacob headed to meet up with Kevin, Becker, and their group to give what aid they could.

Having been asleep for only an hour, it took a moment for Larry to recognize the young man who had awoken him. Daniel, a patrolman who hadn't been out of the academy six months yet, hadn't had to draw his weapon in the line of duty and, he surmised going to be one of the first casualties in this situation.

"The Detective and Mr. Keeler are here, sir. They are requesting your presence at the command tent."

"Yeah, tell them I'll be there in a minute. Coffee still going?" Larry asked.

"Yes, sir." Replied Daniel.

After the young man shut the RV's door, he sat up, slipped his boots on, and grabbed his smokes, firing one up. He wondered how many breaths he might have left before he became a candidate for one of the body bags they had brought. Shaking that thought, he left his camper to meet up with the new arrivals.

He entered the tent and observed that several of the other men had gathered around a table that he assumed had a blueprint or map of the mountain on it. Stopping long enough to take the cup of coffee offered to him by one of the young recruits, he nodded a brief greeting.
"Thanks," he said.

"Names Halo. My friends call me that because of my med flight missions in the service. Real name Richard."

"Yeah, thanks, Halo. You and the other pilot nicknamed 'Ghost.' You're the two we have on standby with the choppers, right?" Larry asked.

"Just the two of us, sir. I believe we're all you'll need." Came the reply.

I'm sure both the military training and medic status will come in handy in the next twenty-four hours. I have a feeling we're all going to be seeing some action soon. Be safe." Larry told him.

"Yes, sir."

Taking an opening at the table across from the old Indian, Larry noticed more than one set of prints, satellite photos, maps, and overlays scattered from one end to the other. At least they were well informed as to the layout of the land. He himself knew this area like the back of his hand.

"Detective, Mr. Keeler," he greeted.

"Larry," Hamby replied while the old man merely raised his hand.

"The beginning of the Flint Mill is about a mile and a half South, back towards Hickory Tree. Also, according to this, it's roughly two miles of steep hiking to the very top, which, by what Keeler claims, is where the final battle, as he calls it, must take place." Hamby informed them.

"Not as I say," Keeler answered, "But as the laws of ancient magic dictate. The exact location is Chivas' original summoning and banishment two-hundred years ago. It is also the place of his recent summoning."

"Isn't there somewhere else a little closer that would serve the same purpose?" One of the other men asked.

"No. That ground has always been, and will forever be, sacred ground. No matter how the land around it has changed, or man has altered it, that piece of land is imbued with magic. It contains many portals to various points in the Netherworld." Keeler answered.

"Okay," Larry spoke up, "Two questions. How do we get this Daemon to go there, and what do we do once it's where you want it to be?"

There were several grunts in agreement and curiosity from those in the crowd, which had grown to three deep all the way around the table. Halo reached for the Aerial map, turning it to face him.

"This shows that a couple hundred yards up there is flat. If that's the case, I can make an air drop of all the materials and weapons needed there. Point me to a few more accessible spots and I can make drops at those as well. It'll save your men a lot of time and heavy labor." The pilot stated.

"That sounds like a good start," Hamby replied to this. "Now, Mr. Keeler, would you be kind enough to begin filling us in on what the rest of us are supposed to do?"

Keeler continued to stare at the maps in silence.

"So far, all we know is you want us to lure the Daemon to that particular spot. I'd like to know How and what you expect the end result to be." Hamby continued.

"I like this map better," Keeler said, pointing at the Aerial map Halo had been looking at. "More detail."

As the old Cherokee stood gazing at it, Larry and the Detective exchanged a questioning glance. A silent question passed between the two. "Did the man even have a plan, or was he just winging it?"

As if reading their thoughts, Keeler pointed North on the map to the starting point of the Josiah trail.

"This would be one of the trailheads to begin herding Chivas up if he tried to come at us from a different direction to gain and edge on us," The old man said. "He would expect us to stick to the main trail, the Flint Mill."

"About three-quarters of a mile up, the Holston Mountain trail crosses, then veers off to join our trail jus a couple of hundred yards below our destination point," Hamby stated.

"Then," Larry said, moving South on the map, "We have an unnamed trail. Listed as the only Trail number forty-nine that goes up and crosses both the Holston and the Flatwoods Trails. We could use that as the alternate Southern trail."

"I say we set up charges on both of those trails as well as the Flint Mill and try to hers the Daemon where we need him," Hamby added.

"Do we have enough explosives and gear to set that up?" Larry asked.

"We do if I call Blair and have him stop by the Highway department and get all they have," Hamby replied.

"Sounds like the beginnings of a decent strategy. Let's work with that. In the meantime," turning his back to the table, "I need more coffee."

****

CHAPTER TWENTY-EIGHT:

WATCHED

Back at Anson Miller's home, Detective Stan Becker paced the kitchen listening to the discussion happening between the others. They were trying to convince Father Ellis that he didn't have to be involved any further if he had any doubts. The pastor would have it no other way though.

Becker was a religious man himself and was pondering the idea of teaming the good Father up with Redwing and Keeler. Stan believed that the Great Spirit of the Cherokee and our God of the Bible were one and the same. As well as the references to Upper Earth and Lower Earth or the Netherworld as Keeler called it, transcribed to be Christianity's Heaven and Hell.

He was thinking of the faithful ministers of old. The ones you only here of in old tales, leaving it to yourself to determine if they could really call down the power of Heaven to smite their enemies. To do that, Ellis would have to be a man of such faith, such conviction and devotion, it was unimaginable in the day and age.

"Are you going to answer that?" Kevin asked him, bringing him back to reality.

Becker picked up his phone.

"Hello. Yeah, we're here. No, nothing's happened on this end yet." Becker continued talking to whom was on the other end as Kevin rejoined the conversation with Father Ellis.

"Hold on a sec," Becker looked at Kevin, "Blair says Jensen and Keeler's nephew Jacob are on the way here. He and Redwing are on the way to join Hamby at the campground. But we need to distract the daemon long enough for them to get set up. May twelve to fourteen hours."

Kevin and Jeff exchanged worried looks. That was an awful long time to keep moving.

"We can try," Kevin answered.

Becker hung up the phone, then turned back to the conversation at the table.

"Why didn't you just send Jensen and Keeler's nephew up to the mountain also? I'm sure we're enough bait." Jeff said wryly.

"I want them here, Becker replied. "I know what kind of man Jensen is; we need him here if things get out of hand. And, I'm anxious to find out more about Jacob; see whether we can count on him in a pinch or not."

Turning to face the Pastor, Becker continued. "Father, I have seen firsthand what this Daemon can do. From what I gather, it not only has immeasurable strength but takes on the forms of both a giant wolf and that of a dragon. With that said, my question for you is this."

Taking a deep breath, letting his last statement sink in, Becker stared Father Ellis in the eyes for a moment. He asked his question then, not knowing if he would get the answer he was seeking.

"Do you have the faith it would take to face something of this magnitude? Do you have the sincerity and the relationship with the Lord like the ones of old, such as Moses and Elijah?

Everyone at the table became as stone. All eyes were on the pastor, awaiting his response. Of course, they expected some half-assed excuse that no one has ever proved the miracles performed in the days before Christ. They were all surprised at the answer they received.

Eyes on the ceiling, Father Ellis cleared his throat and began to speak slowly and deliberately.

"I can't say that I have the faith or the courage to ask God for power such as Moses or the steadfastness of Joshua and Elijah. But I tell you, I commune with my Father above more than most modern -day preachers."

So far, Becker liked this answer. Ellis continued.

"I try to live and fashion myself by the laws commanded in the Bible. They don't change, no matter how the times do. God is the same today as he was yesterday. His commandments are unwavering."

"Do you believe that you can be an asset to this undertaking?" Becker pressed on.

"I do know that I will be a modem of help. You see, I've been praying about this for eight days."

At this statement, the five of them could only stare at one another, trying to figure out if Father Ellis was pulling their leg or if he was half-mad with grief.

"Let me explain," the Pastor said. "Last Thursday, I was in my study when this man entered unannounced. Dressed in old clothes, he smelled like he hadn't bathed in weeks. I thought maybe he came to ask for some help. Instead, he addressed me by my first name and said, 'Do not mourn.'."

Letting that sink in for a moment, he stared at the door – a tear fell. Noting the uncomfortable silence that had crept over the room, he continued.

"I asked what he meant, and he said again, 'Do not mourn.' But he added to it the third time. 'Do not mourn for your loved one; he will be redeemed in Heaven.' Then he told me there was a more pressing trial ahead of me that this led to. That I wasn't to be afraid, for my Father will give me the strength to carry it through. Then, without saying a word, he stood and walked out the door. I tried to follow him in the hall, but he had disappeared." Ellis finished.

"So, you were told a week ago that your son was going to die," Lisa stated.

"In a nutshell, yes. I thought the guy was off his rocker, then, I started having these dreams. They were not comforting." The pastor said.

"All I can say," Jeff chimed in, "is welcome to the team."

****

He left the two females in a somewhat shredded state, but his urges in that department had calmed for the time being. Chivas ducked under the bridge to contact the masters. He knew they would not be happy with his straying from their directives. He also knew they would like the fresh young souls. He would not be scolded too harshly.

The Daemon sat at the river's edge, closed his eyes, and let his mind wander along the spiritual pathways. If any human tried this without years of instruction and honing of their mental abilities, they would be mentally and physically torn apart.

The dark ones must have been eagerly awaiting his contact, they appeared before he had called for their presence.

"We notice that you have taken some liberties for yourself without permission," began the one known as Slayer.

"I have taken nothing except that which presented itself to me," Chivas fired back. "Where are Raven and Tuloc?"

"Watching from the gateway. They are not pleased with your actions. The young female at the summoning – she would not have proclaimed your presence. The other two that rushed you were acceptable fatalities." Kurat the Slayer stated.

"I took what was there. You should be pleased with the extra souls for your collection."

"Yes, but the men in the vehicle that were giving you transport off the mountain? You should have used more discretion," Continued Aveal, the Deceiver.

"Look how quick the authorities were drawn into the path of our doings. Now they are aligned with the Witches who have given them more knowledge of our worlds than anticipated." Kurat said.

"As we speak," the Deceiver resumed, "they gather to trap you and end your journey too soon. Do not underestimate Keeler or the other. They come from great bloodlines with much magic flowing through their veins."

"After two centuries in the Netherworld, doing your bidding when you ask, I have taken a few extra pleasures for myself. As long as the agenda is completed, I believe that I deserve that." Chivas spoke up.

"That is not how we do things, you know this. You, my son, are walking a fine line between praise and punishment. Be careful how far you push it."

"You tell me not to underestimate the old ones," Chivas replied, "What harm can they do to the likes of me with a handful of humans at their side? I will destroy them."

"Keeler was crossing the boundaries between all three worlds long before he should have been able to. He is in collusion with both the Light and Dark realms. His power is not learned; it is infused into his very being." Aveal warned.

"But still," Chivas interrupted.

"Redwing, himself, is a formidable opponent," Kurat took over. "And Keeler's nephew Jacob, he is far beyond the apprenticeship level, he claims. We believe him to have as much capability and skill as his Uncle."

"Bah! They mean nothing to me. I am eons old, created at almost the same time as you were. These humans and witches are as insects to be trodden upon." Chivas boasted.

"Don't take victory for granted is all we ask," Aveal said. "You must finish this task: destroy the witches and the humans as well as those with any knowledge of what you are. Especially the pawn that summoned you. She, above all, now has links to the spiritual realms."

"I'm going to take my time with her, make her feel every ounce of pain due to her for dragging others into my path," Chivas said.

"We will take our leave of you now; you have much unfinished business. I would suggest the next visit you pay be to the younger Miller. Get rid of them." Kurat stated. "If you fail us in this, such misery as you've never known awaits you upon your return."

The Masters shimmered, disappearing into the night in a millisecond, leaving Chivas alone with his thoughts. Shaking the visit off, he then stood. Humming to himself, he brushed his clothes off and began in the direction of the younger Millers.

****

"I feel like an idiot just sitting here watching television while knowing what's happening out there," Jeff remarked.

"So do I, but Becker figures this will be the Daemon's next stop, and we need to act normal to lure it in." It doesn't know it's us instead of Anson and some friends." Kevin said. "Besides, we have to buy Keeler and the others time to set up what trap they have planned."

To exaggerate his point, he kicked back in the recliner and turned up his beer. Father Ellis was still at the kitchen table, deep in his prayers. Lisa was, surprisingly, asleep on the opposite end of the couch. In the meantime, Detective Becker was glancing out of the windows while engrossed in a phone conversation with those on the mountain.

For right now, it was a waiting game. Kevin needed the downtime, considering all that had happened in the last eighteen hours. He had called the hospital to check on Angie's condition. Getting all the information they had for him, he renewed his instructions to phone him in the event of any change.

Lisa had inquired as to her sister's status, and he had informed her that Angie was still in intensive care and still in a coma. Nothing had changed. It was at this news that Lisa had laid her head back and dozed off. Judging from the expression on Jeff's face, he could tell that he hated Angie's predicament but that he was also relieved that Casey had escaped harm and was now safely tucked away out of town.

Kevin looked at his hand, focusing on the wedding band. He remembered all the good times he and his wife had shared, and, some of the hard times as well. It had not been all wine and roses, but they had stuck together, enjoying every minute.

There had been a childless marriage. He had invested all his time in the business and in her education. Now, she was teaching full time as well as coaching the volleyball team while he, well, the business took as much or more time and energy than in the beginning.

His gaze fell on Lisa. Once, his childhood friend through whom he had met Angie. He journeyed back through those memories and found the one happening that had led to all this chaos. If only he had listened to her when she asked him not to take her youngest brother on his first deer hunt. You can't change the past, only deal with the present and make the best of the future.

"Headlights," Becker announced, turning from the window and pocketing his phone. "Looks like it's Officer Jensen and Jacob."

Lisa snapped awake at that statement, and everyone except Father Ellis, who was lost deep in his prayers, went towards the back door in unison. The two new arrivals didn't bother knocking but strode into the kitchen, meeting them halfway to the den.

"Does the suspect, Daemon, I don't know what to call him. But, does he know where this place is?" Jensen asked, Excited. "I think we just passed him walking the road about two miles east of here."

"I'm sure something is guiding him," Lisa answered. "The names were fed to his spirit during the ritual. And so far, he's found his way to their homes. Kevin's, Leonard's…"

She stared at the floor. "I think the rest of them have just been fun and games to him."

"We passed him doing fifty, but he looked exactly like the man that approached us in The Tavern and had the threatening conversation with the old Witches," Jensen said.

"I felt one who was walking with the spirit world. Being a sorcerer myself, I could feel the magic emanating from him. I'm sure he could feel the same coming from me as we passed," Jacob stated.

"If it was him," Becker started giving orders. "We need to get prepared. It won't take long for him to arrive. Jensen, pull your truck behind the barn and get back in here, bishop, go with him. The rest of us will be positioned close to the entrances. Remember, according to Keeler, there's no way we can stop him."

"There's not," Jacob confirmed. "You would become another casualty if you tried."

"Right," Becker continued. "So, for now, we just get him to follow us, lure him away from the mountain for now. Have to give those guys time to set the traps."

"Yeah, but where do we lead it to?" Jeff asked as he and Jensen came back in.

"Thacker's farm. It's two-hundred-plus acres bordering the South fence. Nothing there but woods with some open fields scattered throughout. A couple of ponds, and the river runs through parts of it. Several barns and outbuildings spaced all over it," Kevin responded.

"That's what we have, let's run with it," Becker said. ``We can keep him busy deciding which group to chase, then circle back around after while grabbing the vehicles and moving somewhere else."

"That will give him a little more travel time," Lisa added.

"One other thing," Father Ellis said. "Pray and try to stay alive."

Lisa, Kevin, and Jeff took up position by the doors leading to the side deck while Jensen and Jacob made their way to the French doors in the den. Meanwhile, the Detective was speed dialing Hamby and leading the Pastor to the front window, keeping watch on the road.

The tenseness throughout the dwelling was so thick that you could've cut it with a knife. Each one of them broke out in a cold sweat. The anxiety broke as they heard Becker say those dreaded words into the phone to those at the base camp. "He's here."

****

As Chivas traveled the roads toward the younger Miller's home, he thought about the conversation he'd had only minutes ago with three of the Masters. Their plans weren't on as grand a scale as his. After all, he aspired to gain in the ranks of the Netherworld and do the grunt work for eternity so they could amass more power through the souls he provided.

Of course, he would go along with them to a degree. But, at the same time, he would take a little extra each time, setting a few souls aside for himself. He knew how far the limit could be pushed. He had done it before.

This time, however, he had to destroy those who would seek to banish him again. If that happened, he would wind up back in chains, bound to do their dirty work for them for all eternity. There would be no next chances. The Masters would keep a tight rein on him.

He was still focusing on these thoughts as the blue F-150 passed him. Otherwise, the daemon would have picked up on the aura of magic emanating off the young Native American on the passenger side. It would draw his attention for a moment when the brake lights flashed on for a second, then off as the vehicle sped up.

He blew it off as someone who had been going to offer him a ride, then thought better of it, considering how late (or early in the morning) it was. A few minutes later, he cleared his mind of all thoughts, switching into hunting mode as he neared the property. He had never been told the addresses of the places he was to go. His instincts always led him to the exact spot of his next conquest.

Chivas turned onto the long driveway, sloped slightly upward, with rows of pines on both sides. He stopped halfway up the hill, and he sensed magic in the air. Knowing that the humans that dwelled here would have no education or ability in the true magics, it alerted his intuitions connected with the witchcraft of the world.

His guard rose, eyes both physically and mentally searching for the source. The house. It had to be coming from inside the domicile. All energies he detected were coming from that direction alone. SO, he thought, they are already playing their hand, and this is where it begins. As far as Chivas was concerned, he planned on ending it here as well.

He knew that at least one of the witches was in the home and had sensed the magic about the same time as he. Whoever had tried to lay this ambush was already alerted to his presence. He might as well stay in the driveway as planned, but a casual knock on the door was out of the question.

Instead, he would walk right on past the house and take cover behind a tree, bush, or outbuilding. Whatever happened to be convenient and still allow a good view of the dwelling. He would see what the reaction to this move would be. Then, he would resume the game.

****

"What the hell is that thing doing?" Becker asked as loud as he dared. "The Son-of-a-Bitch just walked right on up the drive into the backyard, then veered off as if he were leaving."

"He's not leaving," Jacob said as he strode back into the kitchen. "He's reassessing. Changing his plan of attack, for he knows this is not normal."

"How so?" The Detective inquired.

"He felt my abilities as soon as I felt his, about the time he left the road onto the driveway. He knows there is a witch or sorcerer in here." Jacob answered.

"Shit."

"I was afraid he would. I tried to mask it as best as I could but, being imbued with magic as his, impossible." Jacob stated.

"Alright," Kevin joined in, "so he's not coming straight in unaware. That's obvious now. How do you think he will approach?"

"I honestly don't know. He will likely observe the house for a few minutes trying to get a number on how many of us are here. What, if any, magical traps are set, then make up his mind how to best catch us off guard. I'll guarantee he's coming in, though."

"Well, the Detective said, "all I know to do is to get back by the entrances and be ready for anything."

****

Chivas settled on a smooth, waist-high rock behind the bushes in the corner of the backyard. If he parted the branches just right, he had a clear view of the windows and doors on this side of the driveway and the rear. Through these windows, he saw movement inside the dwelling.

With a slow grin, he observed the confusion and what appeared to be a hectic discussion caused by his sudden walk-by and subsequent disappearance just as quickly. From what he could see, there were at least four humans in the room, possibly more throughout the home.

There were three exits he noticed on his walk up the driveway. It pays to know the layout of the place you're fixing to wreak havoc on. The Daemon wished he was close enough to hear some of what was being said. He figured they were trying to guess where he had gone and why he hadn't attacked yet. It had to have shaken them up.

He was also trying to measure the level of power that emanated from the home. He could tell it was from a white witch, one that dwelt within both the light and dark realms of sorcery. He couldn't decide if the one that possessed the magic was enough to give him some extra effort that he hadn't counted on. Or, if it was the Native girl that had summoned him to begin with, and she didn't realize the potential in her.

He had promised that one that she would live to witness all his doings until the end, and live she will. This'll be the second set of slayings that she gets to witness first-hand. A promise was made, after all, and he didn't go back on his word.

But, the level of magic he was feeling from there, well, even one consumed by it had to have years of instruction and practice in which to obtain that kind of power. If it were she, he would have felt it the first time he had lain eyes on her. No, it wasn't the girl. Chivas was sure that one of the old ones was in there.

At first, he was going to burst in, catching the younger Miller by surprise and dispatching him in a quick manner. Now, with the interference of these lawmen and the intrusion of the two old witches, his intentions had changed. He would have to destroy them all, a number he nor the masters had counted on.

Yes, the soul count would rise. Of these extras, he could keep them for himself away from the master's reach or knowledge. Souls were pure energy. The more he kept, the more power his immortal self would gain until he could challenge for the position of a master in the dark realm.

Then, he would become one of the high council, answering only to the Grand Master. This most prestigious Daemon was known to the Native Americans simply as The Dark One, to the white man, the name he was most identified as was Lucifer.

But all that was for later. Now, his attention was on the ones in the building. He did know the female was in there, as well as the older Miller. He could smell them. It stood to bare that if those two were here, then that tracker and the other one were in attendance also.

Chivas continued to sit and observe for a time. Finally realizing that he would get no more information at this juncture, he decided on a course of action. Spitting out a thorny rose stem he had been chewing on, the Daemon stood and stretched, overdoing it a bit so at least some in the home noticed him through the windows.

When he was positive their attention was on him, he took two steps forward and was on all fours. His canine senses came to life in an instant. Pristine vision, hearing, and smell combined with the stealth and strength of the most vicious Lycanthrope. The Native American form was no longer visible. Making its way to the front of the house was now the giant wolf.

****

CHAPTER TWENTY-NINE:

SETTING THE TRAP

Larry sat on the tailgate of his truck, packing explosives and blasting caps into both his backpack and duffel bag, when Hamby approached him from the command tent.

"Redwing is here. He's conferring with Keeler, discussing our options, I suppose," the Detective said as he walked up.

"The only option I'm looking at is the one where I kill the son of a bitch for what he did to Neil and the others," Larry replied.

"Regardless of how we do it, that's the result I want also," Hamby said. "But you heard what Keeler has said. That this Daemon is immortal and days when the power existed to kill it is long past."

"That's what he claims."

"According to him, the best we can hope for is to banish it back to the Netherworld or whatever they call it. I figure it's their term for hell," Hamby told him.

"As long as the bastard's in for eternal punishment and torture, I'm fine with that outcome also," Larry snapped back.

"Anyway, I've just gotten off the phone with Becker. You know they're at Anson Millers' place trying to keep that thing away until we get ready for it," Hamby said.

"What does that mean for us now?" Larry asked.

"It means there's no waiting for daylight. It was coming up the driveway as we hung up. The Daemon's there," the detective stated.

"Shit. We've got to get on the ball," Larry said, packing faster. Dynamite, Thermex, blasting caps, fuses and anything else that explodes went into his bags.

"I've got Officer Blair going around gathering everyone up, telling them to hurry and grab their equipment as well," Hamby told him. "We're going to have to begin setting things up by flashlight. Two-man teams."

"I'll be ready in a minute. I'll join you at the main table as soon as I'm finished."

"Fine, I need to get back with Keeler anyway and find out which trail we're going to start on, if not all three. I'm sure Becker will call as soon as he can," Hamby said.

"If there's anything of him left to call," Larry muttered under his breath.

He tried not to imagine what was happening with the group stationed at Anson's house. They were using themselves as bait, and Larry had heard what kind of butchering this monster had done to the victims, Neil included. He prayed that the divine hand would watch over and protect them, ALL of them, through to the end of this nightmare.

He busied himself, loading his gear, hearing the scuffle of those around him doing the same. He heard most of them muttering either quick prayers or blatant string of curse words. Each one builds up their courage in their own way. It was a surprise not one of the original volunteers had left. The group he had here had some balls.

As he finished up, he equipped his utility belt. Larry was going in loaded to the max. He didn't want to waste time with more than an extra trip or two to get re-supplied. That would take time they didn't have to spare.

Satisfied with his packs, he fastened his service belt around his waist, flashlight, extra battery clips for his forty-millimeter, and the pair of Glock nines. He then deposited the forty in a side holster, the Glocks each sliding home into dual shoulder holsters with a few more ammunition clips in his zip-up pants leg pockets.

He took a deep breath letting it out slow as he walked to the command tent where Hamby and the two old witches were gathered around the maps. As he walked away, he reminded the others to restock his truck bed. He would drive that to the trail he was assigned to for quicker re-supplying.

"Mr. Black," Keeler spoke as Larry stepped up to the table, "I was informed that you have prior military experience. That you ran operations in Iraq and Afghanistan."

"He was actually a Ranger, special forces," Hamby volunteered.

Larry rolled his eyes on that one. "Yeah, that was fifteen years and about twenty-five pounds ago."

"Still have it in you, I'm sure," the detective replied.

"As I was saying," Keeler continued, "with your experience and leadership skills, you will head up a unit of ten and begin at the Josiah trail. Rig explosives on both sides no less than eight, but not more than twelve feet apart, spaced at intervals to keep him heading towards the destination."

"Run him up there, you mean."

"Steer him in the direction we want him to go. Do not let him out of your sight," Keeler said. "Of course, you may have to come running and help on one of the other trails should he decide to take them."

"I take it that where Josiah joins the Holston Mountain Trail, we're to rig it the same until it hits the Flint Mill," Larry half-asked.

"Correct. Make sure that everyone is set up with some sort of communication in order to keep all apprised of the progress. Both while setting the charges and during the pursuit," Redwing added.

"Two other teams will be doing the same to the Flint Mill and this trail number forty-nine," Keeler continued. "When you meet at the Holston – Flint Mill crossing, you and five stout men will join Redwing and me to set a perimeter at the ceremonial fire that will be built."

"What about everyone else after the explosives are in place?" Hamby asked.

"The rest will position themselves at strategic places along each trail, readying their weapons and scoping out the lines of fire," Keeler answered.

"I've got two questions for you," said the replacement helicopter pilot. Halo had received an emergency call from home and had to leave. That left them with only one pilot.

"Hurry," Keeler said.

"One, where do you want the airdrops of the weapons and explosives? I can do that, and it will save a lot of time."

"Drop them at a point halfway through each of the trails as well as the intersection of Holston – Flint Mill," Keeler told him.

"Yes. Mr. Keeler, how are you and Redwing going to get up that steep-ass trail to the top, plus cut and gather logs for this fire you say is needed? Neither one of you is exactly a young man anymore," Ghost bluntly stated.

"I believe that we and five more young men will be your first air-drop of the day," the old man answered with a grin.

****

CHAPTER THIRTY:

ATTACKED/JEFF'S DEMISE

etective Becker was peering out the picture window when the wolf stepped out of the darkness of the tree line into the moonlight. He had never seen such an animal in his entire life. This thing was three, maybe four times the size of a normal wolf. Its limbs were lined with nothing but pure muscle and sporting sleek, jet-black fur streaked with grey.

"Oh shit," was all he could say.

The beast stood there a few moments, staring him directly in the eyes. That was what made his insides churn. Not the long, dripping fangs nor the razor-sharp claws. It was those eyes full of hatred. They exuded an immense evil, a pure murderous gaze flowing in excess through two bright, shining silver orbs.

Snapping out of his thoughts, trying to shake the paralyzing fear, the detective backed away from the window. He noticed that Father Ellis had made a beeline to the kitchen, where the rest had gathered at the tone of his voice. With the curtain pulled to the side, all could see the brute clearly, even at that distance.

It seemed as if time had stopped. Becker, reaching the others, could feel the fear emanating throughout the house so thick you could slice it with a knife. For what felt like an eternity, there was no movement either inside or out. It was a stare-down of wills. Waiting to see who would be the first to move. That question was answered in one decisive moment.

All hell broke loose as the beast lunged into the picture window, coming through with a spraying of glass and wooden trim bursting as if a bomb had exploded. There wasn't any plan left to play out as the seven of them split in all directions. Part ran out the back door, the rest out of the side. Nothing on their minds except self-preservation.

Seeing that his prey was trying to escape and also knowing that they couldn't get away from him long, the Daemon slowly advanced across the living room. He made his way into the kitchen, tearing grooves in the furniture and walls as he proceeded.

He knew that they feared him like no other. He wanted to add to what they were feeling as the scent of their distress brought him delight as it filled his nostrils. He almost hated to end it, and this was rather enjoyable.

The four that had been trying to push their way through the side door were almost out as Chivas jumped. He snagged the man in the rear with those deadly talons, hooking him through the leg and dragging the human several feet back into the house. Blood began flowing freely across the floor as his catch let out a scream.

Jacob had halfway kept his wits about him, and, in the back of his mind, he was bringing all his protective spells to the ready. He hoped that he would not stumble over the words to the incantations, praying the magic would not falter. This would be his first battle with anything this sinister. Just as he arrived at the steps leading off the deck, he heard Officer Jensen scream.

Without giving it a second thought, Jacob turned and ran back inside to see that the wolf had the young man on the floor. The animal was hovering over top of him, fangs descending towards his throat. The mage whispered one word, left hand stretched to the heavens with the other pointing at the brute.

A bright blue streak of lightning flared from his fingertips, striking Chivas in the side of that massive head, blowing the surprised animal off his feet and across the room. He grabbed the injured man up, and together, they made it out the door before the Daemon realized what had just transpired.

Jacob shoved the officer into the policeman's Explorer quickly and instructed him to leave immediately. As Jensen fired the engine up, he saw the wolf push through the door frame and onto the deck not 30 yards from the young mage. The last thing he saw, as he headed down the drive towards River Road, was a man and beast eyeballing each other.

"Where did you come from, witch?" the voice of Chivas said through the wolf. The daemon was trying to gauge just how much power this young one wielded.

Jacob, in return, made no attempt to reply. Instead, calling forth an orb of electricity. He lightly passed it from one hand to the other. He was hoping that this show of resistance would give the others more time to retreat further into the woods and over to Thacker's farm.

In Jacob's opinion the group needed to split up again and give this creature several different paths to choose from. This would take as much time as possible for his Uncle and those preparing to fight this monster on the mountain.

This stalemate could only last so long, though, and a decision had to be made. He made it and suddenly hurled the ball of energy at the large canine, striking it full force on his left shoulder blade. The strength of which pushed the massive body back a few feet. Jacob replaced the magical weapon immediately, leaving him at the ready for another strike.

The eyes of the wolf blazed with a smoldering silver as it leaped off the deck and was on the young man in a split second. Chivas intended to take this young upstart's head off with one swing when he was hit in the side by several bullets being fired from the tree line. At this time, a second ball of energy caught him square in the face, momentarily blinding him.

By the time he had regained his sight, all those he had been pursuing had disappeared. Knowing that they could not get far before he caught up with them, he began loping toward the woods and the open fields beyond.

With each stride, his anger grew. Just who in the hell did these puny humans think they were to challenge him? He had destroyed entire villages and wiped out many of the white man's settlements.

All without the least bit of a worthy adversary. By the time he reached the trees, the Daemon had worked himself into a full-blown fury.

****

As the five of them reached the edge of the woods, Detective Becker heard the scream come from the house. Raising his hand to halt the others, he turned to see a flash of light brighten up the dwelling. This was followed by the sight of Jacob half dragging the officer to the county vehicle, shoving Jensen in the driver's side seat, and slamming the door.

"Hold," he said. "Miss Smallwood, take Father Ellis and make your way over to the field. Find a building to take cover in."

"Sure," she said, motioning to the pastor to come with her.

"No, on second thought," Becker changed his mind. "Keep going to the river and follow its banks all the way back around to Dry Branch Road. Walk about a half mile East, towards Bluff city, and find a place to get off to the side."

"What then?" Lisa asked.

"Stay in the weeds or tall grasses. One of us will come find you," came the answer.

"And if none of you live through this?" she asks matter-of-factly.

"If one of us isn't there by daylight, well, you're on your own. I'd say find Keeler and stay with him, Redwing, and Hamby on the mountain," the detective answered.

"Maybe I'll just run and leave town," Lisa said in defiance.

"You know that thing will be coming for you no matter what else happens. And stay away from anyone else's homes, and we don't want more innocent people killed," Kevin chimed in.

"Yeah, that's nice to know," she replied, taking Ellis' arm and leading him off into the trees.

Becker turned around just as the young mage threw the second energy sphere at the wolf. He drew his nine-millimeter, noticing Miller and Bishop had their weapons at the ready as well. Jeff, with his forty-four and Kevin's eyes, lined down the sights of his thirty-o-six rifle. All three of them opened fire on the animal as it advanced on Jacob.

Three guns firing, three clips emptied. The wolf was still on its feet, though temporarily blinded, as the sorcerer got to his feet and ran towards them. When the young man reached them, the foursome took off through the woods, keeping as fast of a pace as they could manage. As they approached the edge of the first field, Becker halted them once more.

"Guys, look, if we stick together, we're an easier target. Four of us, let's go four different directions," he said.

"Yes, that would be best," Jeff agreed. "Which way are you going, detective?"

"Straight down that hill by the barn and veer off to the river. But I will take the opposite direction as Lisa and Father Ellis, hoping to draw him away from them if he comes this way."

"I guess I'll stick to the edge of the trees going west," Kevin said. "Then cut down around the pond and back up to the end of Graybeal Road. Hopefully, I'll be back to Anson's and the truck in an hour." He turned to go his way.

"Hey," Becker said in a harsh whisper, "let's all try and meet back at the vehicles in one piece in an hour. Maybe lure him somewhere else. Too many people live close by."

"I'm headed South-East," Jacob said. "He can feel my presence long before he can smell you. I will try and draw him to me, away from all of you. At least for a time."

With that being said, the twenty-something Native American disappeared into the forest.

"Jeff?" Becker stared at him.

"Yeah. I'll. Well, shoot. I guess I'll split down the area between you and Kevin. I'll still end up coming to the pond behind Kevin and back up to Graybeal Road. That's the only option I have from here," he answered.

"See you at the trucks," the detective said, walking down in the general direction of the barn.

"Sure."

Jeff began walking parallel with the oaks and pines, not exactly having his mind made up where to go. He only knew that this was a nightmare. One that he wanted to wake up from. He didn't deserve this and was beginning to hate everyone and everything associated with this whole situation.

He hadn't traveled but a couple hundred yards when he heard the snapping of fallen branches. Something was approaching, and it didn't care how much noise it made. The time for stealth was obviously over.

Finding a large boulder protruding from the ground ten yards back into the tree line, covered by many fallen limbs, Jeff ducked in behind it. His back tight up against the rock, opposite the direction the noise came from, he chanced a peek around the edge. All of a sudden, the air became as still and silent as a tomb.

Jeff's breathing became shallow as he realized that the beast had somehow snuck up on him. Even with all the commotion it had gotten around him and was now practically on top of him.

He could feel the hot breath on the side of his face and neck, the stench of rot and decay entering his nostrils. Knowing that the end was more than likely near, he felt the wetness spread down the legs of his jeans as he pissed himself. Deep down, he knew that he was as good as dead.

Without hesitating, giving himself the only chance that he could, he jumped up on the opposite end of the boulder, staring eye-to-eye with his executioner. Jeff didn't know if he would be able to make it back out of the trees into the open field or not. It seemed as if he had lost all control of his muscular function, shaking excessively from head to toe, unable to stop.

So far, the animal hadn't moved an inch. It just stood there staring curiously at him. The wolf finally opened its mouth showing off its bone-crushing incisors, jumping at him teasingly. At this, he slowly side-stepped to his right, towards the field.

He felt that it would allow him at least a half-hearted run without the interference of branches slapping at him. He could run at full speed. Oh, he knew it wouldn't be far enough or fast enough, but maybe, just maybe.

"I don't know where you think you're going," the daemon-wolf spoke harshly, stopping Jeff in his tracks. "You won't get far at all. Don't make me chase you, and I'll be quick about it. I have other immediate business to attend to."

With that being said and the overwhelming surprise that the beast could talk, Jeff Bishop lost control of his bowels for the first time in his adult life. Sinking to his knees, knowing that there would be no help this time, no magic to save him, he began to pray. He didn't make it halfway through the Lord's Prayer.

His eyes opened wide at the excruciating pain as the talons penetrated his abdomen. He felt every centimeter of flesh give way as Chivas leisurely sliced upwards through the sternum, continuing up to the base of his throat.

The last thought that crossed Jeff's mind was that he would never see his lovely Casey again. And, the very last thing that he saw as his vision clouded over were those damnable silver eyes.

The man had just taken his last breath when Chivas reverted back to human form, grabbed him by the arms, and began dragging his body back in the direction of the home. He would leave a nice greeting for any that happened to come back that way.

After depositing Jeff's body where it suited him, the wolf reappeared, and the Daemon was back on the hunt.

****

CHAPTER THIRTY-ONE:
STALKED/JACOB'S POWER

Jacob sensed the Daemon's presence before he heard it. He could feel it searching, sending out enchanted waves like a radar, trying to pinpoint magic. Masking his sorcery as best as he could, the young man shifted his course around. He was now hoping to catch the others and let them know where the beast was and which direction it headed.

He broke through a small thicket of pine saplings only to witness Jeff being cut open by the wolf. It was too late to help him, and there wasn't any point in giving the beast another target so soon. He still didn't think that he could fight this otherworldly being off for long with his limited sorcery alone. This thing had eons of magical experience compared to his meager years. The magic was literally embedded into its being from the time it had been brought forth from the depths of hell.

Watching as Chivas changed back to the man-form and drug Bishop's body down the trail, Jacob silently moved to the edge of the wood. He decided to go get the Detective first. They would have to change strategy if the three of them were to make it back to the vehicles alive. Yet, they still had to keep the monster away from the mountain for a time.

It wasn't hard to pick up Becker's trail. The man had left an easy path of flattened grasses through the tall weeds. He followed in the same footsteps as the former had a short time before and twenty minutes later came upon the large barn.

Thirty yards from the structure, he heard a low whistle coming from the hayloft and entered the building, finding and ascending the stairs to join the detective.

"I thought we were splitting up to keep that thing busy chasing different trails for a while," Becker said to him.

"Well, we were. But one of your boys just got himself killed," Jacob answered. "That, to me, was a game changer. This brute isn't fooling around or caring which order he takes us."

"Shit. Which one was it?" The detective asked as he hung his head.

"Jeff. It looked to me as if he had gutted him. Then, for some reason, Chivas dragged him back towards the house.

"Damn. In that wolf shape, it doesn't take him long to run us down, does it?" Becker observed.

"No. And he'll find us fast unless he picks up on the Preacher and the woman and cuts them off first," Jacob stated. "It'll be hard to tell how soon he'll be back onto us. Of course…"

"Of course what?" Becker asked.

"Something you haven't thought about. What if the Daemon decides to return to his other construct, the dragon?" Jacob pondered. "It is

a legend that Chivas has two forms of being other than human to choose from."

"Two? I know the wolf, but what's the other?"

"Dragon. So far, all he's chosen to appear as is the canine form, but if he chooses the flying reptile, we are really screwed," Jacob said.

Silence followed as they both let that line of thought sink in. Both men leaned against either side of the loft door, watching the field and the sky for movement.

"If we're in the open pasture and he's the dragon, that's bad," Becker finally broke into the quietness. "And if he's the wolf, we're fucked in the woods. So, how do we know what to do?"

"Flip a coin?" the mage said sarcastically.

"Maybe we ought to head across here," the detective offered, "hugging this bottom tree line along the river towards the pond. Let's see if we can catch up to Kevin. Then we'll figure out where to go from there."

"Your call."

The two of them eased across the loft to the staircase, taking them as quietly as possible. They stopped at the barn door and, peered out over the meadow and scanned the sky as best as they could. Making their way to the oaks and the brush along the river bank, staying low to the ground. The pair had just made it into a small stand of saplings when a howl broke through the night.

Jacob grabbed the older man by the arm, turning him and guiding his line of sight a little to the left of the building they had just exited. About three hundred yards beyond, up the slope, he could see the stalking form of the beast. It had returned and was following the path made by the detective earlier, straight to the barn.

"I sensed it before I saw it," Jacob stated.

"What do you suggest now?"

"He will have detected my magic by now; that's why he's moving as slow as he is," Jacob said. "He is only being cautious. I think he'll go into the barn and investigate, pick up our trail, and follow it straight here."

"Well, what the hell do you say we do?" Becker asked irritably. "I ask you for suggestions, not what you believe that thing might do. I know we don't want to be here when it arrives."

"The only thing I can think of that might buy us a few minutes is to get in the water and walk as far as we can," Jacob shrugged. "At least until we have to cut back through to go to the pond and try and get up with Kevin."

"Lead on," Becker said as they moved to the water's edge.

The river was crisp and cold as the men moved along in calf-deep water. All the while trying to keep an eye on the few trees between them and the open field. South Holston Dam wasn't generating at that moment, so the river was flowing calmly and leisurely. But, having to move gradually in order to keep from making any splashing noises made seconds feel like hours.

Becker wasn't exactly thrilled about the position they were in any more than he was with the whole damn situation. Yes, the night air was still hot. At least he wasn't in the water on a cold winter's eve, but that opened him up to one of his biggest fears around the lake or river. Snakes.

Mainly the moccasin or copperhead. They all scared the bejesus out of him, but those two stood out in his mind. These thoughts disappeared as Jacob grabbed him by the arm, pulling him to his knees in the water behind some brush.

"What," he began to ask. The other man put his finger to his lips and pointed back downstream.

Straining to see through the brush, Becker couldn't make out anything but the trees from the angle he was having to look from. Feeling a hand on his chin guiding his line of sight further into the trees, he finally saw movement at the edge of the pasture.

It was definitely the wolf. It was loping along, nose to the ground, stopping every few feet to peer around as if it had lost its scent. The two men lay lower in the water, almost completely submerged except for their chests and heads.

They watched as the beast moved around, trying to pick up their trail again. They could tell it was agitated as it raised its head, roaring at the sky, swiping at a four-inch sapling, neatly slicing it in two.

Obviously giving up on them for the time being, the wolf turned and moved off in the direction of the pond. Surely, now it was going for Kevin. Giving the animal a couple of minutes to get out of earshot, hopefully, both men raised to their knees, breathing a sigh of relief.

"Okay," the detective whispered. "What now?"

"Now that he's lost our trail, I'd say that he's definitely going for Kevin," Jacob answered. "I guess we need to circle around and try to beat the Daemon to him. Or, at the very least, get there in time to help him."

"You fended it off once. Do you think you can do it again?" Becker looked at him hopefully.

"Against that kind of sorcery? I can maybe fend it off for a few moments, but I can't really hurt it. I got lucky with the element of surprise that last time."

"Maybe you're better than you think?" Becker said with a smile.

"It is possible that I can hit it with enough to slow it down. Worry him a bit if I can make the beast believe that I'm more than I actually am," Jacob said thoughtfully. "Smoke and mirrors, as you say."

If that's all we've got, we have to go with it."

Catching the thing unaware of our presence would be a big help. But I can't mask my energies and prepare to use them at the same time. It's going to feel me no matter what," Jacob stated.

"Just do the best that you can, son," Becker said, clapping the mage on the back.

The two men left the water. Staying just inside the cover of the wooded area, they began following the Daemon's path.

****

Kevin had worked his way around the lower end of the pond when he heard the howl coming from the direction of the old barn. He knew the wolf was on the prowl, and it was closer than he wished it to be.

Spying the large root system of a downed Oak, he decided to hide behind it for a minute until he could figure out which one of them the thing was following. He had been alright with the night, traipsing around the pasture and on around the pond. But now, the reality that he was out here all alone hit him like a ton of bricks.

Up until a few minutes ago, things had been fast paced with others surrounding him. The talking, making of plans, it all had kept him occupied. Now, it seemed as if the darkness was closing in on him. Not the comforting kind of dark that's there when you're in your tree stand waiting on the first hint of daylight and the deer are moving.

This was a smothering cloak of black that made Kevin think how it must seem in the grave. He felt that it must be like an emptiness that can not be filled. Then, the thought of Angie lying in a coma flooded his mind. He wondered if he would ever get to see her again.

After what seemed like an eternity, Kevin heard a long, deep howl that ended almost like a lion's roar. Then, the sound of a limb snapping as if it were grabbed and ripped off of a tree's main trunk. He knew then that the beast was agitated. Moving his body around quietly, he positioned himself with a good view of the field. He was looking west from the river.

He figured that he couldn't stay here long and told himself that he needed to be on the move now. But at the same time, he was thinking that maybe lying low was the answer. All in all, he reckoned that he was a dad man either way if that thing got him in its sights. It's not a very comforting feeling to have.

His decision was made three minutes later, though, when he observed the Daemon making its way haltingly in his general direction. So, it had either dispatched the rest of them, or it had simply chosen his trail to follow first.

Hiking along the bank of the pond was not an option anymore. He would be in plain sight, and the wolf would be on him in thirty seconds or less. Staying here behind this upturned root system was out also. There was no way the beast would be so careless as to pass right on by. Hell, it would smell him anyway.

The only opportunity left to him was to sneak into the brush and continue on Harrison's land and then cut back around to the house and the relative safety of his truck. To travel as quickly as he needed was going to be damn near impossible without making a bunch of noise. He had to try, though.

Kevin rose up on one knee, gauging the distance between him and the brute. He was hoping to make his move into the thicket undetected. Staying as low to the ground as he could, he emerged from his hiding place. He was moving in what to him was a fairly fast "duck walk" through the high grasses.

Not daring to take the few precious seconds needed to turn and check on the position of his would-be assassin almost cost him his life. For the instant Kevin entered the thicket, the sound of rage exploded behind him. It was then that he stopped to peer back at the wolf's last noted position.

The moment he had the beast in his vision again, it stared back at him. The Daemon burst into movement but only took four steps. On the ground, that is. Kevin never would have believed the occurrence of the next few seconds if he hadn't seen it for himself. It was with horror that he witnessed the new transformation.

The first step the animal took, it sprouted fiery red wings. The second step, its head elongated followed by an instantaneous lengthening of the body. The third paws disappeared into massive feet tipped with solid black fourteen-inch talons. It seemed as if small bolts of electricity flowed around and between these. By the fourth step, the thing was airborne.

Completely frozen in fear and awe, he could do nothing except stare at the horrible yet magnificent dragon flying above him. Oh, it didn't make a beeline for him, as you would imagine. It was toying with him as a cat will sometimes do a mouse as it anticipates the kill.

Flying circles in the night sky above him, the thing looked down on him mockingly as if it was enjoying this new game. After a few lazy passes and intimidating dives, the flying reptile landed approximately thirty yards from him, immediately transforming back to the canine form. An idea formed in Kevin's mind that the Daemon appeared more comfortable in this shape.

Upon hitting the ground, the wolf advanced on him steadily as he moved away from it. He backed into the open space between the brush and the pond, leaving himself exposed. As the beast approached within ten yards of him, Kevin heard running footsteps coming in from behind him. Both he and the Daemon were so intent upon each other that the appearance of the detective and Jacob caught them by surprise.

"Run!" was all he heard as a white-hot bolt of electricity shot through the air, striking the animal in the neck and shoulder.

And run he did. The noise was of no consequence now, so he just put his head down and ran faster than he had in years. However, concern for his friends took over his thoughts and seventy-five yards into his escape, he came to a stop, turning back around to see what was happening. The detective was at his side a second after that.

Both men were breathing hard, but they had a few seconds to let their lungs catch up with the need for air. From the top of the small slope, they witnessed both the young mage and the wolf form of the Daemon staring each other down, waiting to see what the other's next move would be.

"We got lucky," Becker broke the silence. "Caught the damn thing off-guard again."

"Yeah, but how are we going to get completely away from it this time to re-group? Think there's a chance?"

"There's always a chance," the detective answered. "This one's a million to one, but still a chance."

Jacob glanced in their direction and then elected to start backing up toward them, his eyes never leaving the wolf after that. He made it five steps before the animal leaped forward. He retaliated with another, larger electrical bolt, hitting the beast square in the face. It moved a hair backwards.

A split second later, they were looking at the tall Native American visage that had emerged from the wolf's form. The Daemon thrust both his arms and hands forward, shooting its own red bolt at the apprentice sorcerer. Sending back another shot of his own, Jacob was still hit with a glancing blow to the left shoulder, leaving him off balance.

Though slightly injured, he held his own by throwing three consecutive lightning bolts, each one finding its mark. Obviously surprised at the sizable amount of magic flowing through this young one, Chivas retreated back into the thicket, becoming the monstrous wolf once again. He turned back to face the mage.

"I've underestimated you," the thing spoke. "It will not happen again. Enjoy the little time that you have. Use it wisely."

With that being said, the beast simply turned and walked away, disappearing into the thicket.

"Are you hurt?" Becker asked as Jacob joined them.

"Nothing to worry about. A small gash on my shoulder. If he had hit me square on, though, it would have been game over."

"Good," the detective said. "Let's get back to the vehicles and get the hell out of here. The question is, where do we go from here? You know that it's going to follow us. The thing is pissed."

"We can go back to my house," Kevin replied. "He's already been there, of course, but I don't want it to get any closer to the public than need be."

"Good as idea as any," Detective Becker agreed as the men began walking.

****

CHAPTER THIRTY-TWO:

ON THE MOUNTAIN/ PICKING UP

LISA AND FATHER ELLIS

Larry had pulled up to the base of the trail. As he and five others who had ridden with him climbed out of the truck, his phone rang.

"Hello."

"Mr. Black. This is Officer Jensen. I tried Detective Hamby's phone, but there was no answer, and this is very important."

"Go ahead," Larry said.

"Personally, I'm on the way to Bristol Med Center to get stitched up, but I'm okay."

"I take it the Daemon showed up?" Larry said dismally.

"Yeah."

"What happened, Jensen?" Larry ask,

"Long story short," the officer began, "the wolf burst through the window, and we all scattered. I was the last one out. It grabbed me by the leg and hip, cutting me pretty good."

"Well, if it had you, how are you talking to me right now? You should be dead," Larry stated.

"Yes, I should be. But Keeler's nephew shot it with some kind of electricity and stunned it. He helped me out to the truck, and I took off," Jensen explained.

"Where are they now?"

"I'd guess they split up throughout old man Thacker's land. That was the original plan anyway," the officer said.

"Alright. Hopefully, we'll hear from them soon," Larry replied." Get on to the emergency room and then go home. You're out of it."

"Yes, sir."

As he pushed the end call button, Larry hit Hamby's number. No answer. Damn. He shoved the phone in his pocket and slid on his backpack, picking up the duffel bag with blasting caps and such. Joining the others at the trailhead, he heard the helicopter before he saw it.

Ghost had taken the two old witches, Hamby, and the others that would be helping on up to the top along with supplies to get started on that end. He half-grinned at the picture in his mind of the old men being lowered fifty feet or more to the ground. He doubted they were afraid of heights, though. Hell, he doubted they were afraid of anything.

Without hesitation or discussion, he set the men working this route with him at a grinding pace. Now that he had heard what had gone on at Anson's place, he knew that they were running out of time. Spacing the explosives roughly thirty feet apart and ten to fifteen feet off either side of the trail, the men meticulously worked their way up the ridge.

Larry followed behind, rigging up trip wires over and along the path itself. These were then attached to rigs that were activated by c0-2 cartridges akin to certain types of pellet rifles. Only these shot darts tipped with a heavy animal tranquilizer. Since the beast literally came from hell, he didn't hold much hope in the tranqs having much effect.

A short time later, as the sun was coming up, his phone rang. Seeing that it was Detective Hamby, Larry answered.

"Yeah."

"I just saw where both you and Jensen had tried to call. Trouble?" Hamby asked.

"In a nutshell," Larry said, "the thing attacked, Jensen was injured and is on his way to Bristol ER, and the rest of them are scattered over many acres of woods and field."

"I knew it was there. I was on the phone with Becker when it arrived on the property," Hamby informed him.

"Oh, and surprise," Larry continued, "our little apprentice can throw lightning."

"What?"

"Never mind. We're rolling along at a good pace here. We are just about halfway up the Josiah trail," Larry told him. "How's it coming on your end?"

"About the same. Ghost has dropped Keeler, Redwing, and some men at the top and brought me and about a dozen others most of the way here up on #49," Hamby stated.

"What section are you at?"

"Now? We're working our way along the Holston trail towards the Flint Mill. I have Lt Conners and his men at the bottom bringing up to us," the detective informed him.

Okay. I'll meet you at the crossing in a bit," Larry said. "I've got to call Ghost myself and get some more supplies dropped here. Getting low."

"See you later."

Larry paused a minute to watch his people working as if this were any other job. The fact that most of this was so unbelievable it belonged in a fantasy book didn't seem to phase these guys.

"Hell, I don't know if I fully believe it all," he said to himself. They had guts, that's for sure.

Shaking his head and letting out a long sigh, he pulled up the pilot's number and made his call.

****

The trio emerged from the woods once again on Anson's property, all the worse for wear. As they worked their way down the gentle slope of the backyard, Kevin noticed that something looked out of place with his truck. Shielding his eyes against the porch light, it appeared someone was sitting on the passenger side.

"Hey, are you sure Jeff was killed?" he asked Jacob.

"Very. I saw him torn from waist to chest, and then Chivas drug him off. It was too late for me to do anything lest I myself be discovered by the Daemon," Jacob replied.

By the time the men had reached the front of the Z-71, they could see that Jeff was indeed deceased, his chin resting upon his flayed open chest. Kevin grimaced as he opened the door. Blood had run down, pooling in the floorboard. Blood seemed to coat everything on that side of the cab.

"Aw man," Kevin exclaimed as tears ran down his face. "Help me get him to the house. We can at least put him inside."

They laid Jeff's limp form on the couch, standing in silence for a moment.

"Well," Becker started, "Do you think that your house is really the place we should go to next?"

"I don't know. Obviously, there's no safe place for us anymore," Kevin answered.

"Tell me something," the detective said, "I've got to get up the road and see if I can find Lisa and Father Ellis if that thing hasn't already."

"Yeah. Shit, my house," Kevin said. "I'll get the water hose and spray out the truck. Jacob and I will meet you there."

Kevin took a last look at his lifelong friend and went out the door. While he and Jacob were cleaning the blood out of the Z-71, Detective Becker retrieved his Crown Vic and drove in the direction that he thought Lisa and the Pastor should be.

He had driven almost half a mile when he brightened his headlights as he slowed to a crawl. It wasn't long before he spied the man and woman stepping out onto the shoulder of the road.

"We didn't know if you were going to make it or not," Lisa said as she climbed into the front seat.

"I take it you two didn't hear or see anything?" the detective asked.

"No, At least I didn't. He," she pointed at Ellis, "was praying for a few minutes, then began just talking to someone. I thought he'd gone mad."

"I told you that I was speaking with Gabriel. I was not hallucinating," Father Ellis replied. "He told me that we would have divine help when the time arrived."

"Let's hope so," Becker muttered under his breath.

"What happened out there?"

"Your friend Jeff is gone," Becker informed Lisa.

"Gone? What do you mean by Gone? As in, he couldn't take it anymore and ran off?" Lisa ask.

"No. Gone as in dead. The wolf got him before he made it to the field."

"No, no, no," was all she could say, staring out the windshield.

"And the damn thing can turn into a dragon," the detective continued. "We found that out real quick. Plus, Keeler's nephew is a sorcerer. I watched that boy throw bolts of electricity, holding the beast at bay for a minute."

"You're kidding."

"Nope. He's the only reason that we made it out alive."

With plenty of things to think about, the rest of the trip was made in silence until he turned up Kevin's driveway. "What are we doing here?" Lisa asked.

"Just somewhere to go until they're ready up on Holston," Becker answered." I know it's probably the most dangerous place for us right now, but we need to get our shit together somewhere."

"This is really the only place we have left without endangering other's lives," the Father said.

"That too," the detective said. "And we need to communicate with Keeler, Larry, and Hamby, all three, to make sure they realize this thing's coming fast."

"So," Lisa interjected, "We're just gonna hang out inside like sitting ducks, waiting on it to corner us."

"No. We are turning around and staying in the vehicles so that we can at least have a shot at making a getaway," Becker explained. "Although we do have to make sure the Daemon will follow us to Flint Mill. This is our last stop."

He then put in a call to Detective Hamby in order to fill him in on the night's events. With more casualties building up, he stressed that the time frame was getting shorter very fast. They had to be ready soon. When Becker pulled up to the garage, Lisa wanted to trade places with the mage and passenger with Kevin. The switch was made, and Kevin pulled the Z-71 forward to a point about forty feet from the road. The detective backed down and parked window to window with the truck. Cutting off their headlights, they sat in the darkness, watching all around. And waiting.

****

With Larry's men planting the explosives and setting ignition switches in various hidden spots, he was following behind, rigging up other various obstacles for the beast. Tripwires set for deadfalls, a couple of well-placed bear traps, and so on. He planned on giving this thing a hard way to go.

He and his crew were about three-quarters of the way up when his cell phone began vibrating in his pocket. Seeing on the caller ID that it was Kevin Miller, he answered.

"Yeah. What's up?"

"Jeff's dead," came the reply.

Silence. Larry didn't know how to respond to that. He knew the anger and rage that came when the Daemon had murdered his best friend Neil, but he also knew that Kevin and Jeff had been even closer. They were more than business partners, and the two had been inseparable since grade school.

"How/ I mean, what happened?" He asked, although he already knew the answer.

"We split up. Jacob ran up to him as it happened. He was basically disemboweled," Kevin said. "The damned thing put his body in my truck!"

"I don't know what to say, Kev, except that one way or the other, we're going to get this bastard."

"Well, we're just sitting here in my driveway, in the vehicles, waiting. As soon as this thing shows up, it's going to be a hellacious race to you guys," Kevin informed him. "So, I'm just letting you know to be ready as quick as you can."

"We're pushing it now, getting close, though. We'll handle our end, it's those up top I'm wondering about. I haven't heard a single thing from them," Larry replied.

"Don't you think someone should check up on them? This brute is unpredictable as hell. It could start at any time, and there's nowhere else for us to go," Kevin said. "The next leg of the journey is headed straight to you."

"That's comforting."

"Well, I'm getting off here. Don't know when I'll get a chance to check with you again. Be ready." Kevin said as the call ended.

Larry decided he better check in with Hamby to see if he knew anything about the progress of the old mages. He didn't have a clue as to what they were preparing. All he knew was that it was unconventional, some kind of ancient ritual supposed to send this thing back to hell or wherever.

He didn't have much faith in that kind of stuff. To him, magic and rituals were all fantasy that only came to life in some writers' imagination, made into books and shows for entertainment. No, what he believed in was the force of explosives, guns, and knives. Traditional weapons that had saved his life many times overseas. He made the call.

Hamby answered on the second ring.

"Have you heard from Keeler or any of the men at the top?" Larry began.

"Talked to Billy. He says the ceremonial fire or whatever is about laid out and that the old witches are walking around carving symbols into the trunks of the Locust and Cedar trees," Hamby answered. "Hell, I don't know."

"I guess we trust them," Larry said. "It was Keeler's spell that he gave Lisa that brought the Daemon here, to begin with, so he must know something."

"Yeah. I wish things would move along faster, though," the detective stated. "I'm ready for this to be over with."

"Things are going to go quicker in a few minutes, and the sun's coming up. We won't have to work by flashlight."

"Speaking of work," Hamby said, "I'm getting back to it."

"See you soon," Larry said as his eyes began to make out more of his surroundings. "Yeah," he thought, "Things will be easier by the light of day.

He then realized that his crew had been going at it all night. He now split his people up into two groups. Each group takes turns laying against a rock or stump, getting in an hour's sleep, then switching with the others.

If he could keep rotating them like that until the last moment possible, maybe they would be somewhat rested and alert when the time for the real action came. He would take his hours to rest with the second bunch.

****

CHAPTER THIRTY-THREE:
CHIVAS AND LISA'S PARENTS

Chivas could not believe that the young up-start of a mage had taken him by surprise twice, much less in the same hour. It pissed him off that such a thing could happen to him. In his many centuries of being, never had he been halted in his progress by any one person. At first, he had thought it a fluke.

It was at the confrontation at the pond that he felt the true power of the sorcerer. The young one had been unable to mask his abilities in the heat of battle. The Daemon suspected that either the man was one of the immortal ancients that had all but disappeared in the early Earth wars eons ago.

Or, it could simply be that the man did not know his own potential and was just now coming into his powers. Either way, he would have to be dealt with. If that one made it to combine forces with the two old ones, they might make things harder on him. Not that he wasn't confident that he could take them.

His instincts now honing in on his targets, he followed the backroads and fields back to the Millers dwelling. Why they had ventured back there he had no idea, but there would be no immediate attack. The sun was up over the horizon. He'd find a good place to sit and observe them throughout the day. Let the anticipation add to their fear.

The Daemon slowed his pace as he crested the hill behind Kevin's property. Surely, they'd be watching both front and back. He spotted a small set of bushes to the right of the garage and decided upon that as his observation point for the time being.

Making his way slowly down the hill, sliding on his belly like a snake, he eased into position. Satisfied that he had a good vantage point, he settled back against a decorative railroad tie.

After the first hour into the morning sunshine, it was obvious that his lack of appearance was getting them nervous. First, they were on some sort of communication device. Then, two of the men went into the house and returned with food and beverages. They stood at the rear of the car and ate as a group. Still warily watch their surroundings but are a bit more relaxed.

That made him grin. This was good… Letting them think that maybe he's gone on about business elsewhere. Once or twice, the girl had even looked right at the foliage he was concealed behind. She never had a thought of him sitting there, staring her straight in the eyes, About that time, he felt the presence of one of the Masters.

"Chivas. What are you doing?" a voice entered his mind.

"Tor," he said, looking the spirit in the face. "I am carrying out my task. Is it not better to let them wonder through the day, becoming confident in themselves, then suddenly strike after dark?"

"Possibly my son, but this business needs to end soon. The others are laying a trap for you. Don't get led into it blindly," the spirit said as it vanished.

Alone again, he thought the overseers had most likely forgotten his full strengths. He was unbeatable. Chivas would show them. He would show them all. Chuckling to himself as a new idea crossed his mind, he got back as low as possible to the ground and made his way back over the hill.

When there wasn't any chance of being spotted, he stood to his full height and stretched, letting the image flow as quickly as the silver flashed through his eyes – and was on all fours again. With the blood of the wolf racing through his veins, he made better time, arriving at his destination a few minutes later.

Stopping behind the ram-shackled barn, he paused. The Daemon needed to be sure that both parties were home in order for this to work. It would throw more confusion and misery upon his adversaries.

He smiled as Blade Smallwood followed his wife Trudy to the door, giving her a peck on the cheek before returning inside. Mrs. Smallwood walked lightly as she went to the clothesline in the backyard. With her back to him, she never saw the canine sneak up on her.

Trudy had just taken down a bedsheet and begun to fold it when she felt, no, she *heard* the flesh on her back part ways with her spine.

Before she had a chance to utter a sound, claws swung around and across her throat, cleanly removing her vocal cords.

Staring with wonder into the silver eyes of the wolf, an expression of recognition crossed her face as her mind recalled the legends told around the campfires of the reservation she had grown up on.

Once more, the wolf's paw came brutally down, severing her head from her body. As Trudy's corpse hit the ground, Chivas turned towards the dwelling, advancing to the wide-open door and the sounds of the television inside. Once in the entryway, he let out a low warning growl. He at least wanted a little resistance out of this venture.

A bewildered face glanced from the cased opening leading to the next room. Growling menacingly, stepping to the side as if motioning the man on by, the beast sat, fangs bared, and raised a blood-stained paw.

Cautious, Blade Smallwood moved to the door and looked in the direction of the clothesline, only to see his beloved wife of forty-five years sprawled out in a growing pool of blood. Headless.

Driven mad with a sudden rage he had not felt in ages, the elder Smallwood turned and picked up a knife, diving at the beast swinging wildly. Chivas stood and hooked the man by his leg, raking downward, tearing flesh from bone. The man had gone insane. He acted as if he had not even felt the dismantling of his calf muscle as he continued violently slicing in Chivas' direction.

The Daemon casually moved forward, sinking his talons deep into the man's abdomen, lifting him off the floor, and slinging him to the other side of the room. He then padded over to the grievously injured man and, with what sounded to Blade like a laugh, parted his neck from ear to ear.

Satisfied with his handiwork, Chivas then reverted to his human form, smearing blood on his arms, shirt and jeans. Then, to complete the scenario, he walked to the road and flagged down the next car, passing, yelling, and hysterically shouting about murder.

As the occupant of the vehicle drove up to the house, the Daemon mystically was clean and free from the blood on his clothes. Whistling an old tune, he walked back in the direction of the Miller home.

****

The day was passing slowly. The five of them were beginning to wonder if the Daemon had simply tired of them for the moment and went to create havoc elsewhere. And, at the same time, they realized this notion was wrong. It was toying with them. The group knew that the brute could come for them at any time. If it was trying to rattle their nerves, it had succeeded.

Here, it was one o'clock in the afternoon, and still no sign of the beast. Each of them had snuck in at least an hour's sleep or more, taking turns at the look out. Lisa was still asleep in the passenger seat of Kevin's truck when he looked over at the Crown Vic and noticed Becker was in an animated conversation with someone on his cell phone.

The minute the detective hung up, he was out of his car, motioning for Kevin to join him at the back of the truck. Something was up, and it didn't look good. He eased out of the Z-71 as quietly as possible and met Becker at the tailgate.

"Now I know why we haven't seen that thing since before daylight," the detective said.

"Why is that?"

"You might want to wake Miss Smallwood up for this," Becker stated. "I'm not going through this twice. I will tell you this: it's about her parents."

"Shit," Kevin said, walking to the passenger door.

Opening it, he shook Lisa by the shoulder lightly so as not to startle her. As her eyes opened, he gently led her from the vehicle to the waiting detective with a puzzled expression on her face.

"Are you awake," she was asked.

"Enough," came her reply.

"Okay. Listen closely," Becker began, "I was just on the phone with Bill Henson. He's one of our other lead detectives in homicide."

He let that sink in for a moment, watching her facial expressions to see if she might see where this was going – if any idea came to her mind. Apparently, it didn't. She was a blank.

"So, what's that got to do with us, here, in this situation?" she questioned.

"While we've been sitting here waiting on the Daemon, the wolf, or whatever form it's in now, decided to cause more grief and sorrow to our predicament," Becker stated.

"What kind of grief?" Lisa ask. "Who else close to us could it possibly attack?"

"Your parents, Lisa," the detective said with emotion. "It went to their house while we've been here and murdered your mom and dad."

A mournful wail escaped Lisa as she sank to the ground, sobbing uncontrollably. Jacob and Father Ellis, who had heard the conversation earlier as it was being told to Becker the first time, appeared at her side to try and comfort her. The pastor glanced at the other three.

"Could you give me a moment alone with her?" he inquired.

Not knowing what else to do, they moved to the porch, still keeping a watchful eye on their surroundings lest the beast should choose this moment of vulnerability to attack. It would be the perfect opportunity.

"I want to go to them," Lisa whimpered as she buried her face in Father Ellis' shoulder.

"I know my child," he said. "But what would that accomplish except to give this malevolent spirit what it wants? It would have us split up and confused."

"But," she started.

"I understand. But there is nothing that you can do for your parents now, and our strength lies in our togetherness," Ellis tried to explain. "When this is over, will you take me to them and help with the funeral?" Lisa ask.

"Yes, I promise," the pastor answered.

He let the woman cry on his shoulder until the sobbing quieted. He then helped her up off the ground and accompanied her back to the truck, where she climbed back in the passenger seat. She laid her arms on the dashboard, face buried in the crook of them. Father Ellis, seeing Lisa settled in the pickup once again, walked over to the porch joining the others.

"Is she going to be alright?" Kevin inquired.

"Yes, no, I don't know. Are any of us ever going to be the same again?" Ellis Pondered.

"Probably not," Becker chimed in. "I know I won't. There are things that I have seen in the last twenty-four hours that I never thought existed. Things of nightmares that should only be made up around campfires."

"The whiter man has never believed in the spirit world as we do," Jacob added. "We were taught these things from childhood. Especially those of us aspiring to be medicine men or witches."

"Well, we definitely know that it's cunning," the detective continued on, "Divide and conquer, throwing some confusion in the mix while it's at it."

"As smart as this thing is, do you think it's going to hit us now that Lisa's compromised, or is it toying with us, playing a waiting game to see how big of a mistake we'll make?" Kevin asked.

"Hard to tell," Becker replied. "Could go either way. But we can't stay out here in the open much longer. Let's get back in the vehicles where we've at least got a chance to get away from here and lead it to Holston."

Cautiously, the group made their way back to the automobiles and resumed sitting in anticipation. Kevin had been back in his truck only a few seconds when Lisa touched him on the arm, drawing his attention. Her tears had all but dried up, a stern look replaced the sorrow showing on her face. There was a darkness in her eyes.

"If it takes my last breath, I'm going to see that beast returned to hell," She stated.

"We will. For Angie, for your parents, we will," Kevin said.

"No, for all of them," Lisa replied.

Throughout the scene that had just played out, Chivas had observed from behind the corner of the garage. They were none the wiser. He decided that he would stay and watch until sunset. Then he would take action.

****

CHAPTER THIRTY-FOUR:

FINAL PREPARATIONS ON THE

FLINTMILL

The sun had peaked for the day and was beginning its afternoon descent when Larry and Detective Hamby met at the crossing of the Holston and Flint Mill trails. Each had done what they could with the traps and explosives to "guide" the Daemon in the direction they needed him to go. A gauntlet of sorts, as it might be described/.

Larry noticed the detective was on the phone speaking hurriedly as he approached the boulder he was seated upon. Figuring the conversation was with either someone in Kevin's group or one from up top with the two old witches, he sat still, trying to hear what he could of this end of it. Hamby sat beside him, hitting the end button on his Galaxy phone. Slipped it into his shirt pocket, bowing his head, staring at the ground.

"Black," he began. "Do you ever get into something that is a walking nightmare, and it seems as if it will never come to an end?"

"It seems as if that's the situation we're in at this moment, sir," Larry replied.

"Well, it only gets worse as it goes," the detective said.

Larry raised his eyebrows questioningly.

"That was Stan on the phone," Hamby continued. "All day, they've just been sitting in Miller's driveway, waiting. Haven't heard a whisper from the beast until a bit ago."

"And?"

"It seems to have wanted to play mind or emotional games with them. It made another kill elsewhere while they were anticipating an attack on them," Hamby said.

"Shit," Larry shook his head in disbelief. "Who else was tied to us that it could've known about?"

"Miss Smallwood's parents."

"How…. Why?" Larry asked, puzzled.

"Nothing about this creature surprises me anymore," the detective stated. "Apparently, figuring to either lure them or part of them away was one motive Stan and I came up with. Or…"

"Or what?"

"Or the damn thing just likes killing and knew this would rattle their cages more than they already are. It definitely shook Lisa to the core," Hamby said. "Of course, she wanted one of them to take her there, but after careful thought, decided it would be better if they all stayed together."

"Yeah," Larry sighed, "there isn't anything that could be done anyway. I know that sounds bad, but after this is over, she can tend to the funeral arrangements. There's going to be quite a few from this, it seems."

"I hope not too many more. I guess I better call up top and let them know what's going on."

While Hamby made the call, Larry turned on his mic and checked in with the deputies, national guardsmen, and volunteers who were stationed along the Josiah trail. Two to a team, each team fifty to sixty yards apart at the beginning of the trail, then stretched further as the route closed in on their destination.

For now, he told them to make sure each got some kind of rest because it looked as if the expected action was still a couple of hours away. They would all be alerted in plenty of time, as he or Detective Hamby would get word when the other group was Leading/running from the Daemon and were on the way there.

"We're wanted up top with them," the detective announced as he put his phone away once more.

Sighing as he stood, Larry picked his pack up and joined the other man on the final few hundred-yard hike to join the old witches. He glanced around, eyeing the landscape. The ground had begun to lose some of the steepness, gradually leveling off. The trees were thinning out, allowing more daylight in.

He recognized a tree that had held his hunting stand through quite a few outings in the past. This ridge had always held an abundance of deer. Both those that bedded down on the flat run near the crest and those that were traveling through going from feeding area to water and vice-versa.

It seemed weird to him now to know that he had been hunting over what long ago had been an ancient ritual site to the Native Americans. They had inhabited this area for many generations until the white man formed settlements and small towns all around. This, in turn, led to the relocation of the Cherokee to the reservations. Only a few had ventured back, making their homes in the towns as time progressed.

And, of course, most of the lower lands where the villages had been are now underwater with the building of the Dam. What was once only a river and the creeks feeding it was now a several thousand-acre fishing, swimming, and boating haven. Most things left from that time had simply vanished under the gentle waters of South Holston Lake.

Brought out of his revelry by the sounds of preparation, Larry noticed the large stack of both old and fresh-cut cedars laid out for a huge fire. They had all been cut to identical lengths, neatly stacked in some sort of pyramid pattern. Torches were set about every fifteen feet in a semi-circle around the perimeter.

Silver rods and wooden plaques with arcane designs carved in them had been driven into the earth between the torches. The ground had been raked back leaving a clear area around the firepit, symbols etched into the dirt. The grooves had been filled with different colored powders and paints along the triangular-shaped set-up.

"We don't have time to weave the nets from blessed vines," Keeler said as he greeted the two men. "However, I do have some strong netting that I cast an enchantment upon. That might work as well."

"Let's hope so," Hamby replied.

"I knew Chivas would wait until dusk at least, for the night cloaks him better," the old Cherokee witch continued. "But we need more magic here, at the ready to call upon other than just Redwing and myself."

"What can I do?" the detective asked.

"Send Ghost in the helicopter to retrieve Father Ellis. He and I need a little time to confer with the Great Spirit. Or as he is known to the white man, God." Keeler stated.

"Now, as to my need for you," the old Indian turned to Larry, "If you could help me with some information on this surrounding area. I believe you have visited this place often in your youth."

"Sure. Whatever you need." Larry responded.

"And after that….. We wait."

****

CHAPTER THIRTY-FIVE:

FLIGHT

Chivas had sat and watched all of this crap he was going to. His legs and arms had stiffened up. His back hurt from sitting in this position all day. This human form was not good for the prolonged stillness he had required. He needed to be moving.

Standing slowly and stretching, he made sure to stay hidden behind the building. These fools would sit in the vehicles all night if he stayed and allowed them to. It was time to move. Time to end this game. As far as he was concerned, all of them would die between this dusk and the next dawning of day. There would be no tomorrow for them.

First, he needed to unwind. Backing away from the barn, he eased over the hill, being sure to stay out of sight. Once he was on the other side with no chance of being seen, he dropped to all fours. No, for this the wolfen form would not do.

Chivas spread his arms, feeling them elongate into leathery wings. The span was over thirty feet in length from tip to tip. Legs and arms sprouting overly large clawed hands and feet. He felt unrestricted as his face lengthened into a long snout filled with sword-like teeth. The finishing touch was the protective scales forming, overlapping each other in rows to act as a shield.

Launching himself skyward, Chivas flew South. As he felt the air flow over his wings, he raced away from the intended victims. First, he would relax and enjoy the freedom the skies afforded him. He would take a few minutes to unwind from the day's cramped position he had held for so long.

Shortly upon his return, these humans would find out what pure terror he could unleash upon them. Grinning as wickedly as only a dragon could, Chivas aimed for the clouds.

****

Detective Stan Becker was feeling the effects of sitting the day through himself. He was positive the others were just as stiff and sore as he. Getting out of the Crown Vic, he motioned for the rest to do the same. He had received a call a few minutes before inquiring as to an open place where a chopper could land. Becker had, at that time, informed Father Ellis and Jacob that they would be flown onto the mountain.

There they were to join with Keeler and Redwing to finish preparing. The pastor had sat in the back of the car, silently praying and concentrating his mind on the upcoming task. He could only hope that his faith was strong enough, the cause great enough for God to lend him the power and strength that he needed. The five of them now gathered in front of the car and truck.

"Ghost is on his way with the helicopter. Jacob and the good Father are needed at the site with the two old witches ASAP.," Becker began.

"So, us three are still stuck here as bait," Kevin interjected. "I say that we send Lisa on up there as well. She would be much safer with all the firepower there."

"Now hold on a minute," Lisa said. "I started this. I'm not going to run like a frightened child."

"You won't be running. When the shit hits the fan up there, you'll be in as much or more danger than us," Becker told her. "Remember, you did start this. You've got to be high on that things list."

"Besides," Kevin added, "It'll only take the two of us driving the vehicles to lead it there. And we still don't know how we're going to get by it once we get there. Becker and I might bite the bullet before we even get on the trails."

"Thanks for reminding me of that. Asshole," the detective said.

"Yes," Jacob agreed. Looking at Lisa, he continued, "You are needed there with us to fight the spiritual battle more than here. You did ask of Mother Earth and Brother Moon. And *THEY ANSWERED*. That is a feat in itself."

"Okay. I guess you're right," she agreed reluctantly.

"There's the chopper," Kevin stated.

The group watched as Ghost skillfully set the helicopter down in the small clearing to the right of the driveway. Goodbyes were noted all the way around. Jacob and Father Ellis walked on to the bird while Lisa lingered behind a moment.

"You know that I now forgive you for what happened to William," she told Kevin. "I realize that it was an accident."

"Lisa. We don't have to do this now. Tell me when this is over," Kevin said to her.

"See. That's just it. Both or neither of us may not be alive when it ends," she stated. "I need to get this off my chest now or take a chance on never being able to say it."

"Alright," Kevin agreed. "But hurry. You need to go."

"Remember when I asked you not to take William hunting? That I had had a vision? You said I was bullshitting you?" She asked.

"Yes."

"I did have a vision of him dying, but I trusted you and chalked it up to being a bad dream," she continued. "After the funeral, I blamed you when I should have blamed myself as well for letting him go. So, I left."

"What's the point? We have to hurry," Kevin said.

"Damnit. I'm trying to tell you that I realized everything after I left for the summer. When I came back, you and Angie were together," Lisa said. "That brought my rage back to the surface. I believed that not only had you taken my brother away, but my sister as well."

"Okay, Lisa. Apology accepted. Not trying to be an ass, but you've got to go now."

"One more thing," she said. "I was in love with you then and still am. But you have done right by my sister, and I truly regret all the time that we have missed and lost as a family."

Lisa turned and made her way to the waiting helicopter, leaving a puzzled Kevin staring after her.

"Women." Becker patted him on the shoulder. "I'll never understand them either."

****

Chivas had enjoyed his little respite. However, the sun was beginning its evening descent. It was time. The Daemon, in dragon form, circled around and flew in the direction of Millers' farm. He was sure his prey would still be waiting.

"It's almost like slaughtering herded-up sheep," he thought to himself.

As he approached within a couple of miles, he spotted something flying off from the direction of his intended destination. Thinking that it was only a passing aircraft (he had seen several of those with awe and wonder at first), he paid no extra attention to it. His mind was on killing the group, imagining a slow and agonizing death for all. Then, he would track down the old Indian witches, making their demise seem to last a lifetime.

Arriving at the small farm, he witnessed that there were only two men rushing to the vehicles. Puzzled as to where others had gone, he made a lazy circle around the property. He was sure that there wasn't any other way they could have left in the time he was gone.

Maybe one of the lawmen had come and taken the girl to her parent's house, and the priest went with them. It was feasible. He would take a minute and fly back over that scene to make sure.

If that's what had occurred, then he would have to re-think things through and choose another option. One of them entailed killing every living thing on the Smallwoods' property. Which, in turn, would draw much more unwanted attention to himself than he or the Elders wanted. The flyover would draw enough as it was.

It only took a couple of minutes to fly the seven or eight miles between the two farms in a straight flight line. Making slow, agonizing passes over the place, he could neither see nor smell any of his objects of prey. He did, however, receive some yells and looks from the emergency workers there. A few of the lawmen drew their weapons and fired upon him.

Satisfied that the other three were not here, he turned and flew back to Kevin's once again. The thought that three of them had somehow eluded him angered him even more. He hated to lose track of any one of them. Especially the girl that had summoned him from the pit to begin with. Chivas had a special departing planned for her.

Then, realization dawned on him. They had escaped in the flying vehicle. With a burst of speed, he flew in the direction that he had witnessed it go. He would catch it and bring it to the ground. This, he thought, would put a stop to whatever it was they were up to.

****

Detective Becker and Kevin both stopped in their tracks halfway in their vehicles as the dragon flew over and by them. Both men stared in disbelief as they watched it fly in a southerly direction.

"What the hell is that all about?" Becker asked.

"I'll bet you it's going back to the Smallwood place," Kevin responded.

"Why? What's the point? It's already killed Lisa's parents," Becker stated. "There's no reason for it to go there now."

"Let's say that it didn't like the sight of just the two of us here. He knows the others left, and he can't figure out how or why," Kevin said thoughtfully.

"I'd say you're right," the detective agreed. "But what's it going to do when they aren't there either?"

"Son-of-a-bitch is going to come back here and rip us a new asshole. That's what," Kevin stated.

"Well, we have to stay. We're the only ones left to lure that beast up to the mountain," Becker maintained.

"What are we going to do? Just stand here ready to jump in our vehicles when it comes back?"

"Speaking of, here it comes," Stan Becker said as he watched the sky.

The two men stood there prepared for a straight-up attack that never came. On the verge of leaping into his truck, Kevin observed as the Daemon flew at them, then over them. It appeared to be going to the mountain on its own.

"Shit. It's going to try and bring the chopper down," the detective realized. "It figured it out. Now what?"

"Do you have a grenade launcher in the trunk with the other stuff?" Kevin asked.

"Yes," Becker said. "keep one in case of…. Hell, I don't know why, but there's one in there."

"Give it to me, and let's go. We have to turn that thing around," Kevin told him. "We'll take my truck. You drive."

****

CHAPTER THIRTY-SIX:

FACING THE DRAGON

Grabbing not only the grenade launcher, but a couple of fifty caliber rifles and a shotgun for good measure, they sped out of the driveway. Pushing the Z-71 as fast as he dared on the curvy river road, Becker was determined to catch up to the Daemon. By the time they had passed the boat ramp, they had the beast in sight.

Becker ran the stop sign at the Hickory Tree road crossing, actually gaining on the winged serpent. Kevin stuck the Grenade launcher out of the window, taking careful aim. He didn't want to miss. The dragon was almost upon the helicopter.

"Keep it steady as you can," Kevin said.

"This is not exactly a smooth road," Becker replied.

Kevin grunted as he leaned over, putting the crosshairs on the dragon as best as he could. "X marks the spot," he said as he pulled the trigger.

The flying reptile swooped left as the explosion came from behind him. His attention was now drawn to the men in the vehicle. Chivas turned in mid-air much quicker than expected and was on the Z-71 before the detective could react. Flames erupted from the dragon's mouth as he passed overhead.

Paint blistered in the sudden heat as the occupants of the vehicle ducked instinctively. An acrid smell consumed the cab, making both men retch. Kevin reloaded the grenade launcher as the detective pulled the truck to the side. Both men climbed out.

"Where did he go?" Kevin asked as he stared at an empty sky.

"Don't know," came the reply.

They stood there trying to catch their breath and clear their lungs of the acidic stench from the dragon's attack. Less than a minute was all they had, however, as a spot appeared in the distance. It was closing fast.

"Get in. Let's go," Becker yelled as he jumped back in the vehicle.

"Hold on," Kevin said. "I think I can get him."

"Shit."

He laid his arms over the truck bed rails for support. Steadily, he moved the barrel until the crosshairs were laid in the center of the Daemon's chest. It kept coming.

"Any time now," the detective yelled from the cab.

The reptile was now within two hundred yards and closing. One-fifty. One hundred...

"Closer, come on," Kevin muttered to himself. "Steady."

Chivas was bearing down on him fast. It was unnerving to see a beast such as this coming at you. It seemed as if he was smiling even.

Kevin pulled the trigger at about thirty yards. An explosion in the chest area signaled a direct hit. The dragon lost his momentum, crashing into the road, rolling into the trees out of sight.

"Now can we go?" Becker asked, pulling off as Kevin shut the passenger door.

"Hell yes! Go, go, go," came the reply.

****

Hearing the explosion, Larry dropped the netting that he had been hanging around the perimeter of Keeler's so-called ceremony area. He reached for his phone as he jumped on the tallest rock at the edge of the cliff, looking Southward to try and see the cause.

He saw nothing, but he knew something bad was coming this way. It was too early for what he feared. He dialed Becker. It was answered on the second ring.

"Hey! We're on the way," Becker yelled over the phone.

"Things aren't completely ready here," Larry replied. "Steer him off in some other direction for a bit."

"Can't. It spied the helicopter taking off with them and was going to attack it. So we gave chase and distracted it with a grenade," Becker told him.

"So that's what the explosion was," Larry said. "Where exactly are you?"

"Just going by the cutoff to Clear Creek. And coming fast," the detective said.

Larry heard a bang and a grunt, then Kevin's voice in the background. Next came a deafening boom over the phone.

"Son-of-a-bitch," he heard Kevin say.

"Got to go," Becker hollered. "Coming in Hot and fast. Be as ready as you can." The line disconnected.

Larry looked up to see both of the elderly Indian Witches staring at him with understanding.

"The noise. I can feel him. Chivas is on the way." Keeler said as he and Redwing both turned to walk away.

"Where are you going?" Larry yelled.

"To finish preparing," Redwing said. "You should alert the others then, prepare yourself. From this moment on, you'll never be the same."

"If any of us survive," Keeler added. He kept walking towards the firepit. Bending and picking up the jug, the old man began soaking the wood with kerosene while Redwing sprinkled a mixture of herbs and magical components (that's all they would tell him) around the circumference. Larry shook his head.

He raised Ronnie on the walkie-talkie and informed him of the circumstances. Larry then instructed that he should make sure that everyone else knew that the shit was about to hit the fan, to hold their positions. His phone rang. It was Hamby.

"What the hell was that?" Hamby immediately asked.

"The Daemon, or whatever it is, is in dragon form now and was chasing Ghost, Father Ellis, Jacob, and Lisa in the helicopter. So, Kevin and Becker are trying to distract it with a grenade launcher," Larry explained.

"My God!" Hamby exclaimed. "Where are they?"

"On the way here," Larry replied. "Past the entrance to Clear Creek, so you better tell your guys on that side to move in this way and bring everything they have."

"What happens if the beast stays in dragon form?"

"We're screwed," Larry stated.

Hearing the blades of the chopper, he looked up to see Ghost drop the rope ladder in the small clearing, and his passengers begin descending. Jacob was the first off. Father Ellis last. Lisa was in between. Ghost reeled in the ladder and headed the whirlybird back in the direction he came.

"The others have arrived," Larry said.

"I see that," Hamby replied. "Where's Ghost taking the chopper to?"

"I have no idea."

"If he's smart, he's getting as far from here as possible," the detective said.

"Right," said Larry. "I've got to go. "See you soon."

Hitting the end call button, Larry looked around at all the commotion in full force now. Dragon. Shit. He hoped it would change. The wolf form was bad enough, but a fire-breathing reptile? It would be over in a flash.

****

The concussion and surprise at the impact of the projectile from the man's weapon caused Chivas to lose his senses for a moment. He sat up in the middle of some tall brush off in the woods. He had reverted back to human form in his brief unconsciousness. It had to have been for only a couple of seconds. He could still hear the vehicle.

Jumping up, he ran out into the gravel roadway. Catching a glimpse of the tailgate as the vehicle rounded the next curve, Chivas felt a slight twinge in his chest. Looking down, he saw the bruise disappearing from between his breasts.

"What the hell was that?" the Daemon thought to himself. Puny. If that was all they had, he needn't worry. His human form could withstand quite a bit of punishment. But both wolfen and dragon forms could take massive hits. They were almost indestructible.

Stretching out his arms, he took to running. A few steps and he was back in flight. The dragon was on the attack again.

****

"Direct hit," Kevin exclaimed as the dragon crashed into the woods.

"Do you really think that killed it?" Becker asked.

"No, but it sure did stop it for a minute," came the reply.

The detective looked in the rearview mirror as he began around the curve. His heart skipped a beat when he saw the Daemon run into the road. With a sigh, he informed Kevin, "It's already back up. Brace yourself." His phone rang.

The dragon appeared suddenly, smashing into the passenger side of the tailgate. Kevin glanced at Becker, who it seemed was in an excited conversation with someone on the phone. He leaned out of the window once more and took aim. Firing the weapon again.

"Son-of-a-bitch," he hollered as the dragon slowed and dodged this round. He was expecting it. "Step on it," he told the detective as Becker ended the call.

The truck swerved and was almost pushed off the road as the reptile smashed into the bed of the truck. Becker grunted as he fought the wheel, trying to keep the Z-71 on the gravel. Just as they braced for the next anticipated attack, the modified Apache helicopter piloted by Ghost came into view.

The twin 30-millimeter guns underneath the front were blazing, spewing out bullets at a rate of 300 rounds per minute, striking the dragon time after time. The monster hit the ground, rolling as the chopper flew overhead, banking for another run from the side.

Becker brought the Chevrolet to a stop a couple hundred yards up the road. Both men turned to watch out of the rear window. It seemed as though the air attack might be working at first as the spray of ammunition kept the beast pinned to the ground until Ghost passed and banked for a third run at it.

A few seconds to catch its breath and the dragon was up with a roar, taking flight in a mad dash towards the helicopter. It appeared the pilot had noticed the resurgence of the reptile as he sped off to the west, luring the beast away from the others to give them a little more time to finish with the preparations.

"What the hell?" the detective started.

"Ghost knows what he's doing," Kevin yelled. "He's buying us a few minutes. Let's go!"

Becker stepped on the gas, grabbing his phone in the process, and hit Larry on speed dial, switching to the hands-free mode. Kevin was still peering out the back window as the detective began speaking.

"Larry, the dragon's gone after the chopper. Ghost has led it off for a moment, so Kevin and I might just make it there after all."

CHAPTER THIRTY-SEVEN: THE DRAGON AND THE HELICOPTER/ MADE IT TO THE MOUNTAIN

"Good," Larry replied. "I guess you've already passed the Flint Mill trail so you'll be coming up the other one?"

"The Josiah! Yeah," Becker answered. Meet us where it crosses the Holston Mountain trail."

"Listen. When you're running up that trail, watch for the red markers on the trees. Step high. There's trip wires leading to all different kinds of explosives, mines, and traps all up the path," Larry informed him.

"Will do. Getting ready to pull off the road at the entrance now. See you," Becker hung up as he brought the truck to a stop on the side of the road at the trailhead.

Kevin jumped out, grabbing the grenade launcher and his 40-millimeter, stuffing the latter in his waistband along with a couple of extra clips. The detective picked up the 30.06 rifle as well as his service issued 9mm, also grabbing some extra ammunition.

As the two men began to enter the woods, a loud explosion broke the silence of the mountain. Looking back to the west, both could see the smoke rising and a small speck flying in their direction. They only glanced at each other and disappeared into the trees.

****

Chivas was aiming for the hit that would take the vehicle out of action and leave the humans out in the open for him. It would be quick. It would be easy to rid himself of these pesky creatures. Then, he would find the girl and the old Cherokee witches and dispatch them at his leisure.

Just as he was about to make his final dive, he heard the helicopter and the guns. He felt the repeated stinging of the bullets as they hit his thick hide multiple times. The pressure of them causing him to falter. Too many hits, too fast to concentrate.

"Who dares?" He thought to himself.

Then, the chopper was overhead and passed. Chivas slowed his flight and watched as the flying vehicle banked around a grove of trees. He would deal with that one in a minute. But first, back to business.

The dragon veered right and lined himself back up with the truck. As he picked up speed, he set his sights on the passenger side. He aimed to flip it off the left side of the road, where there was a steep embankment. They would not escape him again.

The sound of the machine guns reached his ears once again as the 30-millimeter bullets pelted his side, knocking him off course.

Now. He had to deal with this one now. The human in the air wouldn't let up until he did. With an angered expression he turned from the men in the truck and made chase after the helicopter.

With lightning speed Chivas gained on the nuisance machine rather quickly. Snapping his large jaws at the tail-end he managed to take part of the rear rotor off without too much damage to himself. He would heal in seconds in this form, though.

The copter began swerving, flying erratically from right to left, back, and so on, making it harder to get a hold of. Finally, the pilot tried to turn too sharp going around the top of a ridge and the Daemon snapped his jaws shut tight around the tail. He began slinging his head and body back and forth. It wasn't long before the pilot had no control at all.

Chivas tightened his jaw muscles, sinking his teeth into the metal at the same time spreading his wings akin to a parachute. He could see the man turn to stare with a horrified expression as he rotated in mid-air, letting go of the chopper as he completed his spin.

Metal crunched as the helicopter smashed through the trees, landing with a loud thud. A few seconds later there came an explosion as the fuel tank burst into flames. He was satisfied that the human was dead. He could plague him no more.

"The others have found a place to hide by now," he thought to himself. "I will find them."

The dragon soared slowly over the gravel road, peering off to the sides and into the trees as he went. There were no other roads for a vehicle to turn off on, so he was certain to catch them.

Only a few minutes had passed when he spotted the white Z-71 parked off in the grass. He flew on ahead to see if they had stuck to walking the roadway. After all, there was enough damage to the vehicle that it may not have been able to travel any farther.

After a mile or two and no sight of the men, he began making passes over the trees, venturing further away from the gravel road with each fly-over. There was something in the woods in the area close to the vehicle that made him uneasy. Something out of the ordinary, but he couldn't figure out what it was. He decided to land. Setting down on the gravel behind the vehicle, Chivas changed back to his human form.

He walked up to the truck and peered in the windows. Nothing. He looked underneath. Again, nothing. This was puzzling to him as he knew that the way out was not deeper in the woods. The two humans have played this too smart to trap themselves. Unless they were so shaken up that their minds were not thinking straight, maybe they were confused. Nonetheless, he would track them down and send their souls to the Netherworld.

"Hey, Jackass," a scream echoed from almost at the top of the ridge. It was followed by a bright red flare shooting into the air above the trees. "We're up here, numb-nuts! Come get us!"

Chivas dropped to his hands and knees. The change into the monstrous wolf came almost immediately. He stood there in anger, hackles rising up his back and neck. He stared at the area of the sounds. He was pissed now. The nerve of these pitiless humans. A calming voice came from his right. Three of the masters were with him.

"Don't let your anger interfere with your train of thought my son," the first master spoke into his ear. "That is what they want."

"How can the two of them possibly defeat me? I will tear them apart," Chivas said.

"There are more than just the two," Tulok, the master of war, stated. "Calm yourself. Use your senses."

Doing as he was told, the Daemon took a couple of deep breaths and gathered his thoughts about him. Closing his eyes, he stood still and tried to read the vibes in the air. Turning his head to the top of the ridge, he opened his eyes.

"Magic," he stated. "I can feel old and new magics gathered together. They have laid a trap for me."

"Yes, my son," the first master answered. "Keeler and Redwing are there. As well as a talented apprentice."

"I also sense a different power," Tulok said. "An almost God-like power such as I have not felt in eons. There's also a great power residing in one that does not yet realize that they have it. And even more humans line the path."

"It does not matter," Chivas stated. "I can and will defeat them all. They are no match for me."

"We are limited in what we can do on the mortal plane, but we will help where we can." The first master said.

"I have wasted enough time," the Daemon said. "I go."

The huge wolf entered the woods in the tracks of the humans, disappearing from sight, along the Josiah trail.

****

Kevin and the detective half walked, half ran up the Josiah trail, keeping an eye out for the trip wires and deadfalls. All the while they were letting those stationed along the path know that the beast was close behind.

The pair was a little over halfway when the sound of an explosion boomed across the mountain. Glancing at each other, they knew. Ghost and the helicopter were down. Both men picked up the pace. Damn. How many had to die before this was over?

Ten minutes later they had Larry in sight where the Holston Mountain trail crossed. The look on his face was grim. He was holding an AK 47 in one hand, pistols in his shoulder holster and right side. He had a sword strapped to his left. Standing beside him was Detective Hamby. His expression was one of worry. You could tell both men were tired. Hell, everybody was tired.

"Did you hear?" Larry asked.

"How could you not?" Kevin returned with a question himself.

"We'll mourn the losses later," Becker said. "That thing ought to be here any time."

"He is," Larry stated as he pointed to the sky. They could see the dragon cruising above the treetops in the distance. He retrieved the radio from his belt and began speaking into it, giving last-minute instructions. Hamby approached.

"This is crazy," he said.

"Yep," came Becker's short answer.

"After all this bullshit, are there any charges we can bring on the girl?" Hamby asked.

"She's been through enough," Becker stated. "Besides, what are you going to tell the court? Magic's real? There are beasts from Hell that can appear on Earth? Shit, they'd lock you in an asylum before you could think."

"Yeah, I guess you're right." The other detective agreed as his phone rang. "Hello," he answered and walked off. As he did, Larry re-joined them.

"They're all as ready as you can be for something like this, I guess," Larry said. "Everyone of them knows that there's a chance they won't be alive come morning."

There were murmurs of agreement coming from those stationed in this area. Twenty-some odd men and women, mostly off-duty guardsmen and vets, had the responsibility of this area if the beast made it this far. Which, most knew that it was almost certain that it would.

"Damn!" Hamby exclaimed as he walked back over.

"What now? Larry asked.

"The men at the roadblock at the Hwy 421 entrance said there were news teams gathered there now wanting access," Hamby stated. "They know something big is going on up here."

"I didn't think it would take them as long as it has to figure it out," Becker replied.

"I told them to get some air support to steer off the media helicopters if they happen to think of that," Hamby said. "And I had them re-set the road closure on the Hickory Tree side."

"Well, that's all we can do," Becker replied.

"Well, let's go. We're stationed halfway between here and the area Keeler, Redwing, and the others are at," Larry stated, turning up the rise.

A couple of hundred yards brought the old Indian witches to the edge of their sight. Here, there was a small plateau containing several large boulders. It appeared as if the stones had been brought in and placed where they were. Kevin raised a questioning eye at Larry.

"Yeah. Those rocks are courtesy of Ghost and the chopper. Bless his soul," Larry said. "There have been several things moved and brought in at the behest of Keeler and Redwing."

"I suppose each of us gets a rock?" Becker asked.

"It actually would be better *behind* the stones, but Yes," Larry said, pointing to some weapons and nets piled up in front of the center one. "Grab what you want. It's been placed here for you."

"What the hell are we going to do with nets?" Kevin asked.

"Uh. Well," Hamby began. "Those have been… I guess you'd say enchanted by the two old witches and blessed by Father Ellis. If you can throw one, grab it."

"Excuse me?" Becker said.

"Keeler says that we have to get at least one, preferably two, nets over and around the beast," Hamby informed them. "It's supposed to have the power to help contain it."

"I can't see that happening," Becker replied. "Anyway, I'm no good with a net."

"I'll take one," Kevin said.

Gunfire erupted at the foot of the trail, then an explosion. Then another. Larry's radio crackled to life. "It's here. Oh My God, it's here!" came a voice over the airwaves.

"Hello, Hello!" Larry yelled into the radio.

There was no response, but you could hear the madness, the chaos in the background. Screams came through the speaker, accompanied by a vicious roaring. Then, a crunching sound. Silence. The radio was dead on the other side. The group all assumed most of the people were dead also or would be soon.

Not a word was spoken. Anxious and horrified looks were on each of their faces.

"Fuck it," Kevin said. He took his weapons and a net and walked away towards one of the boulders. The others followed suit.

****

CHAPTER THIRTY-EIGHT:

THE DAEMONS ON THE FLINTMILL

She watched as Kevin, Larry, and the detectives came into view. Lisa also knew there were others stationed along that final hundred yards or so. But here would be where the final battle would take place. This nightmare of her own making would end. One way or the other. A hand touched her shoulder.

"What are they doing up here?" Lisa asked.

"Come, little one," Keeler said softly. "The time is near. We must finish preparing."

She turned and followed the old man over to where the fire would be set and looked around. On her left, Father Ellis was on his knees deep in prayer. Jacob was also kneeling, head bowed. Whether he was praying or concentrating on his spells, she couldn't tell.

To her right, Redwing was pouring some kind of liquid over bundles of arrows and spears. These were for the dozen warriors of a sect that Ghost had flown in with some supplies Keeler had sent him back to the Reservation for. Most of these antique Cherokee weapons and 'supplies' had come from Mohe Stone, the medicine man.

"Here. Look at me, little one," Keeler said.

As she turned to face him, she saw that he was holding two small cups in one hand. With the first two fingers of his other hand, he dipped into one of them and began to smear a colored paste around her eyes. She stood still and let him, knowing he wouldn't take no for an answer anyway.

"The Daemon we face here today is only one of the battles you will face," Keeler said.

"What others are there?" she asked, feeling herself move into a trance-like state. He had captured her full attention with the first words.

"There is something inside of yourself that you have kept buried most of your life," He spoke softly. "You knew things when you shouldn't have. Things have happened around you when you get angered or emotional."

"I don't know what you're talking about," Lisa replied.

"Yes, you do. Deep down, your inner being *Knows*." he continued. "Your grandfather and his father were of the witch clan. Both men and their fathers before them were very powerful sorcerers."

"Were they good or evil? And why didn't my parents tell me of this?" Lisa inquired.

"Your ancestors were of the White order as Redwing and I. Neither good nor evil, but neutral. Acting according to the balance and what is good in the foreseeable future." Keeler told her.

"What does that have to do with me Now?"

"It is time for you to let go. You feel the power you have rising when you are angry or scared. Do not suppress it if and when you feel it today," he instructed as his fingers applied the red paste across her forehead. "Unleash your energy."

"If I do have some abilities, I don't know how to use or control them. It would be utter madness," She said.

"My dear. Madness is what we will need when the time comes," Keeler stated as he finished painting her face. "Now, you are ready for war."

The explosions and gunfire began as she grabbed his arm.

"How do you know I have magical powers?"

Pointing his finger in the direction of the sounds of fighting, he gave her a simple reply.

"You brought that thing to this Earth, didn't you?" he turned and walked from her, smiling.

"Shit," Lisa muttered.

****

Chivas entered the woods, alert to the fact that the humans had laid traps for him. Now that his masters had made him see his errors made in anger and hurriedness, he was once again relying on all his senses. He knew that he had almost lost control.

As the wolf lost sight of the road, he walked at a pace of leisure. His sense of smell was being engulfed with the scent of humans and gunpowder. They were close. He could tell that there were many. He did not know what kind of traps had been set, so he was deciding whether to burst up the trail or err on the side of caution. The circumstances in the next minute or so would determine that.

The beast was busy looking off to the sides and felt, rather than seen, the first tripwire as his front paw broke it. Dirt, wood, and shrapnel engrossed his being as an enormous explosion occurred to his right. Almost immediately several humans stood and began firing weapons. Bullets bounced off his thick hide.

His reflexes kicked in, and he leaped into a group of three on his left. Biting and sweeping his massive claws into the men, ending their lives in mere seconds. Turning to another group of three on the opposite side of the trail, he dispatched them as quickly. His decision having been made, he quickened his pace.

Men and women with various weaponry swarmed out of their hiding places to pelt him with bullets, throw grenades, and set off ground charges. Most of these he tore into, killing some, giving minor injuries to some, and maiming others for life. All the while never losing sight of his main goal.

About halfway up, he ran upon a trap that had been set with a lump of C-4. That detonation took him off his feet. He was momentarily stunned. This gave the individuals in that sector a good chance to try and inflict some damage. About a dozen men attacked him.

Chivas was recovering from the impact rapidly and felt the relentless pinging of the bullets. As he clambered to his feet, the Daemon began swinging his claws back and forth into those crowded around him. Amongst the blood, screams, and ripping of flesh, He started to feel invigorated. The bloodlust was taking over. Stepping over the bodies, he vaulted back onto the main trail, snapping at everything in his way. He was making progress. Taking a moment to look around, he realized that he had almost made it near the top. He could feel the magic in the air emanating from the old (and young) wizards. But most of all… *He could smell her.*

Sure, he had a vendetta against the old witch. That one had gone against the darkness even though he had been commanded to a course of action. But *her*. She, who had thought it a great feat to summon him to this plane. *She* dared set out and bring people in to *hunt him*. It was *she* who had brought in a white man's holy man. *How dare she?*

These things were crossing his mind when the wolf stepped into a small clearing. The stench of those he had been hunting for the past couple of days permeated this place. Miller, he realized.

Closing his eyes, he took in much air through his nose. He smelled all of them. Now, spying on movement at the top of this ridge, he stared at the top. His hackles rose as he recognized most of those at the end of the trail. The priest, the witches, soldiers with many weapons, And her.

In between himself and his main objective was the man named Miller, the detective, and several others that he wasn't familiar with.

Chivas crouched lower to the ground. Gearing himself up for the final battle, the wolf let out a deafening roar and leaped.

****

CHAPTER THIRTY-NINE:

THE FINAL BATTLE/ LISA'S

INHERITED MAGIC

Kevin heard the bellow of the beast before he made it to a bolder. He turned towards the sound, noticing the others had done the same. He watched as the wolf sprang in their direction, only to be swarmed by several men as they came out of hiding. The beast's attackers were firing every weapon they had. The bullets had little effect on the Daemon.

"Hold your ground," Larry yelled as Becker began to move towards the fight. "It'll be our turn in a minute."

The wolf had already dispatched bloodily half of those men while advancing against those remaining. Howls of anger came with almost every breath of the beast. Now, three were left fighting this fiend. One was swiped twenty feet through the air with one gigantic paw while another's head disappeared into the massive jowls.

Dirt exploded high from the ground as the one man who was left accidentally stepped backward, setting off one of the buried land mines. Only a second passed, and the wolf emerged from the smoke and dust at a breakneck speed. There was no point trying to go for cover now.

The creature was on them in seconds. Various weapons began being fired from every direction. For Kevin, time seemed too slow. It was almost like he was in a daydream. Every movement was like watching a bunch of stills put into a frame-by-frame time-lapse. Somebody shoved him. It was Larry. He snapped out of his daze as time sped back up.

"Shoot at the damn thing!" Larry screamed. "Don't just stand there!"

Kevin fired the grenade launcher with a direct hit to the chest. One of many hits the beast had endured without damage. A man he didn't know landed in a heap at his feet, chest ripped open. He pulled the trigger. Nothing. The weapon was empty.

As he was fumbling in his pack for more shells, he heard Hamby shout. Looking up, Kevin watched as Becker advanced on the wolf, emptying out both MAC-11 submachine guns directly into its head and neck. Realizing he was out of ammunition, Becker began a back-step unholstering his forty millimeters.

Chivas leaped forward, and before the detective could get another shot off, the wolf's jaws clamped down on his arm. With a jerk of the beast's head, Becker's forearm was ripped off at the elbow. Blood gushed onto the ground. Another man, a guardsman, ran in to help, and the jaws came down again, snapping together over the man's head. The corpse fell to the ground, and immediately, the beast was on another. By this time, all remaining troops from the Josiah trail had joined in the fray. Around twenty-five to thirty men were attacking the wolf relentlessly. Chivas was returning the favor in brutal fashion.

Detective Hamby and Larry motioned to Kevin that they needed to get to the top with the spellcasters, Lisa and the others. Kevin fired a round and shook his head no.

"Damnit, Miller," Hamby shouted as he began moving up the hill. "Let these guys delay this thing. If we don't go help protect Keeler's group, it's all lost. They're the only ones with a real chance anyway."

Reluctantly, Kevin turned and jogged to the clearing where the Cherokee witches had their ceremonial fire built up. He had not realized the ancient Native American ways, especially in magic, that Keeler had referred to all along. Now, in the few seconds he had to catch his breath, he was astounded when seeing their setup for the first time.

There were more of the supposed 'magic infused' objects placed in different locations, as well as various antique-looking bows, spears, and scythes, as well as some swords. There were not many firearms up here at all. He looked at Jacob, who was only holding a staff, standing on the back side of the fire. Father Ellis was ten feet away and still on his knees praying.

Scanning the entire area, Kevin noticed fifteen or so painted-up Native Americans in loose-fitting garb. All were armed with the weapons of the past. His eyes then landed on Lisa. He had hardly recognized her as she, herself, had her face painted and was wearing

Cherokee clothing resembling that of two hundred years ago. She didn't say a word, only looked at him with an anxious expression.

Keeler and Redwing began chanting in their native language as the wolf burst onto the scene. It was covered in gore. Blood had caked in places, and yet, it still was dripping off its jowls. The eyes stood out more than anything, burning a bright silver. The beast raised its nose in the air as if searching for a scent. It turned its head until its eyes fell upon Lisa. A second later, it bounded in her direction.

****

Lisa had watched the fight below, praying in silence for her friends for everyone. Her heart dropped when she witnessed Detective Becker thrown thirty feet, losing an arm in the process. She watched as Kevin jogged up in the middle of this final place of either hope or despair. Win or lose, this was it.

She didn't say a word as the other three entered this area. She did give each of them what was hoped to be a confident look. And, that's all it would be, a look. She, herself, had serious doubts about the outcome of this endeavor. Keeler had told her that she had some mystical power. She could feel something inside but didn't know how to tap into it or how to use it.

She had memorized the few spells that Keeler and Redwing had given her, but other than that, she had a rifle. She just knew that she did not have a chance. She had started focusing on her inner self when the wolf entered the perimeter. It was searching for something, it seemed. When the creature peered into her eyes, she knew that it was her.

Chivas bounded in her direction but ran into a wall of Cherokee warriors. The old witches chanting became louder. Larry and Detective Hamby fired their Weapons. Kevin's AK-47 was slinging the lead out at an enormous rate. Modern weapons seemed to have no impact on the Daemon.

Slinging bodies out of the way, Chivas fought through the warriors in less than a minute. The animal's claws were swiping at everyone in its way. Larry went down with some vicious slices to his hip and lower ribcage. Detective Hamby took a massive hit to the head, flailing to the ground unconscious.

The old Cherokee witches were still in position. Still chanting, only now both were surrounded with a red and white glow. Jacob held steady with the staff. Lisa still did not know what it was supposed to do.

As the Daemon-wolf came by Hambys' still form, eyes focused on Lisa, Kevin jumped closer, throwing one of the enchanted nets over the beast. Chivas roared with rage, ramming all four claws of one paw deep into his stomach, lifting him two feet off the ground.

Blood ran in streams, quickly soaking Kevin's jeans all the way into his boots. The man's eyes grew wild as he screamed curses into the beast's face. If a wolf could smile, it did so in that moment. Still holding the dying man off the mountain floor, the Daemon turned to stare Lisa in the eyes.

Chivas didn't get the devastating look from her as expected. Instead, the young woman stared back with intense hatred, much to his dismay.

"Now, Little one, Now, Father Ellis," Keeler yelled. And instantly, she knew what the old man had meant about there being an inherent power in her.

Lisa took a step towards the wolf. She raised her left arm and looked to the sky. Her right arm pointed to the Daemon. Father Ellis stepped in beside her. His arms and hands pointing the same. One to the heavens, one towards the beast.

"Mother Earth, Brother Moon," she yelled. "I beseech thee."

"God," Father Ellis yelled at the same moment. "My Father in Heaven, Help me!"

Bolts of lightning came from the sky, striking both Lisa and the pastor in their upraised hands, traveling through their bodies, and erupting from the hands aimed at the wolf. Sparks and flames burst all over the Daemon's body. He shook violently, dropping Kevin's body to the ground.

Keeler and Redwing increased the chanting of the ancient ritual, flames of blue now dancing along their fingertips. They move to stand on either side of Lisa and Father Ellis, who now joins in the chant. Lisa began reciting one of the lyrics Keeler had taught her, overlapping their words with precision inflections of the ancient words.

Jacob stands his ground at the fire, only now the staff has white-hot sparks dancing up and down its entire length. He feels the magic building as the air electrifies and presses down, making it difficult to breathe. He cackles as the old witches release the flames to further engulf the Daemon, who then howls in pain.

The four of them weaving the magical spell circles around in front of Chivas, pushing the beast towards the fire. Its wolfen form begins to shimmer, cracking. Fading in and out until there only remained the human form writhing in agony.

Forced over the rocks lining the fire, the Daemon steps back into the flames. An opening appears on the ground at the center. The gateway. Chivas looks back and sees the entrance to the Netherworld. Seeing his Master just inside, with looks of disappointment and anger on his face, he screams. "NO!"

Feet sliding out from under him, now half in this world, half in his tortured realm, the Daemon tries to push back. Jacob steps into the flames with him, placing the tip of the staff in the center of Chivas' head and pushing down.

With a look of terror, the image of the Daemon disappears into the void as Jacob follows with the staff. The ground closes around the wooden rod as the golden top sinks six inches into the dirt. Jacob quickly inserts an odd-shaped 'key' and turns it counterclockwise. A loud popping noise follows.

The fire had followed the beast into the Netherworld. There were no signs it had ever existed. The two old men sat where they were, exhausted but still in fair shape for their age after all they had been through. Jacob began kicking dirt over the gold top of the staff.

"So, that's supposed to hold it?" Lisa asked.

"It will," Jacob said. "At least until we can find a permanent solution."

"And as long as no one pulls it up," Keeler added.

Lisa looked around at all the injured and dead. Not one of the fighters escaped unharmed. She spied Larry, getting to his knees, crawling over to Hamby to attend to him. Her eyes fell on Kevin's form.

Relieved to see that his hand was moving, she walked over to him. In an instant, she knew that he would not be leaving her alive. His insides were torn through the gashes left by the wolf's claws. He motioned for her to come closer.

"This," he laboriously whispered, "is not all your fault. I forgive you."

"Kev," Lisa started, tears running unchecked down her cheeks.

"Shhh," he managed. "Tell Angie I love her."

"I will," she promised, taking his hand as his breathing became labored, then stopped. He was gone.

Lisa stood and nodded to Keeler, Jacob, and Redwing. She waved at Larry, who had awakened a very sore Detective Hamby, who was now on the phone calling in to dispatch. What kind of story he was going to tell about this one, she couldn't imagine.

She was tired. She had had enough of this. She needed to get to the hospital to be with her sister. Shaking her head, Lisa began the long walk back down the mountain.

****

CHAPTER FORTY:

CLOSURE/ A NEW LIFE BEGINNING

Two months later, Lisa sat in the room with Angie, who was still in a coma. The doctors had told her that there was a slim chance that her sister would come out of it in time. Lisa was a realist, though, and knew exactly what those words had meant.

The damage that had been inflicted upon Angie was tremendous. And, she also knew that it would take a miracle to make it happen. Still, she sat by her side day in and day out, regretting all the time that had been missed.

The doctors had also informed her yesterday that Angie was eight weeks pregnant. What if the baby wasn't Kevin's? What if it had been spawned by that monster? What kind of child would it be? These thoughts ran through her head continuously as she watched the news.

The story of that day on the mountain had been at the top of every news channel list around the country for the first couple of weeks. Now, even two months later, it still was mentioned during each broadcast.

Detective Hamby had spun it as a quiet operation to pin down some terrorist group that went violently array, and the federal authorities and media had bought it. How he got every survivor to agree to it and to give the same statement that fast, she'll never know.

Larry had healed quickly, as had Hamby. Father Ellis had taken some time off from the responsibilities of the church and had left town quietly. It turns out that Detective Becker survived his arm being bit off and was healing from that and a few other injuries. He plans to retire and move to the Midwest.

As far as the Cherokee witches Keeler, Redwing, and Jacob, they made their way back to the reservation. Keeler or Jacob calls every few days to check on her and Angie. When Keeler tries to talk about those days or magic, she changes the subject.

For now, she reflects on the good times with friends gone now. Neil, Becky, and especially Kevin. For her… Life goes on.

****

NINE MONTHS AFTER

I sn't that sad what happened to the Miller woman?" Nurse Cathy asked another.

"Yes," came the other's reply. "To die during childbirth is sorrowful anyway. But she never came out of the coma the whole pregnancy."

"To my knowledge the woman never even knew she was with child," Cathy said.

"With the father dying in that horrible incident on the mountain, what's going to happen to the child?" the other asked.

"To my understanding, the sister is taking custody of the baby boy," Cathy answered.

"Oh. He's such a beautiful baby," the other nurse stated. "And such eyes. Have you seen them?"

"Oh my gosh, yes!" Nurse Cathy exclaimed. "They are so gorgeous, big, bright silver eyes. I've never seen ones like them. They're to die for!"

THE END